ANNA AND MISTER GOD

Mister God, This is Anna

Anna's Book

Anna and the Black Knight

•

Fynn

HarperCollins*Publishers*

HarperCollins*Publishers*
77–85 Fulham Palace Road,
Hammersmith, London W6 8JB

www.harpercollins.co.uk

This paperback edition 2004
1 3 5 7 9 8 6 4 2

Mister God, This is Anna first published by
William Collins & Co. Ltd 1974
Anna's Book first published by
William Collins & Co. Ltd 1986
Anna and the Black Knight first published
HarperCollins*Publishers* 1990
Combined edition first published 1998

ISBN 0 00 716641 9

Printed and bound in Great Britain by
Clays Ltd, St Ives plc

FOREWORD

Many of the personalities that make the most powerful and transforming impression on us in the world's literature are the ones we see only or mostly at second hand, not in their own undoctored words. Plato's Socrates is an obvious example; Boswell's Johnson a rather weaker one. At another level completely, theologians have long pondered the fact that Jesus left no written word of his own and that we rely on four testimonies to him, of very different sorts, not all of which can claim to be eye-witness record.

And perhaps that is appropriate. If you want to see why a personality makes a difference to his or her contemporaries, you need first to understand that difference itself; and this can only be done by means of testimony. Seeing someone through another person's eyes, a person close to them, whose life is really shaped by them, will tell you more than the most accurate third person chronicle. Only a very individualistic age could imagine that the most important truths about someone could be established by a supposedly neutral chronicle.

Fynn is as far as possible from being a neutral chronicler. This is passionately involved reporting. And if a superficial reader skimming the pages starts to imagine that this is a Pollyanna-ish story of a wise and saintly child, which can be relegated to a rather tired genre, they have not begun to see what is being done here. The explosive individuality of Anna is not sentimentally touching but sometimes almost frightening. What is it like to confront a child characterised above all by an undeniable spiritual and intellectual *authority*? It is even harder than an encounter with an adult who demonstrates such authority (and that's hard enough). Fynn leaves us nothing to patronise in Anna (or in himself), but brings us under a merciless scrutiny such as only a child can exercise.

And the point about knowing someone by seeing the effect they have can be taken a stage further. If you want somebody to understand what the major intellects of the world religions mean by God, you could do a great deal worse than introduce them to Anna. The God we encounter here is in no sense simply another inhabitant of the universe who just happens to be more powerful than any other; nor is he an observer of the created scene from an advantaged position, reacting to our behaviour from outside. As the theologians have said, this is a God whose own bliss and beauty and order are simply the ground, the energy and the context of everything, 'more intimate to us than we to ourselves', pressing with a steady loving urge to be manifest to us and so to change us. Anna is memorably sceptical about what happens in church – but in a way that a reader of the gospels will recognise. Religious behaviour that relies on diminishing the human beings involved in it is actually resisting the pressure of God. Anna echoes the incarnate God by saying over and over again, 'Fear not'.

That, I suppose, is why I find these texts so extraordinary, so inexhaustible. I am being asked over and over again whether when I say I believe in God it is actually God that I believe in. Anna's God is of course loving and forgiving, just and holy; but he is so much more than any kind of lawgiver, whether lenient or strict. His law is his being, as the philosophers say; and his being demands of us the utmost in both love and intellect, so that passion for God can open for us the casements of that mathematical and scientific wonder that exhilarates Anna and her chronicler.

C.S. Lewis once wrote about the sort of book that was like a 'mouthwash for the imagination' – clearing out clichés and tired or lazy images and ideas. These books are like that. I hope that a new edition will introduce a new generation to this formidable and astonishing figure – and to the God she lived (and lives) with.

Dr Rowan Williams
Archbishop of Canterbury
December 2003

CONTENTS

MISTER GOD, THIS IS ANNA

INTRODUCTION

Vernon Sproxton

There are good books, indifferent books, and bad books. Amongst the good books some are honest, inspiring, moving, prophetic, and improving. But in my language there is another category: there are *Ah! Books*. This is one of them. *Ah! Books* are those which induce a fundamental change in the reader's consciousness. They widen his sensibility in such a way that he is able to look upon familiar things as though he is seeing and understanding them for the first time. *Ah! Books* are galvanic. They touch the nerve-centre of the whole being so that the reader receives an almost palpable physical shock. A tremor of excited perception ripples through the person.

Ah! Books don't come all that often, at least not my way. André Malraux's *The Psychology of Art* was one of them. It was published just after the war. It was too expensive to buy, but I located a copy of this luminous book in the Manchester Art Gallery; and I had to make several journeys by motor-cycle, often through sleet and snow, until I had finished it. From time to time I wanted to get up on the table and proclaim its truth to all around me, or slap my desk-neighbour over the back and say, 'There you are; just get hold of that!' Once I nearly did but, just in time, I noticed that he was reading a text on the structure of plastics. By now, of course, I know that some people can get as much aesthetic pleasure out of contemplating the formula for a long molecule as others do from beholding a mural by Piero della Francesca. Technologists have their *Ah! moments*, too!

Ah! Books give you sentences which you can roll around in the mind, throw in the air, catch, tease out, analyse. But in whatever

3

way you handle them, they widen your vision. For they are essentially Idea-creating, in the sense that Coleridge meant when he described the Idea as containing future thought – as opposed to the Epigram which encapsulates past thought. *Ah! Books* give the impression that you are opening a new account, not closing an old one down.

So for me, at any rate, this is an *Ah! Book*, and has been since the manuscript first came my way; from the very first sentence, too. 'The diffrense from a person and an angel is easy. Most of an angel is in the inside and most of a person is on the outside.' A few seconds' thought and then – the tingle in the mind. I remembered the poet Norman Nicholson, as a young man on the cricket field, newly come to T. S. Eliot's use of common speech in poetry, incanting between overs, 'The young man carbuncular arrives ... on whom assurance sits as a silk hat on a Bradford millionaire.' That was a sentence which gave a fresh look to language. This was one which gave a fresh look to holiness.

It was the repristinizing of religious language which struck me forcibly when the manuscript of this book first came into my hands; except, of course, that there was by no means what a publisher calls a manuscript. There were a few pages hesitantly and anonymously offered by a friend of the author who wished to remain humbly and unobtrusively in the background. But these were enough to show that, whoever he was, the writer, though by no means an accomplished literary man, had a quick eye for the human scene, a warm regard for his fellows and, above all, a mind of great originality which appeared to have either escaped from or never been subjected to the processing which normally marks people who write about such matters. I read those first few pages over and over again until I was pursued by Fynn and Anna as a kind of literary puzzle. I tried to make an *Identiwrit* picture of the author and his background: a man certainly thinking his way through to the frontiers of thought; a scientifically trained parson or a theologically astute scientist; in any event someone who was attempting to communicate a message of some sort, and was finding that purely logical forms would not bear the burden of his meaning; an inventor of a mini-myth. For *Alice in Wonderland* read *Anna in Bethnal Green*. Whoever he was, the few dog-eared pages sharpened the appetite for more. I could hardly wait for following chapters, which arrived in dribs and drabs, and I began to feel for all the world like the young T. B. Macaulay walking from Cambridge to meet the London coach bearing the next instalment of the Waverley Novels. (Much to the disgust of his father, incidentally, who believed that novels were no fit occupation for a scholar and a gentleman!) There grew in me a mastering curiosity to meet the author, if only to confirm my guesses.

We met. And I was wrong – at least in large part. Fynn disguises nobody but Fynn. At the time of writing I have known him for a couple of years. But there is another way in which I have known him all my life. For there is about him that transparent vulnerability which makes for a total and immediate correspondence with anyone who is prepared to throw prejudices to the wind and celebrate life as a lump of mysterious and joyful awe. But all the speculation about a trained scientist or theologian with imaginative leanings and communication problems was pretty wide of the mark. Fynn, thank God, was not *trained* as either of these. Intelligent to the eyelashes and with a gargantuan appetite for knowledge, Fynn was early advised to eschew (may his adviser rest in peace) universities and other institutions for the purveying of processed thought. So most of his formative thinking took place far from the quads and colleges and punted rivers amongst the small streets, warehouses, and canals of the East End. But with his modest job and his Woolworth's do-it-yourself laboratory he produced thought to which few PhDs have approximated. If in doubt, thumb through the theses lodged in the libraries of the universities: 'Four Methods of Washing a Cup', 'The Social Life of the Sperm Whale', 'The Water-absorbing Properties of Pink Geraniums'! It is no disrespect to sperm whales, or for that matter tea-cups and geraniums, to say that Fynn has produced something qualitatively different from PhD-thinking and which would probably not have emerged if during those critical years he had had to attend twice-weekly tutorials on logical positivism which was then raising its ayry-fairy head.

Fynn is a large man; tall, and once on a day enormously strong; and not only physically large but mentally very masculine, with a bold aggressive intelligence compounded of that mixture of credulity and scepticism which is always prepared to abandon well-trodden ground for intellectually virgin territory. But on the other hand he has a strongly developed feminine side which can only be described as skin stretched over tenderness. I remember sitting with him one night talking about his early experiments with mirrors and Meccano. (Now he uses computers made up from surplus W.D. junk.) And then he started discussing people who were maladjusted or had fallen on bad times and with whom he had worked for a large chunk of his life. And he did so with such deep insight and total acceptance that his attitude could only be described as love. As I watched and listened my mind began to search around for some historical person of whom he reminded me: who also had had little formal education, and whose feminine and masculine streaks co-existing made an inner dialectic which produced a creative vitality. At last, as the night folded us in a brotherhood of discussion and debate, the name dropped out of the memory. It was that of Leonardo da Vinci.

Fynn has suffered: suffered not only physically, mentally, and emotionally; but has also suffered spiritually in that total solitariness, isolation, and abandonment which, however close one's friends and relatives may be, becomes a terrifying experience for the lonely being. The men of the Middle Ages were right to describe it as 'a dark night of the soul'. Fynn is still partially disabled from a psycho-physical injury. But he is now in process of throwing away his crutches with an almost insolent, hilarious impudence, relying on his own grit and gumption, and the grace and goodness of his fairly recently acquired wife. And all this makes Fynn the sort of person who gives you the impression that though he has been tossed about by life his feet have firmly touched the bottom.

So Fynn is the author of this book; and he is who he was, and who he is. He has an address and a telephone number. He is pretending to be nobody other than himself. But a very real and permanent part of his being is – Anna.

Now, to tell a plain and honest tail, I did not need convincing that the East End had bred and moulded Fynn. I knew the East End thirty years and more ago and the cameos he makes of that rich, gay, almost voluptuous life are cut from the flesh. That marvellous Cockney Mum, the soft-hearted brassy Venus de Mile End, the garrulous Night People; I knew and loved such people by the hundred.

But Anna ... She was qualitatively different, and she had me puzzled, not so much because of her flamboyant precociousness, but because I needed a good deal more documentation of her uniqueness. To begin with, I found it hard to believe that anyone could have existed at that age who was so untouched by the constraining type of education available at that time, and whose precocity took the form of devastating challenges to the received way of construing things; and more so, when her nascent philosophy went to the heart of some problems of spiritual perception and the nature of being which are precisely contemporary. And I questioned the intimate physical relationship between Fynn and Anna which, even in these permissive days, will undoubtedly be offensive to many well-meaning ladies who are in good standing with the executive committee of the Mothers' Union.

But these problems began to resolve themselves as soon as I met Fynn. There is another quality about him which transcends his masculinity and femininity; the only word I can use to describe it is Innocence. No doubt he is touched by original sin, whatever that may mean, and many of the things that frail flesh is heir to. He is not amongst the ever-sanctified. But there is about him a touch of that engaging, wide-eyed, winsome innocence which mankind must have had before the Fall, and which would permit a youth and a young girl to snuggle up in bed together in a way which was completely innocent (there the word is again) of any sexuality. In fact the simple honesty of their relationship reminded me of the practices of the *subintroductae* – those virgins who slept with the early Christian fathers without intercourse taking place – which had to be abandoned in the fourth century because Cyprian and others were worried about SCANDALS; and of which Charles Williams writes in *The Descent of the Dove* (London, 1939 and 1950, p. 13): 'It was one of the earliest triumphs of "the weaker brethren", those innocent sheep who by mere volume of imbecility have trampled over many delicate and attractive flowers in Christendom. It is the loss, so early, of a tradition whose departure left the Church rather over-aware of sex, when it might have been creating a polarity with which sex is only partly coincident.'

The other credibility problems resolved themselves when I realized that Fynn lives on dialectic. It is not simply that he has a great appetite for dialogue with people. He gives the appearance of being in a kind of reciprocal tension with all phenomena all the time. He is a man of furious intellectual energy. It is as though his mind is processing data (and not only that of number) at every moment and perceiving and printing out new and significant patterns of relationships.

It was into this dialectical orbit that Anna fortuitously swam, and suddenly found her spirit lifted up to see the world with different eyes from other children and to refuse the blinkers which both school-ma'am and parson had readily to hand in their pre-packed word-parcels. If Fynn needed Anna, Anna also, and just as specifically, needed Fynn. And it stands to reason that the problems which they teased away at together were the problems which obsessed Fynn. And it also follows that the problems which have preoccupied him over the intervening years have naturally become contemporary. In other words this dialectical relationship shaped the Anna story. An analogy from the Christian story casts some light upon this problem.

The first three Gospels represent the words and deeds of Jesus which the early Church found useful and necessary for their domestic life of living, and teaching, and explaining. With the passage of time the continuous use made the *form*. So Fynn, continuously reflecting on and remembering and re-evaluating his life with Anna, within the context of his own intellectual growth, *formed* the Anna story and its meaning. Just as the Fourth Gospel is a theological work, where perhaps one pregnant sentence spoken by Jesus (like, 'I am the bread of life') is expounded by putting words into the mouth of Jesus, so, it seems to me, Fynn has taken an Idea of Anna, expressed in a lapidary way and, grasping its meaning, has worked out its significance so that the *Ah!* of it makes a dramatic impact on bears of very little brain like me.

Even so, some readers may remain incredulous. They will ask, 'Is it true?' Now I happen to believe that it is true in the way they are asking the question. But then I know Fynn. I have seen the documents in the case: the notes, the drawings, the essays, the music. But there is a sense in which the relics have nothing to do with the truth of this, any more than the *truth* of the myth of the Garden of Eden would be enhanced by the discovery of a fossilized apple with a couple of bites taken from it!

What is Truth? Pilate raised the question and wisely declined to answer it, realizing no doubt that all political truth is necessarily tainted. But Søren Kierkegaard did make an attempt at answering the same question; and many people have found it satisfying as a rough-and-ready measure for that kind of truth which cannot be measured on the laboratory bench. *The truth*, he wrote, *is what ennobles*. It is, in other words, that which makes you a better being. It is in that realm that the truth of *Mister God, This Is Anna* is finally to be found. It is an ennobling tale which greatly widens our perception and touches the heart. And it does so in a way which defies the processes of logic. We cannot find words to explain how it works its spell. But, as Solzhenitsyn wrote in his Nobel prize speech, 'Not everything has a name. Some things lead us into the realm beyond words ... It is like that small mirror in the fairy tales – you glance in it and what you see is not yourself; for an instant you glimpse the Inaccessible, where no horse or magic carpet can take you. And the soul cries out for it.'

This book has the same kind of transporting magic. Fynn and Anna, with their mirror-book and all their other simple impedimenta, allow us to glimpse the Inaccessible. They would never have won a Nobel prize for literature. They do, however, make me congratulate myself on having joined the human race. Above all they put back the *Ah!* into that mixture of mess and marvel which makes the mystery of our mortal life.

CHAPTER ONE

'The diffrense from a person and an angel is easy. Most of an angel is in the inside and most of a person is on the outside.' These are the words of six-year-old Anna, sometimes called Mouse, Hum or Joy. At five years Anna knew absolutely the purpose of being, knew the meaning of love and was a personal friend and helper of Mister God. At six Anna was a theologian, mathematician, philosopher, poet and gardener. If you asked her a question you would always get an answer – in due course. On some occasions the answer would be delayed for weeks or months; but eventually, in her own good time, the answer would come: direct, simple and much to the point.

She never made eight years, she died by an accident. She died with a grin on her beautiful face. She died saying, 'I bet Mister God lets me get into heaven for this', and I bet he did too.

I knew Anna for just about three and a half years. Some people lay claim to fame by being the first person to sail around the world alone, or to stand on the moon, or by some other act of bravery. All the world has heard of such people. Not many people have heard of me, but I, too, have a claim to fame; for I knew Anna. To me this was the high peak of adventure. This was no casual knowing; it required total application. For I knew her on her own terms, the way she demanded to be known: from the inside first. 'Most of an angel is in the inside', and this is the way I learned to know her – my first angel. Since then I have learnt to know two other angels, but that's another story.

My name is Fynn. Well that's not quite true; my real name doesn't matter all that much since my friends all called me Fynn and it stuck. If you know your Irish mythology you will know that Fynn was pretty big; me too. Standing about six foot two, weighing some sixteen stone odd, close to being a fanatic on physical culture, the son of an Irish mother and a Welsh father, with a passion for hot saveloys and chocolate raisins – not together, I may add. My great delight was to roam about dockland in the night-time, particularly if it was foggy.

My life with Anna began on such a night. I was sixteen at the time, prowling the streets and alleys with my usual supply of hot dogs, the street lights with the foggy haloes showing dark formless shapes moving out from the darkness of the fog and disappearing again. Down the street a little way a baker's shop-window softened and warmed the raw night with its gas-lamps. Sitting on the grating under the window was a little girl. In those days children wandering the streets at night were no uncommon sight. I had seen such things before, but on this occasion it was different. How or why it was different has long since been forgotten except that I am sure it was different. I sat down beside her on the grating, my back against the shop-front. We stayed there about three hours. Looking back over thirty years, I can now cope with those three hours; but at the time I was on the verge of being destroyed. That November night was pure hell; my guts tied themselves into all manner of complicated knots.

Perhaps even then something of her angelic nature caught hold of me; I'm quite prepared to believe that I had been bewitched from the beginning. I sat down with 'Shove up a bit, Tich.' She shoved up a bit but made no comment.

'Have a hot dog', I said.

She shook her head and answered, 'It's yours.'

'I got plenty. Besides, I'm full up', I said.

She made no sign so I put the bag on the grating between us. The light from the shop-window wasn't very strong and the kid was sitting in the shadows so I couldn't see what she looked like except that she was very dirty. I could see that she clutched under one arm a rag-doll and on her lap a battered old paint-box.

We sat there for thirty minutes or so in complete silence; during that time I thought there had been a movement of her hand towards the hot-dog bag but I didn't want to look or comment in case I put her off. Even now I can feel the immense pleasure I had when I heard the sound of that hot-dog skin popping under the bite of her teeth. A minute or two later she took a second and then a third. I reached into my pocket and brought out a packet of Woodbines.

'Do you mind if I smoke while you're eating, Tich?' I asked.

What?' She sounded a little alarmed.

'Can I have a fag while you're eating?'

She rolled over and got to her knees and looked me in the face. 'Why?' she said.

'My Mum's a stickler for politeness. Besides, you don't blow smoke in a lady's face when she's eating', I said.

She stared at half a sausage for a moment or two, and looking at me fully, she said, 'Why? Do you like me?'

I nodded.

'You have a fag then,' and she smiled at me and popped the rest of the sausage into her mouth.

I took out a Woodbine and lit up and offered her the match to blow out. She blew, and I was sprayed with bits of sausage. This little accident produced such a reaction in her that I felt that I had been stabbed in the guts. I had seen a dog cringe before, but

never a child. The look she gave me filled me with horror. She expected a thrashing. She clenched her teeth as she waited for me to strike her.

What my face registered I don't know, perhaps anger and violence, or shock and confusion. Whatever it was, it produced from her the most piteous whimper. I can't describe this sound after all these years, no words are fitting. The feeling I can still taste, can still experience. My heart faltered at the sound, and something came undone inside me. My clenched fist hit the pavement beside me, a useless gesture in response to Anna's fears. Did I think of that image then, that image which I now think of, the only one that fits the occasion? That perfection of violence, that ultimate horror and bewilderment of Christ crucified. That terrible sound that the child made was a sound that I never wish to hear again. It attacked my emotional being and blew a fuse.

After a moment or two I laughed. I suppose that the human mind can only stand so much grief and anguish. After that the fuses blow. It did with me, my fuses blew in a big way. The next few minutes I know very little about – except that I laughed and laughed, then I realized that the kid was laughing too. No shrunken bundle of fear – she was laughing. Kneeling on the pavement and leaning forward with her face close to mine, and laughing – laughing. So very many times in the next three years I heard her laughter – no silver bells or sweet rippling sounds was her laughter, but like a five-year-old's bellow of delight, a cross between a puppy's yelp, a motor-bike, and a bicycle pump.

I put my hands on her shoulders and held her off at arm's length, and then came that look that is entirely Anna's – mouth wide open, eyes popping out of her head, like a whippet straining at the leash. Every fibre of that little body was vibrating and making a delicious sound. Legs and arms, toes and fingers, the whole of that little body shook and trembled like Mother Earth giving birth to a volcano. And what a volcano was released in that child!

Outside that baker's shop in dockland on a foggy November night I had the unusual experience of seeing a child born. After the laughter had quietened off a bit, but while her little body was still thrumming like a violin string, she tried to say something, but it wouldn't come out properly. She managed a 'You – You – You –.'

After some little time and a great deal of effort she managed 'You love me, don't you?'

Even had it not been true, I could not have said 'No' to save my life; true or false, right or wrong, there was only one answer. I said 'Yes'.

She gave a little giggle, and pointing a finger at me, said, 'You love me,' and then broke into some primitive gyration around the lamp-post, chanting 'You love me. You love me. You love me.'

Five minutes of this and she came back and sat down on the grating. 'It's nice and warm for your bum, ain't it?' she said.

I agreed it was nice for your bum.

A moment later: 'I ain't arf firsty.' So we upped and went along to the pub just down the road. I bought a large bottle of Guinness. She wanted 'one of them ginger-pops with the marble in the neck'. So she had two ginger-pops and some more saveloys from an all-night coffee stall.

'Let's go back and get our bums warm again,' she grinned at me. Back we went and sat on the grating, a big un and a little un.

I don't suppose that we drank more than a half of the drinks, for it seemed that the idea of a fizzy drink was to shake it vigorously and then let it shoot up into the air. After a few showers of ginger-pop and a determined effort to do the nose trick, she said,

'Now do it to yourn.'

I'm sure even then that this was not a request but an order. I shook hard and long and then let fly with the stopper and we both were covered with frothy Guinness.

The next hour was filled with giggles and hot dogs, ginger-pop and chocolate raisins. The occasional passer-by was yelled at: 'Oi, Mister, he loves me, he do.' Running up the steps of a nearby building she shouted, 'Look at me. I'm bigger than you.'

About ten-thirty that evening, whilst she was sitting between my knees having an earnest conversation with Maggie, her rag-doll, I said, 'Come on, Tich, it's about time you were in bed. Where do you live?'

In a flat, matter-of-fact voice she exclaimed, 'I don't live nowhere. I have runned away.'

'What about your Mum and Dad?' I asked.

She might have said the grass is green and the sky is blue. What she did say was just as factual and effortless. 'Oh, she's a cow and he's a sod. And I ain't going to no bleeding cop shop. I'm going to live with you.'

This was no request but an order. What could you do? I merely accepted the fact. 'Right, I agree. You can come home with me and then we will have to see.'

At that point my education began in earnest. I'd got myself a large doll, but not an imitation doll, a real live one and, from what I could make out, a bomb with legs on. Going home that night was like coming home from Hampstead Heath, slightly tiddled, a little dizzy from the merry-go-round I'd been on, and not a little bewildered that the beautiful doll I'd won on the shooting-range had come to life and was walking beside me.

'What's your name, Tich?' I asked her.

'Anna. What's yours?'

'Fynn,' I said. 'Where do you come from?'

I didn't get an answer to this question, and that was the first and last time she didn't answer a question – I gathered later the reason for this. It was because she was afraid that I might have taken her back.

'When did you run away?'

'Oh, three days ago, I think.'

We took the short way home by climbing over the 'cut' bridge and crossing over the railway yards. This was always my way in because we lived next to the railway and it was convenient, to say nothing of the fact that it meant I didn't have to get Mum out of bed to open the front-door.

We got into the scullery by the back-door and then into the kitchen. I lit the gas. For the very first time I saw Anna. God only knows what I expected to see; certainly not what I did see. It wasn't that she was dirty or that her frock was about ten sizes too big; it was the mixture of ginger-pop, Guinness and her paint-tin. She looked like a little savage, smears of various coloured paints all over her face and arms, the front of her frock a complete riot of colour. She looked so funny and so tiny, and her response to my bellow of laughter so reduced her to her cowering self again, that I hurriedly picked her up to the level of the mirror over the mantelpiece and made her look. Her delicious little giggle was like closing the door on November and stepping out into June. I can't say that I looked much different that night. I too was covered in paint. 'A right pair', as Mum later said.

In the middle of all the giggles there was a thump, thump, thump on the wall. That was Mum's signal. 'That you? Your supper's in the oven and don't forget to turn the gas off.'

Instead of the usual, 'OK, Mum, won't be long', this night I opened the door and yelled down the passage, 'Mum, come and see what I've got.'

One thing about Mum, she was never fussed about anything, she took everything in her stride. Bossy, the cat I brought home one night, and Patch the dog, eighteen-year-old Carol, who stayed with us for two years, and Danny from Canada, who stayed about three years. Some people collect stamps or beer-mats; Mum collected waifs and strays, cats, dogs, frogs, people and, as she believed, a whole host of 'little people'. Had she been confronted that night with a lion she'd have made the same comment – 'The poor thing.' One look when she came through the door was enough. 'The poor thing,' she cried, 'what have they done to you?' And then, as an afterthought, to me, 'You look a right mess. Wash your face.' With that, Mum flopped on to her knees and put her arms around Anna.

Being embraced by Mum was like tangling with a gorilla. Mum had arms like other people have legs. Mum had a unique

anatomical structure which still puzzles me, for she had a
fourteen-stone heart in a twelve-stone body. Mum was a real lady
and wherever she may be now she'll still be a lady.

A few minutes of 'ooh's' and 'aah's', then things began to get
organized. Mum heaved herself upright, and with a passing shot
to me to 'get those wet clothes off the child', flung open the
kitchen door, yelling, 'Stan, Carol, come here quick!' Stan's my
younger brother by two years; Carol was one of the waifs or
strays that came and went.

The kitchen and the scullery suddenly erupted – a bath
appeared, kettles of water on gas-rings, towels, soap; the kitchen
range was filled with coal; and there was me trying to undo
sundry hooks and eyes on Anna's clothing. And suddenly there
she was, sitting cross-legged on the table as raw as the day she
was born. Stan said 'Bastard!' Carol said 'Christ!' Mum looked a
bit grim. For a moment that little kitchen blazed with hatred for
someone; that poor little body was bruised and sore. The four
older people in the kitchen were ready to bash someone and for
a time we were lost in our own anger. But Anna sat and grinned,

a huge face-splitting grin. Like some beautiful sprite she sat there, and I believe for the very first time in her life she was entirely and completely happy.

The bath completed, the soup downed and Anna resplendent in Stan's old shirt, we all sat around the kitchen table and took stock of the situation. Questions were asked but no answers were forthcoming. We eventually decided that the day had had enough questions asked. The answers could wait until tomorrow. While Mum went to work getting Anna's clothes clean again, Stan and I made up a bed on an old black leather sofa next door to me.

I slept in the front room, a room stuffed full of aspidistras, a tall-boy with the precious pieces of cut glass displayed on the top, one bed, and sundry bits and pieces scattered around. My room was separated off from the next room by a large baize curtain hung on big wooden rings that slid back and forth with their clack, clack, clack. Behind the curtain was Anna's sofa-bed. Outside my bedroom window was a street lamp and as the window was only covered by lace curtains the bedroom was always

well lit. As I said, our house was right next to the railway, with trains passing all day and all night, but you got used to that. In fact after nineteen years the rumble and rush of the passing trains was more of a lullaby than a noise.

When the bed had been made and all the night preparation attended to, I went back into the kitchen again. There was the little imp enthroned in a cane chair, swaddled in blankets, drinking a cup of hot cocoa. Bossy was sitting on her lap giving a fair imitation of Houdini trying to wriggle out of a strait-jacket, and Patch at her feet, beating time with his tail on the floor. The hiss of the gas-lamp, the bright firelight, the little pools of water on the floor, all turned that little kitchen into a Christmas scene. The Welsh dresser, the shining pots and the black-leaded kitchen-range, with its brass fire-irons and guard, seemed to sparkle. In the midst of it all sat the little princess, clean and shining. This little thing had the most splendid, the most beautiful, copper-coloured hair imaginable, and a face to match. No painted cherub on some church ceiling was this child, but a smiling, giggling, squirming, real live child, her face alight with some inner radiance, her eyes like two blue searchlights.

Earlier in the evening I had said 'Yes' to her question, 'You love me, don't you?' because I was unable to say 'No'. Now I was glad that I had been unable to say 'No', for the answer was 'Yes. Yes. Yes.' How could anyone fail to love this little thing?

Mum gave a bit of a grunt and her usual 'Well, we had better get to bed or we won't be worth anything tomorrow.' And so I picked up Anna and took her along to her bed. The bedclothes were already pulled back and I put her down and made as if to tuck her up, but this was all wrong.

'Ain't you gonna say your prayers?' she asked.

'Well, yes,' I replied, 'when I get to bed.'

'I want to say mine now with you,' she said. So we both got down on our knees and she talked while I listened.

I've been to church many times, and heard many prayers, but none like this. I can't remember much about her prayer except that it started off with 'Dear Mister God, this is Anna talking', and she went on in such a familiar way of talking to Mister God that I had the creepy feeling that if I dared look behind me he would be standing there. I remember her saying, 'Thank you for letting

Fynn love me', and I remember being kissed goodnight, but how I got to bed I don't know.

I lay in bed in some confusion wondering what had hit me. The trains rattled on their way, the fog swirled round the street lamp. It may have been an hour that I had lain there, possibly two, when I heard the clack, clack of the curtain rings and there she was standing at the end of my bed quite visible in the lamplight. For a minute or two I lay there thinking that she was just wanting to reassure herself, when she moved around to the head of my bed.

I said, 'Hi, Tich!'

'Can I get in?' she said in a whisper – she didn't wait for my 'if you want to', but slid in beside me and buried her head in my neck and cried silently, her tears warm and wet on my chest. There was nothing to say, nothing to do but to put my arm around her. I didn't think I would sleep, but I did. I awoke to the sound of stifled giggles, Anna still beside me giggling like a fiend, and Carol, already dressed, standing there giggling, with a morning cup of tea in her hand. All this in less than twelve hours.

CHAPTER TWO

During the next few weeks we tried to find out by a bit of cunning questioning where Anna lived. The gentle approach, the sideways approach, the sneaky approach, all proved to be useless. It seemed quite possible that she had just dropped out of heaven. I was ready to believe this to be true, but Stan, being much more practical than me, didn't agree at all. The only certain thing we knew was that she wasn't going to no bleeding cop shop. By this time I was sure that I had initiated this idea. After all, you don't find an orchid and then put it in the cellar. It wasn't that any of us had anything against the cops, far from it. In those days cops were more like official friends, even if they did clip you round the ear with a glove full of dried peas if they caught you up to any funny stuff. No, as I said, you can't lock a sunbeam in the dark. Besides, we all wanted her to stay.

By this time Anna was a firm favourite down our street. Whenever the kids played team-games like four sticks everyone wanted Anna on their side. She had a natural aptitude for all games: whip tops, skipping, fag cards. What she couldn't do with a hoop and a skimmer wasn't worth doing.

Our street, twenty houses big, was a regular United Nations; the only colours in kids we didn't have were green ones and blue ones, we had nearly every other colour. Our street was a nice street. Nobody had any money, but in all the years I lived there, I can never remember anyone's front-door being shut in the daytime, or, for that matter, for most of the night either. It was a nice street to live in and all the people were friendly, but after a few weeks of Anna the street and the people in it took on a buttercup glow.

Even our boss-eyed cat, Bossy, mellowed. Bossy was a fighting tabby with lace-edged ears who regarded all humans as inferiors, but under Anna's influence Bossy started to stay at home more often and very soon treated Anna as an equal. I could stand by the back-door and yell myself silly for Bossy, but he wouldn't budge for me, but for Anna, well, that was a different thing. One call and he simply materialized with an idiot grin on his face.

Bossy was about twelve pounds of fighting fury, and I've got the scars to prove it. The cat's-meat man used to leave the meat under the knocker, wrapped up in newspaper. Bossy used to lurk in the dark passageway, or under the stairs, waiting for someone to reach up for the cat's meat, at which moment he would launch himself like a fury, all teeth and claws, using whatever was available to get up to his meal. If a human leg or arm could be used to claw his way up to the meat, Bossy would use it. Anna tamed him in one day. She lectured him with an admonishing finger on the vice of gluttony and the virtues of patience and good manners. In the end Bossy could make his meal last for about five minutes, with Anna feeding him bit by bit, instead of the usual thirty seconds. As for Patch the dog, he sat for hours practising beating new rhythms with his tail.

In the back-garden was an odd collection of rabbits, pigeons, fan-tailed doves, frogs, and a couple of grass-snakes. The back-garden, or 'The Yard' as it was called, was for the East End a fairly sizeable place. A bit of grass and a few flowers and a large tree some forty feet high. All in all Anna had quite a lot to practise her magic on. But no one fell under her spell more completely or willingly than me. My work, which was in oils, was not more than five minutes' walk away from home, so I was always home for dinner at about 12.30. Up to this time the answer to Mum's question as to what time I would be home that night as I left for the afternoon's stint had been 'Some time before midnight'. Now things were different. I was seen off by Anna from the top of the street, kissed wetly, promising to be back about six in the evening. Knocking-off time usually meant a few pints in the pub on the way home and a few games of darts with Cliff and George, but not now. When the hooter went I was off home. I didn't run exactly but walked very briskly.

That walk home was a pleasure; every step was one step nearer. The road I had to travel curved to the left in a gentle arc, and

I had to walk just more than half the distance before the top of our turning came into sight, and there she was. Come rain or shine, snow or icy wind, Anna was always there, not once did she miss this meeting, except – but that comes later. I doubt if ever lovers met more joyously. When she saw me coming round the bend of the road she came to meet me.

Anna's ability to polish any situation was truly extraordinary. She had some uncanny knack of doing the right thing at the right time to get the most out of an occasion. I've always thought that children ran towards those they loved, but not Anna. When she saw me she started to walk towards me, not too slowly, but not too quickly. My first sight of her was too far away to distinguish her features; she might have been any other child, but she wasn't. Her beautiful copper hair stood out for miles, there was no mistaking her.

After her first few weeks with us she always wore a deep-green ribbon in her hair for this meeting. Looking back, I feel sure that the walk towards me was deliberate and calculated. She had grasped the meaning of these meetings and seen almost instantly just how much to dramatize them, how long to prolong them in order to wring out their total content. For me this minute or two of walk towards her had a rounded-off perfection; no more could be added to it, and nothing could be taken away without completely destroying it.

Whatever it was she projected across that intervening space was almost solid. Her bobbing hair, the twinkle in her eyes, that enormous and impudent grin, flicked like a high-voltage charge across the space that separated us. Sometimes she would, without any words, just touch my hand in greeting; sometimes the last few steps transformed her, she let everything go with one gigantic explosion, and flung herself at me. So many times she would stop just in front of me and hold out her closed hands. I learned rapidly what to expect on these occasions. It meant that she had found something that had moved her. We would stop and inspect whatever the day's find was – perhaps a beetle, a caterpillar, or a stone. We would look silently, heads bowed over today's treasure. Her eyes were large deep pools of questions. How? Why? What? I'd meet her gaze and nod my head; this was enough, she'd nod in reply.

The first time this happened, my heart seemed to come off its hook. I struggled to hold on. I wanted to put my arms around

her to comfort her. Happily, I managed to do the right thing. I guess some passing angel nudged me at the right moment. Unhappiness is to be comforted, and so perhaps too is fear, but these particular moments with Anna were moments of pure and undiluted wonder. These were her own and very private moments which she chose to share with me, and I was honoured to share them with her. I could not comfort her, I would not have dared to trespass. All that I could do was to see as she saw, to be moved as she was moved. That kind of suffering you must bear alone. As she said so simply, 'It's for me and Mister God', and there's no answer to that.

The evening meal at home was more or less fixed. Mum, being the daughter of an Irish farmer, was given to making stews. A large black iron pot and an equally large black iron kettle were the two most used utensils in the kitchen. Often the only way one could distinguish the stew from the brew was that tea always came in large cups and stew was put on plates. Here the difference ended, for the brew often had as much solid matter in it as did the stew.

Mum was a great believer in the saying that 'Nature grows cures for everything'. There wasn't a weed, or a flower, or a leaf that wasn't a specific cure for some ailment or other. Even the outside shed was pressed into use for growing cobwebs. Some people have sacred cows or sacred cats, Mum had sacred spiders. I never quite understood the reasoning concerning spiders' webs, but all cuts and abrasions were plastered with spiders' webs. If spiders' webs were not available there were always fag papers under the clock in the kitchen. These were well licked and stuck over the cut. Our house was littered with bottles of juices, dried leaves and bunches of this, that and the other, hanging from the ceiling. All ailments were treated the same way – rub it, lick it, or if you can't lick it, spit on it, or 'Drink this, it'll do you good'.

Whatever the value of these things, one thing was certain, nobody was ever ill. The only time the doctor entered our house was when something was suspected of being broken, and when

Stan was born. No matter that the brew, or to give it its full title, 'the darlin' brew', and the stew looked the same, they tasted wonderful and meals were certainly man-sized.

Mum and Anna shared many likes and dislikes; perhaps the simplest and the most beautiful sharing was their attitude towards Mister God. Most people I knew used God as an excuse for their failure. 'He should have done this', or 'Why has God done this to me?', but with Mum and Anna difficulties and adversities were merely occasions for doing something. Ugliness was the chance to make beautiful. Sadness was the chance to make glad. Mister God was always available to them. A stranger would have been excused for believing that Mister God lived with us, but then Mum and Anna believed he did. Very rarely did any conversation exclude Mister God in some way or other.

After the evening meal was finished and all the bits and pieces put away Anna and I would settle down to some activity, generally of her choosing. Fairy stories were dismissed as mere pretend stories; living was real and living was interesting and by and large fun. Reading the Bible wasn't a great success. She tended to regard it as a primer, strictly for the infants. The message of the Bible was simple and any half-wit could grasp it in thirty minutes flat! Religion was for doing things, not for reading about doing things. Once you had got the message there wasn't much point in going over and over the same old ground. Our local parson was taken aback when he asked her about God. The conversation went as follows:

'Do you believe in God?'

'Yes.'

'Do you know what God is?'

'Yes.'

'What is God then?'

'He's God!'

'Do you go to church?'

'No.'

'Why not?'

'Because I know it all!'

'What do you know?'

'I know to love Mister God and to love people and cats and dogs and spiders and flowers and trees', and the catalogue went on, '– with all of me.'

28

Carol grinned at me and Stan made a face and I hurriedly put a cigarette in my mouth and indulged in a bout of coughing. There's nothing much you can do in the face of that kind of accusation, for that's what it amounted to. ('Out of the mouths of babes ...') Anna had bypassed all the non-essentials and distilled centuries of learning into one sentence – 'And God said love me, love them, and love it, and don't forget to love yourself.'

The whole business of adults going to church filled Anna with suspicion. The idea of collective worship went against her sense of private conversations with Mister God. As for going to church to meet Mister God, that was preposterous. After all, if Mister God wasn't everywhere, he wasn't anywhere. For her, church-going and 'Mister God' talks had no necessary connection. For her the whole thing was transparently simple. You went to church to get the message when you were very little. Once you had got it, you went out and did something about it. Keeping on going to church was because you hadn't got the message, or didn't understand it, or it was 'just for swank'.

After the evening meal I always read to Anna, books on all manner of subjects from poetry to astronomy. After a year of reading, she ended up with three favourite books. The first was a large picture-book with nothing in it but photographs of snowflakes and frost patterns. The second book was Cruden's *Complete Concordance*, and the third, of all the strange books to choose, was Manning's *Geometry of Four Dimensions*. Each of these books had a catalytic effect on Anna. She devoured them utterly, and out of their digestion she produced her own philosophy.

One of her pleasures was my reading to her that part of the concordance given over to the meaning of proper names. Each name was read in strict alphabetical order and the meaning given. After each name had been tasted and thought over she

30

made her decision as to its rightness. Most times she shook her head sadly and disappointedly; it wasn't good enough. Sometimes it was just right; the name, the person, the meaning, all fitted perfectly for her and, with a burst of excitement, she would bounce up and down on my lap and say, 'Put it down, put it down.' This meant writing the name in large block capitals on a slip of paper, which she would stare at with complete concentration for a minute or two and then place in one of her many boxes. A moment to compose herself, and, 'Next one, please.' So we would go on. Some names took all of fifteen minutes or more to decide one way or the other. The decision was made in complete silence. On the occasions when I moved to a more comfortable position, or started to speak, I was reprimanded with a tilt of the head, a full-blooded stare and a small finger placed gently but firmly on my lips. I learned to wait patiently. It took us about four months to work through the section on proper names, moments of high excitement and moments of low disappointment, none of which I understood at that time. Later I was let into the secret.

Since our first meeting God had been given the title Mister God; the Holy Spirit, for some reason only known to her, was given the name Vehrak. I never heard her use the name Jesus. Whenever she referred to Jesus it was as Mister God's boy. One evening we were working our way through the J's and came eventually to Jesus. I had hardly got the name out before I was stopped by a 'No!', a wagging finger and 'Next one, please.' Who was I to argue? I pressed on. The next name on the list was JETHER. I had to pronounce this three times, and then turning to me she said, 'Read what it says.' So I read:

'JETHER meaning he that excels or remains, or that examines, searches, or a line or string.'

The effect of this was electric, catastrophic. With a blur of movement she had slipped off my lap, twisted about to face me and stood crouched with hands clenched, the whole of her being shaking with excitement. For one horrifying moment I thought she was ill or having a fit, but that wasn't the explanation. Whatever the explanation was it went deeper than anything I could understand. She was filled with joy. She kept saying, 'It's true. I know it. It's true. It's true. I know it.' With that

31

she fled out into the yard. I made to go out after her but Mum put out a hand and held me back, saying, 'Leave her alone, she's happy. She's got the eye.' Half an hour passed before she returned. Without a word she climbed on to my lap, gave me one of her special grins and said, 'Please write the name big for me tonight,' and then went to sleep. She didn't even wake up when I put her to bed. It was months before the word epilepsy faded from my thoughts.

Mum always said that she pitied the girl that I married, for she would have to put up with my three mistresses – Mathematics, Physics and Electrical Gadgetry. I would rather read and practise these subjects than eat or sleep. I never bought myself a wrist-watch or a fountain-pen, and very rarely did I buy new clothes, but I never went anywhere without a slide-rule. This device fascinated Anna and soon she had to have a slip-stick of her own. Having mastered the whole business of counting numbers, she was soon extracting roots with the aid of her slip-stick before she could add two numbers together. Users of slip-sticks soon fall into a stable method of using this device. It's held in the left hand, leaving the right hand free to hold the pencil; the 'cursor' can be moved with the thumb and the sliding-scale tapped against the work-bench. One of my particular pleasures was seeing the copper-crowned diminutive child doing her 'workings out', as she called it – looking down from a height of six foot or more and saying, 'How you doing, Tich?', seeing her head screw round and upward and watching one delicious wiggle start from her toes, pass up her body, to be tossed off the top of her head in a foam of silky copper thread, with a grin of absolute joy.

Some evenings were given over to piano-playing. I play a fairly good honky-tonk piano, a bit of Mozart, a bit of Chopin, and a few pieces like 'Anitra's Dance' just for good measure. On the top of the piano were several electronic devices. One device, the oscilloscope, held all the magic of a fairy wand for Anna. We'd sit in this room for hours on end playing single notes, watching the green spot on the 'scope do its glowing dance. The whole exercise of relating sounds that one heard with the ears to the visual shape of those sounds actively seen on the little tube's face was a source of never-ending delight.

What sounds we captured, Anna and I! A caterpillar chewing a leaf was like a hungry lion, a fly in a jam-jar sounded like an air-ship, a match being struck sounded like an explosion. All these sounds and a thousand more were amplified and made available, both in sound form and visible form. Anna had found a brand new world to explore. How much meaning it had for her I didn't know, perhaps it was only an elaborate plaything for her, but her squeals of delight were enough for me.

It was only some time during the next summer that I began to realize that the concepts of frequency and wavelength were meaningful to her, that she did, in fact, know and understand what she was hearing and looking at. One summer afternoon all the kids were playing in the street when a large bumble-bee appeared on the scene.

One of the kids said, 'How many times does it flap its wings in a minute?'

'Must be millions,' said another kid.

Anna dashed indoors humming a low-pitched hum. I was sitting on the doorstep. With a few quick prods at the piano she had identified the note, her hum and the drone of the bee. Coming to the door again, she said, 'Can I have your slip-stick?' In a moment or two she shouted out, 'A bee flaps its wings such-and-such times a second.' Nobody believed her, but she was only a few counts out.

Every sound that could be captured was captured. Meals began to be punctuated with such remarks as, 'Do you know a mosquito flaps its wings so many times a second? or a fly so many times a second?'

All these games led inevitably to making music. Each separate note had by this time been examined minutely, and a sound depended on how many times it wiggled per second. Soon she was making little melodies to which I added the harmonies. Little pieces of music entitled 'Mummy', 'Mr Jether's Dance', and 'Laughter' soon began to echo around the house. Anna had begun to compose. I suppose Anna only had one problem in her little life – the lack of hours per day. There was too much to do, too many exciting things to find out.

Another of Anna's magic carpets was the microscope. It revealed a little world made big. A world of intricate shape and pattern, a world of creatures too small to see with the naked eye; even the very dirt itself was wonderful.

Before all this adventuring into these hidden worlds, Mister God had been Anna's friend and companion, but now, well this was going a bit too far. If Mister God had done all this, he was something larger than Anna had bargained for. It needed a bit of thinking about. For the next few weeks activity slowed down; she still played with the other children in the street; she was still as sweet and exciting as ever, but she became more inward-looking, more inclined to sit alone, high in the tree in the yard, with only Bossy as her companion. Whichever way she looked there seemed to be more and more of everything.

During these few weeks Anna slowly took stock of all she knew, walking about gently touching things as if looking for some clue that she had missed. She didn't talk much in this period. In reply to questions she answered as simply as she could, apologizing for her absence by the gentlest of smiles, saying without words, 'I'm sorry about all this. I'll be back as soon as I've sorted this little puzzle out.' Finally the whole thing came to a head.

She turned to me. 'Can I come to bed with you tonight?' she asked.

I nodded.

'Now,' she replied.

She hopped off my lap, took my hand, and pulled me to the door. I went.

I haven't told you Anna's way of solving problems, have I? If Anna was confronted with a situation that didn't come out easily, there was only one thing to do – take your clothes off. So there we were in bed, the street lamp lighting up the room, her head cupped in her hands, and both elbows firmly planted on my chest. I waited. She chose to remain like that for about ten minutes, getting her argument in its proper order, and then she launched forth.

'Mister God made everything, didn't he?'

There was no point in saying that I didn't really know. I said 'Yes.'

'Even the dirt and the stars and the animals and the people and

the trees and everything, and the pollywogs?' The pollywogs were those little creatures that we had seen under the microscope.

I said, 'Yes, he made everything.'

She nodded her agreement. 'Does Mister God love us truly?'

'Sure thing,' I said. 'Mister God loves everything.'

'Oh,' she said. 'Well then, why does he let things get hurt and dead?' Her voice sounded as if she felt she had betrayed a sacred trust, but the question had been thought and it had to be spoken.

'I don't know,' I replied. 'There's a great many things about Mister God that we don't know about.'

'Well then,' she continued, 'if we don't know many things about Mister God, how do we know he loves us?'

I could see that this was going to be one of those times, but thank goodness she didn't expect an answer to her question for she hurried on: 'Them pollywogs, I could love them till I bust, but they wouldn't know, would they? I'm million times bigger than they are and Mister God is million times bigger than me, so how do I know what Mister God does?'

She was silent for a little while. Later I thought that at this moment she was taking her last look at babyhood. Then she went on:

'Fynn, Mister God doesn't love us.' She hesitated. 'He doesn't really, you know, only people can love. I love Bossy, but Bossy don't love me. I love the pollywogs, but they don't love me. I love you, Fynn, and you love me, don't you?'

I tightened my arm about her.

'You love me because you are people. I love Mister God truly, but he don't love me.'

It sounded to me like a death-knell. 'Damn and blast,' I thought. 'Why does this have to happen to people? Now she's lost everything.' But I was wrong. She had got both feet planted firmly on the next stepping-stone.

'No,' she went on, 'no, he don't love me, not like you do, it's different, it's millions of times bigger.'

I must have made some movement or noise for she levered herself upright and sat on her haunches and giggled. Then she launched herself at me and undid my little pang of hurt, cut out the useless spark of jealousy with the delicate sureness of a surgeon.

'Fynn, you can love better than any people that ever was, and so can I, can't I? But Mister God is different. You see, Fynn, people can only love outside and can only kiss outside, but Mister God can love you right inside, and Mister God can kiss you right inside, so it's different. Mister God ain't like us; we are a little bit like Mister God, but not much yet.'

It seemed to me to reduce itself to the fact that we were like God because of some similarities but God was not like us because of our difference. Her inner fires had refined her ideas, and like some alchemist she had turned lead into gold. Gone were all the human definitions of God, like Goodness, Mercy, Love and Justice, for these were merely props to describe the indescribable.

'You see, Fynn, Mister God is different from us because he can finish things and we can't. I can't finish loving you because I shall be dead millions of years before I can finish, but Mister God can finish loving you, and so it's not the same kind of love, is it? Even Mister Jether's love is not the same as Mister God's because he only came here to make us remember.'

The first salvo was enough for me; it all needed a bit of thinking about, but I wasn't going to be spared the rest of her artillery.

'Fynn, why do people have fights and wars and things?'

I explained to the best of my ability.

'Fynn, what is the word for when you see it in a different way?'

After a minute or two scrabbling about, the precise phrase she wanted was dredged out of me, the phrase 'point of view'.

'Fynn, that's the difference. You see, everybody has got a point of view, but Mister God hasn't. Mister God has only points *to* view.'

At this moment my one desire was to get up and go for a long, long walk. What was this child up to? What had she done? In the first place, God could finish things off, I couldn't. I'll accept that, but what did it mean? It seemed to me that she had taken the whole idea of God outside the limitation of time and placed him firmly in the realm of eternity.

What about this difference between 'a point of view' and 'points to view'? This stumped me, but a little further questioning cleared up the mystery. 'Points to view' was a clumsy term. She meant 'viewing points'. The second salvo had been fired. Humanity in general had an infinite number of points of view, whereas Mister God had an infinite number of viewing points. When I put it to her this way and asked her if that was what she meant, she nodded her agreement and then waited to see if I enjoyed the taste. Let me see now. Humanity has an infinite number of points of view. God has an infinite number of viewing points. That means that – God is everywhere. I jumped.

Anna burst into peals of laughter. 'You see,' she said, 'you see?' I did too.

'There's another way that Mister God is different.' We obviously hadn't finished yet. 'Mister God can know things and people from the inside too. We only know them from the outside, don't we? So you see, Fynn, people can't talk about Mister God from the outside; you can only talk about Mister God from the inside of him.'

Another fifteen minutes or so were spent in polishing up these arguments and then, with an 'Isn't it lovely?' she kissed me and tucked herself under my arm, ready for sleep.

About ten minutes later: 'Fynn?'

'Yes?'

'Fynn, you know that book about four dimensions?'

'Yes, what about it?'

'I know where number four is; it goes inside me.'

I'd had enough for that night, and said with all the firmness and authority I could muster: 'Go to sleep now, that's enough talking for tonight. Go to sleep or I'll paddle your bottom.'

She made a little screech, looked at me, and grinned and squirmed in closer to me. 'You wouldn't!' she said sleepily.

Anna's first summer with us was days of adventures and visits. We visited Southend-on-Sea, Kew Gardens, the Kensington Museum and a thousand other places, most times alone, but sometimes with a gang of other kids. Our first excursion outside the East End was 'up the other end'. For anyone not familiar with that term it simply means west of Aldgate pump.

On this occasion she was dressed in a tartan skirt with shirt-blouse, a black tammy, black shoes with large shiny buckles and tartan socks. The skirt was tightly pleated so that a twirl produced a parachute-like effect. Anna walked like a pro, jumped like Bambi, flew like a bird, and balanced like a daring tightrope-walker on the curbs. Anna copied her walk from Millie, who was a pro, head held high, the slight sway of body making her skirts swing, a smile on her face, a twinkle in her eye, and – you were defenceless. People looked and people smiled. Anna was a burst of sunlight after weeks of gloom. Of course people smiled, they couldn't help it. Anna was completely aware of these glances from passers-by, occasionally turning her head to look at me with a big, big grin of pleasure. Danny said she never walked, she made a royal progress. Her progress was halted from time to time by her subjects: stray pussies, dogs, pigeons and horses, to say nothing of postmen, milk-men, bus-conductors and policemen.

As we walked west of Aldgate pump the buildings got grander and bigger and Anna's mouth opened further and further. She walked round and round in small circles, she walked backwards, sideways and every way. Finally she stopped in bewilderment, tugged at my sleeve, and asked, 'Does kings and queens live in them and are they all palaces?'

She didn't find the Bank of England very impressive, nor for that matter St Paul's; the pigeons won hands down. After a little talk we decided to go into the service. She was very uncomfortable, fidgeting about the whole while. As soon as the service was over we hurried outside and made straight for the pigeons. She sat on the pavement and fed them with great pleasure. I stood a few paces off and just watched her. Her eyes flicked from place to place, at the doors of the cathedral, the passers-by, the traffic and the pigeons. Occasionally she tossed her head in disapproval of something. I looked about me to see what it was that affected her so much. There was nothing that I could see which would account for her mood.

After some months I could now read her distress signal accurately. That sharp little toss of the head wasn't a good sign. To me it always looked as if she was trying to dislodge some unpleasant thought in the same way that one might shake a money-box to get the coins out.

I went over to her and stood waiting. Most times just being near her was all the trigger she needed. The move towards her wasn't in order to give her counsel. Long ago I had given that up. Her reply to the question, 'What's up, Tich?' was invariably the same: 'I can get it, I think.' On those occasions when she couldn't get the answers, then and only then would she ask questions. No, my reason for moving over to her was simply that my ears were at the ready if she needed them. She didn't, and that was a very bad sign.

From St Paul's we moved off towards Hyde Park. After all these months I was beginning to be rather proud of the fact that more and more I was learning to think along with Anna. I was beginning to understand the way she thought and the way she said things. This particular afternoon I had forgotten, no, not forgotten, hadn't realized one simple fact. It was this. Up to now Anna's visual horizon had been one of houses, factories, cranes and a toppling inwards of structure. Suddenly there were the open, and to her, the very open, spaces of the park. I wasn't ready for her reaction. She took one look, buried her face in my stomach, grabbed me with both hands, and howled. I picked her up and she clung to me like a limpet, arms tight around my neck and legs around my waist, sobbing into my neck. I made all the appropriate noises, but this didn't help much.

After a few minutes she took a sneaky look over her shoulder and stopped crying.

I said, 'Want to go home, Tich?' and she shook her head.

'You can put me down now,' she said.

I think I had expected her to give one whoop and gallop off across the grass. A couple of hearty sniffs and a moment or two to gain her composure, and we started off to explore the park, but she held on to my hand very tightly. Like any other child, Anna had her fears, but unlike most children she recognized them. And with this recognition came the realization that she could go on in spite of them.

How can any adult know the exact weight of that fright? Does it mean that the child is timid, alarmed, anxious, petrified, or frozen stiff with terror? Is a ten-headed monster more frightening than an Idea? If she hadn't exactly mastered her fear, whatever it was, she had got it well under control. By now she was prepared to let go of my hand, to make a little sortie after something that interested her, always looking back to make sure I was there. So I stopped in my tracks and waited for her. She was still a little bit scared and she knew that I was aware that she was scared too. The fact that I stopped whenever she let go of my hand brought forth a grateful little smile of acknowledgement.

My mind flipped back to the time when I was her age. My mother and father had taken me to Southend-on-Sea. The sight of the sea and the press of all those people was like being hit by a bus. I had been holding my father's hand when I first had a sight of the sea, and then, suddenly, I was holding a stranger's hand. I can't remember very much except that then and there the world came to an end. So I did have some inkling of her fears, whatever they were.

Her little explorations were slowly bringing things back to normal. She'd return with her usual treasures, different shaped leaves, stone, bits of twigs, etc. Her enthusiasm could not be restrained any longer.

Suddenly I heard the gruff shout of a park-keeper. I turned, and there she was, kneeling in front of a flower-bed. I had forgotten to tell her to Keep off the Grass. Anna would not have given way to Lucifer himself and certainly not to a park-keeper. Having negotiated one catastrophe, I didn't want to face another. I ran and scooped her into my arms and stood her down on the pathway.

'He,' she said indignantly, pointing an accusing finger, 'told me to get off the grass.'

'Yes,' I replied, 'you're not supposed to be on this bit of grass.'

'But it's the best bit,' she said.

'See those words.' I pointed to the notice. 'They say "Keep off the grass".'

She studied the notice with great concentration as I spelt out the words for her.

Late that afternoon, while we were sitting on the grass eating chocolate, she said, 'Them words.'

'What words?' I asked.

'Them words that say to keep off the grass – them words are like that church we went to this morning.'

Then it all became apparent. Like the flower-beds the church service had been to Anna nothing less than a notice saying 'Keep off the grass'. She couldn't get at the best bits. To be inside a church, not at a church service, but simply to be inside, was for Anna like visiting a very, very special friend, and visiting a very special friend is a happy occasion, and that, surely, is a good enough reason to dance. Inside a church Anna danced; it was the best bit. Church services, therefore, like the 'Keep off the grass' notices, did not allow her to have the best bit. I smiled as I pictured the kind of service that Anna would have liked. I'm not so sure that Mister God wouldn't have preferred it too!

Having started to unburden herself, she pressed on with, 'You know when I cried?'

I grunted my attention.

'It didn't half make me small, so small I nearly got lost.' This in a small and far-off voice, and then, zooming back from an infinity of space and landing with a thump on my chest, she went on triumphantly, 'But I didn't, did I?'

It was some time towards the end of this first summer that she made two most startling discoveries. The first was seeds – that things grew from seeds, that all this beauty, these flowers, these trees, this lovely grass, came from seeds, and moreover that you could actually hold these seeds in your hands. The second major discovery was writing, that books and writing in general had a much more exciting aspect to them than merely being the machinery for telling stories. She saw writing as a portable memory, as a means of exchanging information.

These two discoveries started off a frenzy of activity. Anna's thought-processes and bodily activity were such that on occasions it was very nearly possible actually to see the pictures in her mind.

The first day she held flower seeds in her hand was such a time. There was no need for words; her actions and thoughts

spoke for themselves. There she was in front of some wild flow-ers, kneeling down with a sprinkling of seeds in her hands. Her eyes located her thoughts; she looked at the seeds and her brow furrowed. She looked over her shoulder into the distance and her eyes popped in amazement, back to the seeds, back over her shoulder. Finally she stood up, looked outwards, where to I do not know – and slowly turned a full circle. By the time she faced me her inner lamps had been turned full on.

I didn't have to be told what was going on in her head; it was plain to see. The sharp needle of her thoughts had sewn together this flower-filled scene that we now occupied with the bare patches of land in the East End. Of course seeds could be transported from one place to another – so – why not do it? She looked at me with large question-marks in her eyes, and without a word I gave her my clean pocket-handkerchief. She spread this on the ground and with infinite care shook the seed pods. The white handkerchief was soon covered with the dark grains of the seeds.

This activity of collecting seeds was one that I saw thousands of times; never once was she violent with any seed pod, and on each and every occasion came the moment of decision: 'Have I taken too many?' 'Are there enough left?' Sometimes the decision could only be made after a careful inspection of the seed pods. If she decided she had taken too many she would then proceed to portion out those seeds she had collected, sprinkling very care-fully some portion back on the land again. Mister God went up about ten points in her estimation with regard to these seeds as she said, 'Ain't Mister God wonderful!'

Anna was not only deeply in love with Mister God; she was proud of him. Anna's pride in Mister God grew and grew to such dimensions that in some idiot moment I wondered if Mister God ever went pink with pleasure. Whatever feelings people have had about Mister God over the many centuries, I'm very sure of one thing, nobody has ever liked Mister God more than Anna.

These excursions into the realm of seeds meant that a large supply of envelopes was carried with us and a large pouch was fixed around Anna's waist. The pouch was fixed on to a rather splendid beaded belt made for her by Millie. Millie was one of the dozen or so pros who had a house at the top of the street. Millie and Jackie were, according to Anna, the two most beautiful young ladies in the whole world. Between this young prostitute and Anna there developed a mutual-admiration society. Just in passing, Millie had the rich name of the Venus de Mile End.

Anna's other major discovery of that summer grew into a very complex activity, for our house suddenly blossomed with little blue notebooks and slips of paper. When confronted with something new, Anna would accost the nearest passer-by, and hold out notebook and pencil, with a 'Please write that down big, please'.

CHAPTER THREE

This request to 'write it down big' often produced a somewhat startled reaction. Anna's presentation on these occasions was like a stick of dynamite with a very, very short fuse and it frightened some people. To be confronted by a red-headed five-year-old kid, to have a notebook and pencil thrust into your hand and to be requested to 'write it down big' was for a lot of people unnerving to say the least. People shied away with that kind of look; they replied with 'Buzz off, kid', 'Don't bother me, kid', but Anna expected this sort of thing and pressed on regardless. Anna's ship of discovery was now fully under way. True, it might leak a bit here and there and the seas of knowledge could become a little rough at times but there was no turning back. There were things to be discovered and Anna meant to discover them.

Many and many an evening I would be sitting on the steps smoking a fag and watching her asking people to 'write it down big', enjoying her search for knowledge. One particular evening, after a row of refusals on the part of passers-by, Anna began to sag. I reckoned it was about time to dish out a few words of comfort. I levered myself off the steps and crossed the road to her.

She pointed to a broken-off stump of an iron railing. 'I want somebody to write about that, but they don't see it.'

'Perhaps they are too busy,' I suggested.

'No it ain't. They don't see it. They don't know what I mean.'

This last reply was uttered with a kind of deep and inward sadness; it was a sentence that I was to hear more and more. 'They don't see it. They don't see it.'

I had read the disappointment on her face and knew what to do – or thought I knew. This was the kind of situation that I figured I could handle. I picked her up and held her close to me.

'Don't be too disappointed, Tich.'

'Not disappointed. Sad.'

'Never mind,' I said, 'I'll write it down big for you.'

She wriggled herself out of my arms and stood on the pavement, her hands fiddling with the notebook and pencil, head bowed and with tears on her cheeks. My mind raced around in circles. A number of methods of approach jostled each other. Just as I was about to 'put it all right again' that passing angel fetched me a crack on the skull again. So I remained silent and waited. She stood there in utter dejection. I knew for certain, I told myself, knew for certain that she wanted to run to my arms, knew that she wanted comforting, but she just stood there wrestling inwardly. Trams clanked on their way, people shopped, barrow-boys shouted their wares, and there we stood, me fighting against picking her up and she staring at some new picture painted on her mind.

At last she looked up and her eyes met mine. It suddenly got cold, and I wanted to hit somebody. I knew this look, I had seen it before in other people and it had happened to me more than once. Like some monstrous iceberg appearing out of the fog the word formed, welling up from deep inside me, haloed with tears but none the less clear to see. Anna was mourning. All the doors of her eyes and heart stood wide open and that lonely cell of her inmost being stood plain to see.

'I don't want you to write nuffink.' She tried out a smile but it didn't work too well, and with a sniff she continued, 'I know what I see and I know what you see, but some people don't see nuffink and – and –.' She threw herself into my arms and sobbed.

On that evening in a street in East London I stood with a child in my arms and looked into that lonely cell of humanity. No book-learning, no lecture has shown me more than those few moments. Lonely the cell may be, but dark never. It wasn't dark behind those tear-filled eyes, but a blaze of light. And God made man in his own image, not in shape, not in intelligence, not in eyes or ears, not in hands or feet, but in this total inwardness. In here was the image of God. It isn't the Devil in humanity that makes man a lonely creature, it's his Godlikeness. It's the fullness of the Good that can't get out or can't find its proper 'other place' that makes for loneliness.

Anna's misery was for others. They just could not see the beauty of that broken iron stump, the colours, the crystalline shapes; they could not see the possibilities there. Anna wanted them to join with her in this exciting new world but they could not imagine themselves to be so small that this jagged fracture could become a world of iron mountains, of iron plains with crystal trees. It was a new world to explore, a world of the imagination, a world where few people would or could follow her. In this broken-off stump was a whole new realm of possibilities to be explored and to be enjoyed.

Mister God most certainly enjoyed it, but then Mister God didn't at all mind making himself small. People thought that Mister God was very big and that's where they made a big mistake. Obviously Mister God could be any size he wanted to be. 'If he couldn't be little, how could he know what it's like to be a ladybird?' Indeed, how could he? So, like Alice in Wonderland, Anna ate of the cake of imagination and altered her size to fit the occasion. After all, Mister God did not have only one point of view but an infinity of viewing points, and the whole purpose of living was to be like Mister God. So far as Anna was concerned, being good, being generous, being kind, praying, and all that kind of stuff had very little to do with Mister God. They were, in the jargon of today, merely a 'spin-off'. This sort of thing was just 'playing it safe', and Anna was going to have none of it. No! Religion was all about *being* like Mister God and it was here that things could get a little tough. The instructions weren't to be good and kind and loving, etc., and it therefore followed that you would be more like Mister God. No! The whole point of being alive was to *be* like Mister God and then you couldn't help but be good and kind and loving, could you?

'If you get like Mister God, you don't know you are, do you?'

'Are what?' I questioned.

'Good and kind and loving.'

This last comment was delivered in her throw-away tone of voice as if it were insignificant and irrelevant. I knew this one of old. Either you had to pretend it hadn't happened or start asking questions. A moment or two of hesitation on my part as I watched the grin spread from her toes and explode in one short sharp hoot of mirth and I realized that she had sprung the trap. She had something to say and had forced me into asking the question. If I hadn't done it then I would have had to sooner or later so...

'OK, Tich. What's all this goodness and kindness and loving lark then?'

'Well,' and the tone of her voice slid down the roller-coaster of excitement, shot up the other side and took off. 'Well, if you think you are, you ain't.'

From my position at the bottom of this particular class I asked, 'How come?'

I thought I had got the drift of this conversation and reckoned I was waiting for her about two steps ahead. She had signalled a right turn and I was waiting for her, but suddenly she took a left-handed U-turn and sped back against the oncoming arguments. Thrown off balance by this sudden switch, I could do no more than walk back to where she was waiting.

'Right. Give!' I said.

'You don't expect Mister God *knows* he is good and kind and loving, do you?'

I don't suppose I had ever given this a moment's thought, but put like that there was only one answer to give, even though I wasn't convinced of the truth of it.

'I guess not,' I replied, with some hesitation.

The question 'Why?' got stuck somewhere between my brain-box and my vocal chords. I should have known that the whole of this conversation was leading to some conclusion, some idea, some statement that satisfied her completely. She gathered herself, holding her excitement in check.

Suddenly, with an explosive gasp, she said, 'Mister God don't know he is good and kind and loving. Mister God is – is – empty.'

Now I'll accept that the stone that bruises my toe isn't really there. I don't mind entertaining the idea that everything is an illusion, but that Mister God is empty simply goes against the grain. It stands to reason that Mister God is full! Full of knowing, full of love, full of compassion – you name it, and he is full of it. Why God is like some – some gigantic Christmas stocking full of good presents, inexhaustible, showering untold and unnumbered presents upon his children. Damnation, of course he's full! That's what I was taught and that's how it was – or was it?

I got no more from Anna that day or for several days after. I stewed in my own juice. The idea that Mister God was empty milled around in my brain. Of course it was ridiculous but it just stuck there. As a picture formed in my mind, I got more and more embarrassed and more and more ashamed. I hadn't seen this picture with such clarity before, but there he was, Mister God all dressed up in a dress-suit, top-hat and a wand, producing rabbits out of a hat. You put up your hand and asked for a motor-car, a thousand pounds, or what you will, and Mister God waved his magic wand and out it all came. In the end I saw my picture of Mister God – a kindly, benevolent and bewhiskered MAGICIAN.

A few days later, after a lot of wondering how came this idea that Mister God was quite empty, I asked the question that had puzzled me for days.

'Tich! What's with this Mister God being empty stuff?'

She turned to me eagerly. I distinctly got the impression that she had waited for this question for days but could do nothing until I had seen my picture of Mister God the great magician.

'When the world went all red through the bit of glass, and the colour from the flower.'

I remembered that all right. We had talked about transmitted light and reflected light: that light took on the colour of the glass through which it was transmitted, that the colour of the yellow flower was due to reflected light. We had seen the colours of the spectrum with the aid of a prism, we had looked at Newton's coloured spinning disc and had mixed all the colours of the spectrum back to white again. I had explained that the yellow flower absorbed all the colours of the spectrum, with the exception of yellow, which was reflected back to the viewer. Anna had digested this bit of information for a while and then had come back with:

'Oh! Yellow is the bit it don't want!' and after a little pause, 'So its real colour is all the bits it do want.'

I couldn't argue with this since I couldn't be sure what the heck a flower would want anyway.

All these bits of information had been taken in, mixed with various bits of coloured glass, shaken well and worked into her particular framework. It seemed that each and every individual was issued at birth with various bits of glass labelled 'Good', 'Bad', 'Nasty', etc., etc. People got into the habit of slipping these bits of glass over their inward eye and seeing things according to the colour and label of the glass. This we did, I was given to understand, in order to justify our inner convictions.

Now Mister God was a bit different from a flower. A flower that didn't want the yellow light was called yellow by us because that is what we saw. You couldn't say the same thing about Mister God. Mister God wanted everything, so he didn't reflect anything back! Now if Mister God didn't reflect anything back, we couldn't possibly see him, could we? So as far as we were concerned, so far as we were able to understand what Mister God was, we simply had to admit that Mister God was quite empty. Not empty because there was truly nothing there, but empty because he accepted everything, because he wanted everything and did not reflect anything back! Of course you could cheat if you wanted to; you could wear your bit of coloured glass marked 'Mister God is loving' or the bit marked 'Mister God is kind', but then, of course, you would miss the whole nature of Mister God. Just imagine what kind of an 'object' Mister God must be if he accepts everything, if he reflects absolutely nothing back. This, said Anna, is being a REAL GOD. This is what we were being asked to do, throw away our pieces of coloured glass and see clearly. The fact that Old Nick was busy turning them out by the million made things a bit difficult at times but that was the way things were.

'Sometimes,' said Anna, 'growed-ups make kids have bits of glass.'

'Why would they want to do that?' I asked.

'So they can make the kids do something they want them to.'

'You mean frighten them?'

'Yes. To do something.'

'Like God will punish you if you don't eat up your prunes?'

'Yes, like that. But Mister God don't care if you don't like prunes, do he?'

'I guess not.'

'If he did punish you for that he would be a big bully, and he ain't.'

Most people are lucky if they ever discover the world in which they live. Anna had discovered unnumbered worlds through her 'bitsa coloured glass', optical filters, mirrors and garden witch balls. The only problems with these many worlds was that more often than not you soon ran out of words to describe what you saw. I can't ever remember Anna using the words 'noun' or 'verb', and certainly she couldn't tell an adjective from a ham sandwich, but she very soon came to the conclusion that the most haz-ardous aspect of writing or talking was the use of descriptive words. She'd go along with the statement that 'A rose is a rose is a rose' – well almost go along with it – but that 'Red is red is red' was something else again.

The problem with words got further complicated by Mrs Sussums. Mrs Sussums had met us in the street. Mrs Sussums was in fact Aunt Dolly, an aunt by marriage, and Aunt Dolly had one great passion in her life. This was eating nut toffee. She ate it in enormous quantities, continuously, and consequently her face always looked somewhat deformed by the presence of a large lump of toffee. If one was critical of Aunt Dolly it was because she always insisted on kissing everybody, not once but many times. Taken separately, the toffee-eating and the kissing were manage-able, but together, well – it could become a bit dangerous.

We didn't manage to dodge the kissing. We were instructed to 'open our mouths' and something about the size of a slab of toffee was popped in, that is to say about half of it went inside, the rest had to stay outside and wait.

After years of toffee-eating Aunt Dolly's face muscles had developed quite remarkable strength which enabled her to talk in spite of the glue strength of the toffee. Holding Anna at arm's length, she said, 'My, isn't she big!'

I shifted gear with the toffee and managed, 'Ga gig, guite gig!'

Anna came out with something that sounded like 'Gok gum gockle', which I hoped was translatable.

Aunt Dolly bade us goodbye and went on her way. We sat on a wall and coaxed the toffee into a manageable size and position.

Before Aunt Dolly's arrival we had been walking along the street, or rather, we had been progressing along the street in a somewhat crazy way. You see, we had invented a game which could make a couple of hundred yards' walk take about two hours. Somebody was the 'caller' and the other person was the 'doer'. The idea was that the 'caller' would name some object on the ground, say a matchstick, and the 'doer' would stand upon it. The 'caller' would then name some other object and the 'doer' would have to reach this other object in one step or leap. Hence the somewhat erratic progress; there was no guarantee what direction the 'doer' would take. We restarted our game. We had gone a matter of twenty yards or so in as many minutes when Anna stopped.

'Fynn, we both be "doers" and I'll be "caller" too.'

So off we set, Anna doing the calling and we both the doing, only this time it was different. No giggling this time, no squeaks of 'I've found one, I've found a tram-ticket.' This time it was altogether too earnest. Anna muttered to herself at every step, 'little step' hop, 'little step' hop, 'big step' hop, and then stopped. Looking back over the last step, she turned her head to me and said:

'Was that a big step?'

'Not very.'

'It was for me.'

'That's because you're just a tich.' I grinned.

'Auntie Dolly said I was big.'

'She probably meant you were big for your age,' I replied.

As an explanation this didn't satisfy her one bit. The game stopped dead. She turned towards me, hands on hips. I could see her thinking apparatus itching with the woolliness of words.

'It don't mean nuffink,' she said, like a judge putting on the black cap.

'Well it does,' I tried to explain. 'It means compared to a lot of little girls of five and a bit years of age, you are bigger than most.'

'Well then, if them girls was ten I would be littler, wouldn't I?'

'Could be.'

'If I was the only one I wouldn't be littler or bigger, would I? I'd just be me, wouldn't I?'

I nodded my agreement. I could feel the tide coming in again, I could feel her working up to something, so I tried one last sentence before I was submerged.

'Look, Tich, you don't use words like "bigger" or "lovelier" or "smaller" or "sweeter" unless you've got some other thing to compare them with.'

'Then you can't then, not always.' There was a note of confidence in her voice.

'Can't what?' I asked.

'Can't compare, 'cos,' and Anna fired her salvo of big guns, ''cos Mister God. There ain't two Mister Gods so you can't compare.'

'People don't compare Mister God with themselves.'

'I know,' she giggled at my efforts to defend myself.

'So what are you getting all fuzzed up about then?'

''Cos, 'cos they compare themselves with Mister God.'

'Same difference,' I replied.

'Ain't.'

I reckoned I had won this particular exchange since my questions had forced her into a wrong move. After all, she had agreed that people didn't compare Mister God with themselves so it followed that they didn't compare themselves with Mister God, and I told her so. Preparing to move to the top of the class on this particular exchange, I launched my unsinkable man-o'-war with:

'You said people *did* compare. You should have said that people *didn't* compare.'

Anna looked at me. I hurriedly manned the guns. I knew that I was right but I was going to be prepared, just in case. Anna looked, and my unsinkable man-o'-war just disappeared. I can remember feeling bad that she had handcuffed herself with her own arguments, feeling bad that it had been to some extent my fault and feeling bad that I had enjoyed winning this exchange. She moved close to me and put her arms around me and burried her head in the base of my chest. I thought how tired she must be with all this thinking, how disappointed she must feel because she 'hadn't got it'. All the doors of my storehouse of comfort and love opened wide and I hugged her. She gave a little wiggle to signify that she understood.

'Fynn,' she said quietly, 'compare two with three.'

'One less,' I murmured in a fug of contentment.

'Um. Now compare three with two.'

'One more.'

'That's right, one less is the same as one more.'

'Uh-huh,' I grunted, 'one less is the same as – HEY!'

Suddenly she was ten yards away, doubled up with mirth and hooting like a banshee.

'It isn't the same,' I yelled after her.

'It is, too,' she bellowed.

I chased her home through the stalls and barrows of the market street. I didn't catch her. Being so much smaller than me, she got through places that I couldn't squeeze through physically or, for that matter, mentally either.

That evening, sitting on the railway wall watching the trains go by, I said, 'I suppose that was a bit of your famous glass?'

She made a noise that I took to be 'Yes'. After a little pause I continued with, 'How many bits of glass are you lumbered with?'

'I got millions, but they're all for fun.'

'What about the bits you can't get rid of?' I went on.

'I have.'

'Have what?'

'Got rid of them.'

The completely matter-of-fact tone with which she uttered this last statement robbed me of my next sentence. Buzzing around in my brainbox were such ought-to-be-said sentences as 'Pride goes before a fall' and 'The Devil rides the backs of those who are certain.' I had this nice adult feeling that I 'ought' to take her down a peg or two, she 'ought' not to make such remarks. After all, the only reason such corrective remarks were jostling around in my head was that it was good for her. I wanted to say these things for her benefit. It was my duty to say such things, and this gave me a nice warm virtuous and comforting feeling. The angel flew on his way without fetching me the usual crack on the skull so I knew that I was safe. I'd got the green light so I could proceed. My stew of platitudes, proverbs and general good advice had got to the 'fast-rolling boil stage', so I opened my mouth to deliver all this wisdom. Trouble was it didn't come out, instead I asked:

'You reckon you know more than Rev Castle?'

'Nope.'

'He got bits of glass?'

'Yes.'

'How come you haven't got bits of glass?'

The shunting engine on the railway line marshalled its charges with a blast of steam and a whoop: a couple of toots of warning, a rheumaticky squeal of its joints, and it shoved. The trucks woke up and passed the message down the line: 'Ting-bong-tibang-bing-bong-bang-ti-clank.' It reached the end of the line and then back to the engine came the message, 'OK, we're all awake, quit that blasted whistling.' I grinned as I thought that the tank-engine and Anna might be related in some way. They both had the same sort of technique. The engine shoved the trucks and Anna shoved me into asking the kind of questions she wanted to answer.

She didn't need to think about the answer to my question 'How come you haven't got bits of glass?' She'd had it ready for a long time, simply waiting for the right moment to deliver it. She didn't make a fuss about delivering it either: 'Oh, 'cos I ain't frightened.' Now, that's probably the most missable sentence that can be uttered. Missable because that's what it's all about. Missable because it is too damned expensive, missable because the price of not being frightened is trust. And what a word that is! Define it how you like, and I'll bet you'll miss the main point! It's more than confidence, more than security; it doesn't belong to ignorance or, for that matter, to knowledge either. It is simply the ability to move out of the 'I'm the centre of all things' and to let something or someone take over. And as for Anna, she had simply moved out and let Mister God move in. I'd known about this for a long time.

I like mathematics. I see it as the most beautiful, most exciting, most poetic, and the most sublime of all activities. I have and have had for many years a little plaything, a toy, something I like to consider and something which sparks off ideas in me. It is simply two circles of heavy copper wire linked together like two links of a chain. I play with this so often that at times I am quite unaware that I have it in my hands. On one occasion I was holding it so that the circles stood at right angles to each other.

Anna pointed to one of the circles and said, 'I know what that is – that's me.' 'And that's Mister God,' she said, pointing to the other. Mister God goes right through my middle and I go right through Mister God's middle.'

And that's how it was. Anna had grasped that her proper place was in God's middle and that God's proper place was in her middle. That might be a little difficult to come upon for the first time but the taste of it gets nicer and nicer, and of course Anna's "Cos I ain't frightened' was completely without blemish. This was her structure, her satisfactory picture of how things were, and I envied her.

It wasn't very often that Anna was taken completely off her guard. But on one particular occasion I actually saw a spoonful of

spotted dick and custard arrested in mid-air. It happened like this.
Ma B had a pudding shop. Ma B was one of Nature's miracles; she
was taller when she was lying down than when she was standing
up. I suppose it was because she ate her own puddings.

Ma B had reduced the English language to real basic stuff. She
had the use of two sentences: 'What's yours, ducks?' and 'Fancy
that!' What Ma B lacked in the way of the melody of the language
she made up for by orchestration. 'Fancy that!' could be orches-
trated to signify surprise, indignation, horror, or any feeling or
mixture of feelings appropriate to the moment. When Ma B
wheezed out, 'What's yours, ducks?' the request for 'two of meat
pud and two of pease pud' was often followed by such juicy bits
as, 'What do you think of Missis So-and-So's eldest?' This is where
'Fancy that!' came in so handy. Perhaps Missis So-and-So's eldest
had upped and died, and 'Fancy that!' was suitably draped in
black, or perhaps Missis So-and-So's eldest had gone off with the
lodger, and 'Fancy that!' was another way of saying 'I knew it all
along', but 'Fancy that!' it always was. As for 'What's yours,
ducks?' Ma B was no snob. 'What's yours, ducks?' had a universal

quality about it; it applied equally to sixteen-stone dockers, vicars, tram-drivers, kids and dogs. Danny had a theory that Ma B had eaten so much of her own suet puddings that her vocal chords had got gummed up with suet and the only two utterances that could find their way out were 'Fancy that!' and 'What's yours, ducks?'

Ma B's pudding shop sold every kind of pudding; meat puds, suet puds, with or without fruit, dumplings, with or without fruit – every conceivable kind of stodge pudding Ma B sold. As an incentive to buy her wares, the sauces were free: jam sauce, chocolate sauce, custard, and gravies of all sorts in great cauldrons. The only time that this suet-pudding heaven of happiness was ever marred, and it happened two or three times an hour, was when some little urchin tried to swipe a free bit of pudding. Ma B shifted her twenty stone and brought the ladle down with a crash, but the little hand had long since gone. Ma B wasn't a very good shot with her ladle. Not only did the waving of this lethal weapon shower everybody with custard or whatever sauce she had last used it for, but the blow often landed on and did some lasting damage to an innocent suet pudding on the counter. Those in the know stood well back or even sat at the 'Seating Provided For', as the notice on the shop-window read.

The evening of the arrested spotted dick we were seated at the tables. There were six of us. Anna and her two special buddies Bom-Bom and Tick-Tick, Danny, a young French Canadian, Millie, the Venus de Mile End, and me. We'd got through our pease pud and steak and kidney pud and we were on to the spotted dick course when the table next to us was occupied by two young men in uniform – French *matelots*. I don't know what led up to the remark, nor will I vouch for its complete accuracy, but suddenly:

'Mon Dieu,' dit le matelot, 'le pudding, il est formidable!'

Anna's spoon stopped in mid-air. The mouth opened to receive the spotted dick opened further with astonishment, eyes that had been glazed with gustatory pleasure were suddenly prised wide open with question-marks.

Danny answered the unasked question. ''S French,' he said, with his mouth full.

'What's he say?' asked Anna in a whisper.

'He said the pudding was 'orrible,' laughed Bom-Bom.

But this was no time for jokes, and Anna did not join in the general laughter. She lowered her spoon to the plate, and as if some colossal offence had been made against her, she said, 'But I don't know what he's talking about.'

Now my French is limited to *papillions* being *belle, vaches* eating grass and the *pleur* being wet. In spite of this I managed to tell Anna that French was spoken in France, that France was another country and was generally that way, waving my hand in an eastward direction. I managed to convince her that this was no visitation of angels speaking the language of heaven and that in fact Danny could speak French as well as he could speak English. She digested this bit of information more readily and easily than she digested Ma B's spotted dick.

'Can I ask him?' she whispered.

'Ask him what?' I queried.

'To write what he said?'

'Sure.'

With paper and pencil at the ready Anna went off to ask the *matelot* to 'write it down big – about the pudding'. Happily one of the *matelots* spoke English so she didn't need my help. Two cups of tea later she came back to our table and even managed an '*au revoir*' in response to their leaving.

The excitement of this meeting lasted for a day or two. The fact that there were more people in France speaking French than there were people in England speaking English was a bit of a shock.

A few days later I took her to the public library and showed her text-books of various languages but by this time Anna had distilled her astonishment and had tucked it in an appropriate corner of her mind. As she explained to me later, it was not really surprising when you got to think about it; after all, cats speak cat language and dogs speak dog language and trees speak tree language. So it wasn't really surprising that the French people spoke the French language.

I had been a little taken aback at Anna's reaction to hearing the French language spoken. She certainly knew of other languages;

she could speak rhyming slang and back slang, and used a lot of Yiddish words in her own speaking. She was able to talk to Tick-Tock in sign language. This was necessary since Tick-Tock had been born deaf and dumb. Braille had intrigued her and my own interest in ham radio had revealed to her the mysteries of the Morse code. What I did not know at the time of this French encounter was that she was already immersed in the problem of languages. Her reaction to the French language had been more on the lines of 'What, another one?'

It seems that two questions had germinated in her mind concerning language. The first was 'Can I make a language of my own?' the second being 'Just what is a language?' The first question was well on the way to being solved. One evening I was shown the 'working out' of this adventure. One of the many shoe-boxes was taken from the cupboard and placed on the kitchen table; it contained notebooks and many sheets of paper.

The first sheet of paper to be taken from the box showed a simple column of numbers on the left-hand side of the page and on the right-hand side the word or words corresponding. The fact that it was possible to write '5 apples' with a numeral and 'five apples' as a word was, I was told, very important. If all numerals could be written as words, then it followed that all words could be written as numerals. A simple substitution of the first twenty-six numbers in place of the twenty-six letters obviously did the trick, but writing 'God' as '7.15.4' really didn't help very much.

Objects could be used as substitutes for letters or the names of the objects could be used. A reading primer had shown that 'A is for Apple', and of course the implication was that 'Apple is for A'. If 'Apple is for A', and 'Pear is for P', and 'Lemon is for L', and lastly, 'Elephant is for E', then the word 'Apple' could be represented with the line of objects – Apple, Pear, Pear, Lemon, Elephant.

Sheet after sheet of paper showed that Anna had experimented with words, numbers, objects and codes until she had finally come to the conclusion that the problem about inventing a language wasn't that it was very difficult, far from it. The difficulty was, how do you choose amongst so many possibilities? What she did come up with, however, was an adaptation of the Morse code. As this consisted only of dots and dashes it was pretty plain to see that any two distinct things could be used. As Mister God had been thoughtful enough to provide a left foot and a right foot – well, these could be used to talk with. A hop on the left foot was to be taken as a dot, a hop on the right foot as a dash. Both feet on the ground was the end of a letter. We got quite good at this kind of communication and could converse over quite large distances. For close work the scheme was adapted to treading on a line of a paving-stone for a dot and treading in the middle of the stone for a dash. By holding hands and pressing either with the little finger or the thumb we developed a very intimate and private means of conversing. In all, Anna produced nine different variations of this system.

I got caught up with her enthusiastic approach to this form of communication and produced two buzzer belts. The buzzer belt was simply a belt with two buzzers riveted on to it. When the belt was worn one buzzer snuggled under the left ribs and the other under the right ribs. The serious drawbacks to this method were, firstly that the buzzers tickled and made her laugh, secondly that the whole business of being wired up with bell-pushes, batteries and connecting wire was a bit tedious, and thirdly that the first time we used it in the street we managed to trip up a couple of innocent people who, to say the least of it, were not amused, but definitely not, so we scrapped that method.

The question 'Just what is a language?' was a little more tricky to work out. In the course of her 'workings out' Anna had come to the conclusion that in the realm of numbers there was one number which was far more important than any other number.

This was the number 1 – important because any other number could be made up by adding sufficient numbers of ones. True, there was a tricky way out. You could, of course, use signs like 5 or 37 or 574 instead of saying 'One plus one plus one plus one, etc'. This method merely saved you time; it didn't alter the argument that 1 was the most important number. Like numbers, words also had a most important word and this word naturally enough was 'God'. Anna saw the 'most important number 1' as the apex of a triangle – only her triangle was standing on that apex! Number 1 had to bear THE WEIGHT of all the other numbers.

Words were different. Words seemed to stand on piles of other words. These other words served the purpose of explaining the use and the meaning of the word on the top. The word 'God' stood on the top of the pile that contained all the other words and somehow or other you were expected to climb to the top of this pile to understand the meaning of the word 'God'. This was a daunting idea. The Bible, the Church, the Sunday school were all busy building this colossal mountain of words and it was doubtful if anyone could climb to the top of such a pile.

Fortunately good old Mister God had, in his wisdom, already solved the problem for us. The solution of the problem did not lie with WORDS but with NUMBERS. The number 1 bore the weight of all the other numbers so it must be wrong to expect words to bear the weight of the meaning of the word 'God'. No! It must be that 'God' is the word that bears the weight of all the other words. So the pyramid idea of words with 'God' on the top is WRONG SIDE UP; so turn it UPSIDE DOWN. That's better. Now the whole pyramid of words is standing on its apex like the numbers. The apex of the word 'pyramid' is 'God', and that must be right because now the word 'God' carries the weight and meaning of all the other words.

Anna showed me her 'workings out'. One sheet contained an 'upside-down triangle' standing on the point labelled '1' – this was the numbers triangle. One sheet showed a triangle standing on the point labelled 'God', and the last sheet in the shoe-box showed a triangle standing on the point marked 'Anna'!

'Ha,' I said, 'you've got a triangle all to yourself I see!'

'No. Everybody has got one.'

'Oh. What's it mean then?'

'It's for when I die and Mister God asks me all them questions.'

'What about it?'

'Well, I've got to answer them all by myself. Nobody can do it for me.'

'I see, but what does the triangle mean?'

'That I have got to be—'

'Responsible?' I suggested.

'Yes, responsible.'

'Yes, I see. You mean you've got to bear all the weight like those other triangles do?'

'Yes, of the things I've done and the things I've thought.'

Each word was underlined with a nod of satisfaction. She left me in the silence of her full-stop.

It took a little time for all this to sink in, but it was true. We've all got to bear the weight of our own actions. We've all got to be responsible – either now or later. We've got to answer Mister God's questions all by ourselves.

CHAPTER FOUR

There was no doubt about it, Anna's arrival had caused a fair degree of upheaval in the house, given me lots of problems to deal with, and caused a lot of heartache. From the very beginning I had seen her as someone who was a little unusual. Perhaps it had just been the unusual way we had met. The first few weeks had shown me that she was certainly no baby angel, no changeling, in fact not even a sprite. No, she was at least a hundred per cent child, complete with the giggles, dirty face and breathless wonder. She went flat out after each day, as busy as a bee, as inquisitive as a kitten and as playful as a puppy.

I suppose to some extent all children have a touch of magic about them – like some mysterious living lens they seem to have the capacity to focus the light into the darkest and gloomiest of places – and this one had it in a very high degree. Perhaps it's the very newness of the young, or perhaps it's just because the shine hasn't worn off, but they can and do, if you give them half a chance, make a dent in the toughest armour of life. If you're very lucky they can dissolve away all those protective barricades so carefully erected over years of living. Lucky, did I say? Well, if you can take in your stride being twenty years of age and naked, then you are lucky. If you can't, then it's hell. I've seen other people knocked right back on their heels at some of Anna's comments. It wasn't that her remarks were all that clever and penetrating, it was just that she made herself so vulnerable. This made people hesitate as to the next step. This was a trick that she had learned – make people hesitate by whatever means you have at your disposal, fair or foul. And Anna was not above using tricks if they achieved her aim. Make people hesitate, and your remarks have a better chance of being looked at, being seen again. I suppose on the whole I didn't do too badly, considering. I didn't give in without a struggle. Letting your soul, or whatever fancy name you like to give it, out of its cage and into the daylight is perhaps the hardest thing anyone can do.

The hoarding down the Broadway displayed in large red lettering: 'Do you want to be saved?' I wondered just how many people would say 'Yes' to that. Had it read 'Do you want to be safe?' millions of people would have said, 'Yes, Yes, Yes, we want to be safe', and another barricade would have gone up. The soul is imprisoned, protected, nothing can get in to hurt it, but then it can't get out either. Being 'saved' is nothing to do with being 'safe'. Being 'saved' is seeing yourself clearly. No 'bitsa coloured glass', no protection, no hiding, simply seeing yourself. Anna never said anything about being saved, never to my knowledge attempted to save anybody. I don't suppose she would have understood this way of putting things, for this was my interpretation. But Anna knew full well that it was no use playing things safe, you simply had to 'come outside' if you wanted to make progress. 'Coming outside' was dangerous, very dangerous, but it had to be done; there was no other way.

It wasn't very long after Anna had come to live with us that I tried to tie a label on her. I suppose it was for my own satisfaction and comfort, but thank God she wouldn't stay labelled. After the first few weeks of delicious enchantment with Anna I found myself faced with two problems, one of which was fairly immediate and easy to understand; the other grew more slowly and was very difficult to understand. Neither of these problems was easily solved, in fact it was over two years before I felt that I had the answers. The solution to both problems came at the same instant.

My first problem was, exactly what was my relationship with Anna? I suppose I was old enough to be her father, and for some time I wore that role without any great success. Perhaps the part of a big brother was a better bet, but that didn't fit either. I saw myself variously as father, brother, uncle, friend. Whatever I called myself seemed to leave an emptiness which needed to be filled. Nothing happened for a long time.

The other problem was, what exactly was Anna? A child certainly, a very intelligent and a very gifted child, but what was she? Everybody who came into contact with Anna recognized in her some strangeness, something that marked her as different from other children. 'She's fey,' said Millie. 'She's got the "eye",' said Mum. 'She's a bloody genius,' said Danny. The Rev. Castle said, 'She's a very precocious little girl.' This certain strangeness in Anna gave some people an uneasy feeling, but her innocence and sweetness acted like a balm, soothing away suspicions and fears. Had Anna been a mathematical genius all would have been well; she could have been written off as a freak. Had she been a musical prodigy we could all have cooed with delight, but she was neither of these things. Anna's strangeness lay in the fact that her statements were so often right, and as time went by they became more and more often right. One of our neighbours was quite convinced that Anna could see into the future, but then Mrs W was like that. Mrs W lived in a world of tarot cards, tea-leaves and premonitions. The fact however remained that Anna was so often right in her predictions that she appeared to be some sort of diminutive prophet, or East End oracle.

Certainly Anna had a gift but it turned out to be nothing spooky, nothing out of this world. In a very deep sense it was at once as mysterious as it was simple. She had an immediate grasp of pattern, of structure, of the way that bits and pieces were organized into a whole. Unexplainable as this gift might be, it was always well and truly earthed in the nature of things. As simple and as mysterious as a spider's web, as ordinary as a spiral sea-shell. Anna could see pattern where others just saw muddles, and this was Anna's gift.

The day that the horse and cart got its back wheel stuck in the tram-lines produced half a dozen willing helpers.

'All together, lads. When I say "heave", all heave together. Ready? Heave!'

We all heaved like mad. Nothing happened.

'Once again lads. Heave!'

We all heaved once again; same result – nothing.

After a few minutes of heaving and cussing, Anna tugged at my coat. 'Fynn, if you put something across the line under the wheel and something so it won't go back again, and then push, it's easier and the horse can help.'

With the help of a flat iron bar and a few bits of timber we pushed and the horse pulled. The wheel came out as sweetly and as easily as a cork out of a bottle. Someone thumped me on the back. 'Good lad, that was a good idea of yourn.' How could I say that it wasn't my idea? How could I say it was hers? I just accepted the praise.

Yes, it was true, Anna certainly had a lot of luck. Such moments as these gave me great pleasure and pride in her achievements; but there were also moments of great anguish when she seemed to overstep the mark, moments when her remarks, her statements, her claims, seemed to me to be so rash, so wildly out, that I felt compelled to say something. She took it all without comment. I felt like a heel and I didn't get it right for a long time.

Now Anna accepted the concept of the atom as easily as a canary-bird accepts bird-seed, accepted the size of the universe and its billions of stars without batting an eyelid. Eddington's estimate of the number of electrons in the universe was admittedly a fairly large number, but nevertheless very manageable. It wasn't very hard to write down a number bigger than that, and Anna knew full well that numbers have the capacity for going on and on and on. Anna soon ran out of words to express very large numbers, and this was becoming more and more important. The word 'million' was adequate for most things, 'billion' came in handy on occasions, but if you wanted to use a word for a very, very large number, well, you just had to invent one. Anna invented one, a 'squillion'. A 'squillion' was a very elastic sort of a word; you could stretch it as far as you liked. Anna was beginning to have need for such a word.

One evening we were sitting on the railway wall, just watching the trains go by and waving to anyone who would wave back. Anna was drinking her 'fissy' lemonade when she started to giggle. It's difficult to describe the next few minutes. If you want some kind of a picture, I suggest you try to drink 'fissy' lemonade, giggle, and develop the hiccups. I waited until the giggles had died down, until the hiccups had stopped, waited until the toss of the head had settled her hair back into place.

'Well,' I said, 'what's so funny, Tich?'

'Well – I just thought I could answer a squillion questions.'

'Me too', I replied, without any surprise.

'Can you do it too?' She leaned forward with excitement.

'Sure! Nothing to it. Mind you, I might get about half a squillion wrong.' I'd taken careful aim with this remark but it fell wide of the mark.

'Oh,' the disappointment was obvious, 'I get all my answers right.'

This, I thought, is the time for a bit of the old guiding-hand stuff; a bit of correction wouldn't come amiss.

'You can't. Nobody can answer a squillion questions right.'

'I can. I can answer a squillion squillion questions right.'

'That's just not possible. Nobody can do that.'

'I can – I really can.'

I took a deep breath and turned her to face me, quite ready to scold her. I was met by a pair of eyes, calm and certain. It was obvious that she thought she was correct.

'I can teach you,' she continued.

Before I had a chance to utter another word she was off.

'What's one add one add one?'

'Three, of course.'

'What's one add two?'

'Three.'

'What's eight take away five?'

'Still three.' I wondered just where this was getting me.

'What's eight take away six add one?'

'Three.'

'What's a hundred and three take away a hundred?'

'Hold it, Tich! Of course that answer's three, but you're cheating a bit, aren't you?'

'No, I'm not.'

'It looks like it to me. You're just making these questions up as you go along.'

'Yes, I know.'

'Why, you could go on asking that kind of question until the cows come home.'

Her grin exploded into a roar of laughter and I wondered what I had said that was so funny. It was the tilt of the head and the grin that made me realize what I had said. If asking questions till the cows came home wasn't the same as a squillion questions, what was it? Just in case the lesson hadn't been rammed home far enough, she turned the thumbscrew one last turn with, 'What's a half and a half and a half and a—' I put my hand over her mouth, I'd got the message. I didn't give the answer, I wasn't supposed to. With the ease and matter-of-factness that a mother shows when patting up baby's burps, she finished off with, 'And how many question sums is "Three" the answer to?'

Duly chastised, I answered, a little uncertain as to what garden path I had been led up, 'Squillions.'

By this time I had looked away and was busy waving to the passing trains as if nothing had happened. After a moment or two she put her head on my shoulder and said, 'Ain't it funny, Fynn, every number is the answer to squillions of questions?'

I suppose it was at that point that my education began in earnest. For quite some time I just didn't know which way was up or down or if I was coming or going. I had been taught the good old-fashioned method of question first, answer second. Now I was being taught by a half-pint red-headed demon that almost every sentence, grunt, number or utterance was the answer to an unuttered question. I suppose it is possible to fault this method of approach, but now I'm stuck with it, and it's very usable. Very gently, but with great excitement, I was instructed in the method of walking backwards. Keeping my eye firmly fixed on the answer, I was encouraged to walk backwards until at last I bumped into the question. Patiently it was pointed out to me that the answer 'Three' was very important and useful because it led back to 'squillions' of questions. The more questions an answer led back to, the more useful that answer was. The interesting thing about this method, I was told, was that some answers led back to a very few questions, and some answers led back to only one question. The fewer questions an answer led back to, the more deeply important were those questions. When an answer led back to only one question, then you'd hit the jackpot.

As I was slowly initiated into this upside-down world I found myself positively enjoying the kind of answers that led back to 'squillions' of questions. That the number nine stood as the answer to 'squillions' of unasked questions I found myself getting more and more excited about. I too could answer 'squillions' of questions right. At this aspect of the upside-down world I found myself somewhere near the top of the class, constructing questions of such complexity that I would have hesitated to try to solve them had I not known the answer from the beginning. At the other end of the scale, the end where an answer led back to only one question, I was at the bottom of the class. Uncertain, hesitant and most unwilling to state the question.

Taking a stroll one evening with me and playing an unending solo game of hop-scotch on the paving-stones, Anna suddenly flung over her shoulder without stopping her game, 'Fynn, say "In my middle".'

As a very obedient pupil, I chanted, 'In my middle.'

From ten yards ahead of me she yelled, 'Wot?'

I stopped dead in my tracks, filled my lungs with the necessary, and yelled: 'In my middle.'

Little old ladies with their shopping baskets hurriedly crossed over the road with sidelong glances at me. Young girls giggled and children made those sorts of signs that indicated that I had a screw loose somewhere. Whatever activities or thoughts these good people had been engaged in were rudely interrupted by a six-foot-plus, fifteen-stone young man suddenly standing still

and yelling fit to wake the dead, 'IN MY MIDDLE.' Sympathetic looks and such remarks as 'He must be bonkers', 'You never can tell by looks, can you?' were aimed in my direction. How could they possibly have known that I was conversing with that leaping, prancing demon red-headed kid now some thirty or forty yards away? Obviously the man was having some kind of a seizure. At all these reactions to my yell my mouth fell open and I gaped like a stranded goldfish, my eyes stood out on stalks. I must indeed have looked bonkers. With a flood of embarrassment I rapidly pulled up my anchors, slammed my legs into top gear and fled down a side street, around the block and braked hard in front of Anna, who was still spring-heeling it on the spot.

'Oi!' I panted. 'You with me?'

My mentor – or was she my tormentor? – still continued with her demented yo-yo act. I put both hands on her head and pressed her to a stop with, 'Hold it, your engine's still running. Cease. You'll curdle your brains.'

She ceased, and said, 'What's the BIG question, Fynn?'

'How the heck do I know?' I answered, looking back down the street, half expecting to see white-coated men bearing down on me with strait-jackets.

'You're frightened.' She took my hand and we went on our way. It wasn't an accusation, just a matter-of-fact observation. We came

72

to the canal bridge and Anna said, 'Let's go down the cut.' I picked her up and leaned over the bridge, holding her at arm's length, and dropped her the five feet or so on to the tow-path. This was our usual method of getting down to the cut; we never ever used the stairs about twenty feet away. We mooched along down the tow-path, said 'How do' to a couple of horses, plopped a few stones into the canal and sunk a baked-bean tin. We searched for a handful of skimming stones and skimmed for about half an hour, managed to bounce a few stones on to the opposite tow-path with one bounce and pressed on down the path. We came to a moored barge and clambered on board and sat up at the front end with our legs dangling over the side. I rescued a fag from my coat pocket and straightened out the kinks, searched for and found a match. Anna lifted up her foot and I scraped the match alight on the sole of her shoe. I lit the fag and took a long drag.

We lay there side by side on the barge, soaking up as many ultra-violet rays as managed to stagger through the steam and smoke of the surrounding factories. I was dreaming of my nice white yacht sailing through the Mediterranean, the steward bringing me cool pints of bitter and lighting my specially made monogrammed cigarettes. The sun was shining in a clear blue sky and the fragrance of exotic flowers wafted across the waters. Beside me lay this enchanting child, happy and contented, radiating sweetness, as innocent as a summer's morning. Little did I know that this miniature angel was busy stoking up her questions-and-answers boiler, waiting for a good head of steam. Little did I know that she was busy sharpening up her scalpels, saws and cold chisels, weighting the haft of her sledge-hammers. Halfway through my second glass of bitter my beautiful white yacht struck a mine and sank instantly. My comfortable couch was now the metal deck of a barge, my pillow a coil of tarred rope, my monogrammed cigarette was a dead and drooping fag, and the sweet smell of flowers wafting across the Med. was the soap factory working overtime. The golden sun in the clear blue sky was peering watery-eyed through the sulphurous clouds from the chimney-stacks.

'You empty in yer middle?'

I closed my eyes tightly, hoping that another yacht would pick me up. Already it was beginning to take shape. I could see the news placards: 'Dramatic Sea Rescue', 'Young Man Rescued after 21 Days at Sea – Exclusive Story'. I was beginning to like this; I fitted the part well.

'Oi!'

My right ear exploded and all my dreams fled out of my left ear. A good hard prod with an elbow and my empty brainbox filled up with reality again.

'What? What's up?' I said, prising myself up on to my elbow.

'You empty in yer middle?' I didn't know if that was a question or a statement.

'Course I'm not empty in my middle.'

'Wot's the question then?'

I thought that I knew what she wanted me to say, but I wasn't going to say it, she could stew. I chewed it over for a few moments and framed the question, 'Where is Anna?' On second thoughts I decided that this particular question was a bit too dangerous so I said, 'Where is Millie?'

She grinned at me and I felt that at any moment she would pat me on the head and pop a sweetie into my mouth for the good little pupil that I was.

ANNE

'And wot's the question to the answer, "In Mill's middle"?'

Ha! I'd already worked that one out. A 24-carat foolproof question-stopper, a real doozie, one that she hadn't bargained on, one that she couldn't wriggle out of. With great care and deliberation I replied, 'The answer "In Mill's middle" leads back to the question "Where is sex?" ', and added to myself, 'and now, you little perisher, get out of that!'

She didn't have to get out of it – she never got into it. Without the flicker of an eyelid, without the catch of a breath, she pressed on. Her questions and proddings were like the waves breaking on the seashore; as one rolled up the sandy shore, so millions of others were being formed far out at sea. They were rolling in relentlessly and nothing could stop them. So it was with Anna's questions and proddings. In the depths of her being questions were being formulated, boiling up to spill out of her mouth, out of her eyes, out of every action, nothing could stop them, but nothing. It was as if every occasion inside her was destined to meet its companion occasion outside her.

She started to say, 'What is the question to the answer, "In the middle of sex"?'

I reached out my hand and silenced her question with a finger on her lips. 'The question is,' I said, ' "Where is Mister God?" '

She bit my finger – hard – and looked at me. Her eyes said, 'That's for keeping me waiting.' Her lips said 'Yes'.

I lay back again on the deck of the barge and thought about what I had said. The more I thought about it the more did I come to the conclusion that it really wasn't bad at all, in fact it was pretty good. I liked it. At least it prevented all the fuss and pother of pointing up there and saying that's where God is, or pointing out among the stars and saying that God is there! Yes, indeed, I liked it very much – only –.

The 'only' didn't get resolved for quite a few days. Even then 'teacher' had to lead me gently by the hand and explain in words that this idiot could understand. You see, I had got to the point where I could, without any undue hesitation, give the question to the answers, 'In the worm's middle', 'In my middle', 'In your middle.' I'd even stopped getting het up about the question to the answer, 'In the tramcar's middle.' The question was 'Where is Mister God?' So far so good. Everything in the garden was lovely, except perhaps for one tiny, irrelevant and unimportant fact. I was ringed about with an unclimbable, impenetrable couldn't-see-the-top-of range of mountains.

The names of these towering peaks were: The worms in the GROUND; I'm HERE; your're THERE; the tramcars moving DOWN the street. I had got stuck with all these multitudinous and varied things which had got 'middles' in which Mister God was! The whole universe it seemed was strewn and littered about with sundry THERES and various HERES. Instead of some whole and big Mister God sitting around in a heaven of umpteen dimensions, I was now faced with a vast assortment of little Mister Gods inhabiting the middles of everything! Perhaps all these middles contained bits of Mister God which had to be put together like some gigantic jigsaw puzzle.

After it had all been explained to me, my first thought was for poor old Mohammed. He had to go to the mountains, but not Anna. She neither went to the mountains nor did she fetch the mountain to her – she merely said 'Scat'. And they scatted. Mind you, although I knew by now that the mountains were not really there, and that I could move about freely and unhampered, there are occasions, not many I'm glad to say, when I get the distinct feeling that I've been brought up pretty sharpish-like by a clunk on the head. It certainly feels as if I have walked into a mountain, even though I can't see it. Perhaps one day I shall be able to walk about freely, without ducking occasionally.

As for my problem about the HERES and the THERES, the explanation went like this:

'Where are you?' she had said.

'Here, of course,' I replied.

'Where's me then?'

'There!'

'Where do you know about me?'

'Inside myself someplace.'

'Then you know my middle in your middle.'

'Yes, I suppose so.'

'Then you know Mister God in my middle and your middle, and everything you know, every person you know, you know in your middle. Every person and everything that you know has got Mister God in their middle and so you have got their Mister God in your middle too – It's easy.'

When Mr William of Occam said, 'It is vain to do with more what can be done with less', he had invented his famous razor, but it was Anna who sharpened it!

Trying to keep up with Anna and her ideas could be a very exhausting business, particularly because I had finished with my schooling, or so I thought. Here was I, all nicely stacked up with Ideas of what was what, and I was being made to unstack them again, and sometimes it wasn't all that easy. Like the time I was introduced to the idea of sex!

One of the great advantages of living in the East End was sex. In those days it was spelt with a small 's' and not with a big 'S'. By 'advantage' I mean that nobody spent half their life wondering if they were born in a beehive or a bird's-nest. The whole of the birds-and-bees saga was out, but definitely. Nobody was in any doubt as to their origins. One might have been conceived under a gooseberry-bush, but born, never. Most of the kids were familiar with the good old-fashioned four-letter Anglo-Saxon words before they could even count to four or knew what a letter was. Those were the days when the said Anglo-Saxon words were used as nouns and verbs and not as adjectives; when sex with a little 's' was as natural in its right place as the air we breathe. It hadn't got the self-importance of a capital 'S', nor for that matter its problems. Perhaps it was because we learnt about it so early on in our lives that it rarely got snagged up. Perhaps it's only when you learn about it late in life that you begin to spell it with a capital 'S'. This is nothing to do with sex with a small 's' or a capital 'S'. This is to do with Anna's discovery of SEX, the kind that you spell with all capitals.

It wasn't that there was anything wrong with the ordinary run-of-the-mill sex stuff, it was all perfectly understandable. After all, babies were babies, whatever else you called them. Kittens are babies, lambs are babies, and what about baby cabbages? One thing they all seemed to have in common was the fact that they were new, brand new; they were, as Anna said, 'Borned', or in other words had been brought forth! If this were true, and it certainly appeared to be true, then what about ideas? what about stars? what about mountains, and such like? You couldn't argue with the statement that words brought forth new ideas; could it be that words were something to do with sex? I don't know how long Anna had been mulling over this problem, it may have been for months. One thing was certain, she hadn't sorted anything out, otherwise I would have had the full blast of her discoveries.

It was a happy coincidence that I happened to be around when she made her breakthrough. It happened one Sunday afternoon after a not very successful Sunday-school meeting. Danny and I were holding up the lamp-post, chatting to Millie. The street was full of kids playing high-jimmy-knacko and skipping games, and four or five of the little ones were playing with a yellow balloon. The balloon game did not last very long as a balloon is not made to withstand the combined weight of five kids lying on it. It burst. Millie charged off to mop up the tears and to give general comfort to one and all. Danny was roped in to be the cushion for the next team to be 'downsy' in the high-jimmy-knacko game. Anna had stopped the never-ending chant of a ball-bouncing game and had picked up the burst balloon. She drifted over towards me and sat on the curb by the lamp-post. In a kind of reverie she was pulling the remains of the balloon into various shapes.

Suddenly I heard it. It was the sound of Anna's tongue slapping against the back of her teeth, it was a sign that her thinking apparatus was working overtime. I looked down. Anna had got one

end of the burst balloon trapped by her foot to the pavement. Whilst she was stretching it with the one hand, she was poking it with her right index finger.

'That's funny,' she murmured. Her unblinking eyes solidified this experiment like some twentieth-century Medusa.

'Fynn?'

'What's up?'

'Will you pull this for me?'

I got down beside her and was handed the burst balloon.

'Now pull it for me.'

I stretched the balloon for her and she stuck her finger into it.

'That's funny.'

'What's funny?' I asked.

'Wot's it look like?'

'Looks like you're sticking your finger into a burst balloon.'

'Don't it look like a man's bit?'

'I suppose it does, kind of.'

'Looks like a lady's on the other side,' she said.

'Oh! Does it? Let's have a look.' I looked, and it did in a way.

'That's funny, that is.'

'Well, what's so funny about it?'

'If I only do one thing,' she poked her finger into the balloon again, 'it makes a lady's and a man's. Don't you think that's funny, Fynn? Eh?'

'Yes. Two for the price of one. That's funny.'

She went off to play with the other kids.

It must have been about three o'clock in the morning when she stood beside my bed.

'Fynn, you awake?'

'No.'

'Good, I thought you were asleep. Can I come?'

'If you want to.'

She slid into bed.

'Fynn, is church sex?'

I was awake, very much so!

'What do you mean, is church sex?'

'It puts seeds in your heart and makes new things come.'

'Oh!'

'That's why it's Mister God and not Missis God.'

'Oh, is it?'

'Well, it might be. It might be.' She went on, 'I think lessons is sex too.'

'You'd better not tell Miss Haynes that.'

'Why not? Lessons put things in your head and some new things come.'

'That's not sex, that's learning. Sex is for making babies.'

'Not always, it ain't.'

'How d'you make that out?'

'Well, if it's on one side it's a man, if it's on the other side it's a lady.'

'One side of what?' I asked.

'I don't know. Yet.' She paused for a few moments. 'Am I a lady?'

'Almost, I reckon.'

'I can't have babies though, can I?'

'Well, not quite yet.'

'But I can have new ideas, can't I?'

'You sure can!'

'So it's like having a baby – a bit – ain't it?'

'Could be.'

The conversation stopped at this point and I lay awake for about thirty minutes or so and then must have fallen asleep. Suddenly I was being shaken and Anna was asking me:

'Asleep, Fynn?'

'Not now, I'm not.'

'If it's coming out it's a lady and if it's going in it's a man.'

'Is it? – What is?'

'Anything.'

'Oh, that's nice.'

'Yes! Ain't it exciting?'

'Breathtaking.'

'So you can be a man and a lady at the same time.'

I got the idea that she was trying to put over. All the universe has got a SEX-like quality about it. It is seminal and productive at the same time. The seeds of words produce ideas. The seeds of ideas produce goodness knows what. The whole blessed thing is male and female at one and the same time. In fact, the whole thing is pure SEX. We've taken one aspect of it and called it 'sex', or made it self-conscious and called it 'Sex'. But that was our own fault, wasn't it?

CHAPTER FIVE

The first two years with Anna were for me years of pleasure, years of pride and of amusement in the things she had said and done. People often said, 'Guess what Anna said today', or 'Guess what Anna did this morning', and I'd chuckle at the audacity of the child. The gap of years that separated Anna and me was a good place to laugh from. That laughter was warm and loving. That laughter was after all a little higher up the ladder of understanding and one can afford to be generous from these high places. The ladder was crowded, we were all forging ahead for one reason or another. We had all of us wrestled with our various problems; we had solved them to some extent. Of course we could chuckle, of course we could be generous. We could, from our elevated position, give advice to those struggling below.

This was the first two years, though they weren't wasted years. Anna cast her pearls about and I picked up a good many, but not all of them. I left too many of them lying about, and the feet of thirty years have trodden them into the ground. I'm told that every second of our life is somehow registered in our brains. I find that a comforting thought, but in what chamber, in what convolution do these pearls lie? I've never found the key to unlock these memories, but sometimes it happens. I find another pearl, some happening or some word, and the memory comes back.

I shudder to think that for two years I was content to eat the stale bread of learning when right under my nose Anna was busy baking new and crusty ideas. I suppose I thought that a loaf ought to look like a loaf. To me 'loaf' and 'bread' were synonymous and at that time I hadn't the sense to see the difference. In some part of my mind I can still detect a feeling of shame, a flicker of anger, and a sense of wasted time from that moment when I realized that the important word was 'bread', that bread could be baked into an infinity of shapes. I hadn't the sense to see that the shape of the loaf had nothing to do with the food value of the bread. The shape was nothing but a convenience. But my education had been too much concerned with the shapes. At odd moments I find myself angered when I ask the question, 'How much of what I was taught was a matter of convenience?' But I ask nobody. There's nobody there to give me an answer. What a stupid waste of time even to ask such a question. The answer lies ahead of me, not behind me. Anna has left her map of discovery behind, some parts pretty thoroughly explored, some parts only hinted at, but most parts of the map have arrows of direction on them.

The evening I discovered the nature of my relationship to Anna was the same evening I began to grasp what she was, or at least to see the way she worked.

It was early winter and dark. We had the kitchen to ourselves, and the shutters were closed. The gas-lamp hissed its light into the room, the kitchen-range, newly banked up with coal, spluttered its erratic candles of flame through the fire-bars. On the kitchen table a half-finished radio set, boxes of bits and pieces, a methylated spirit lamp, a soldering-iron and a clutter of tools, valves, and what have you. Anna was kneeling on a chair, elbows on the table, her chin resting in her cupped hands. I was at the opposite side of the table, my attention divided, like all Gaul, into three parts: the radio set I was making, Anna, and the shadows on the wall. As the coal in the kitchen grate warmed up, the trapped gases escaped, and ignited. The brilliant flame imprinted Anna's shadow on the wall, exhausted itself, and went out; another took its place and cast another shadow.

The explanation was simple enough, but the effect somehow defied the explanation. The shadow was there by the picture, then it was there by the doorway, then there on the curtains. The shadow pulsated in the flickering flame as if it had a life of its own, it vanished and appeared somewhere else. There was no movement between one position and another. It came and went.

It looked – how can I say it? – it looked as if the shadow was play-ing. My eyes moved from one shadow to another, then to three at the same time, then nothing. A few seconds later two shadows. Something itched deep inside me, but too deep to look at. Anna looked up, saw, and grinned. The merry-go-round inside me twirled but nothing happened. Whatever had nudged had disap-peared, leaving behind a hole in some part of me.

The radio grew bit by bit in silence, except for the sizzle of the soldering-iron as it was plunged into the flux. Tests were made and at last the valves were plugged in and the batteries connect-ed. A last look, and we switched on – nothing! It was just one of those things which happen from time to time. The meter set to the right voltage range, one or two measurements – Ah! that's probably the fault. Unsolder this, set the meter to current reading, insert the meter into the circuit, switch on. Of course it was one of those silly mistakes, soon rectified. Anna's hand was on mine, her brow furrowed in thought.

'What you done with that?' She pointed to the meter.

'I've just found out what is wrong.'

'Please do it all again.' She wasn't looking at me, her eyes were riveted on the meter: 'From where you used that just now.'

'D'you mean put the fault back after I've taken all this trouble to find it?'

She nodded. So I put the fault back.

'Now what?' I asked.

'Now do wot you did before, but talk,' she commanded.

'But, sweetie,' I cried, 'if I talk about what I'm doing, you won't be able to understand a word.'

'Don't want to understand no words. It's somfink different.'

'First I set this meter to read voltage on this range, then I attach the meter across this resistance to measure the voltage at this point.' My finger stabbed at the various bits as I spoke their names. 'Now we move on down to here and do the same thing all over again and the meter registers the right voltage.'

Getting to the faulty part, I hooked up the meter and Anna noted that the meter reading was very different.

'That's where it is,' I exclaimed. 'Now if I unsolder this bit here and put the meter to read current we'll just see what happens.'

I unsoldered, saying, 'Now we put the meter in the circuit and, Bob's your uncle, no current.'

The hands came forward again and I nodded. She unhooked the leads carefully and slowly hooked them back again. No current. Replacing the faulty part, I switched on again, made a few adjustments and listened to the music.

Some time after two o'clock in the morning I was wakened by the clack, clack of the curtain rings. By the light of the street lamp I could see Anna standing there. It was strange how the noise of those curtain runners always kicked me wide awake; strange, considering the fact that we almost slept on the railway lines with express trains running in one ear and out of the other, but the slightest jiggle of those runners and I was wide awake. After two years Bossy and Patch had elected themselves as Anna's bodyguard, a kind of advance guard scouting out possible danger that might harm their little mistress. Bossy, the old show-off, always way out in front, had already landed on my chest, whilst Patch,

with lesser courage, excused himself by continually looking back
to see if Anna was still coming.

'You awake, Fynn?'

'What's up, Tich?'

'Full up!'

'Oh.'

A little sob brought the guards tramping up my chest in order
to size up the situation.

The sniffs lasted a few moments longer whilst I thumbed
through the events of the last day or so, trying to figure out the
possible reason for the tears.

'Did you put it in the middle?' she asked at last.

'Did I put what in the middle?'

'That bit at the end, when you undid it.'

'Oh yes, I remember. When I unsoldered the circuit.'

'Yes. Did you put the box in the middle?'

'Yes,' I said, getting the drift of the conversation, 'I suppose it
was like putting it in the middle. Why?'

'Well, it's funny.'

'Hilarious,' I admitted. 'But how is it funny?'

'Like church and Mister God.'

'Oh sure, that is funny, that is.'

'But it is. True. It is.'

At two o'clock in the morning my brain cogs are apt to be a
little slow at reacting. Obviously this was one of those times.
Fuelling up to meet this situation meant getting up and it was too
darn cold, so I lit a fag. The fumes hit my brain and I coughed
awake my engine. I put my brain into bottom gear, the church and
Mister God being like repairing a radio was obviously going to be
a tough hill to climb, and at that time in the morning I wasn't at
all sure where my brakes were. Nothing was going to stop it, so
resigning myself to the inevitable, I invited her to proceed with,
'All right, so going to church is like mending a radio. I agree.
I agree, only tell me about it slowly – nice and slowly.'

'Well, first you put the box outside, then you put the box
inside. That's like people in church – they keep outside and they
ought to go inside.'

'I wish you'd tell me exactly what's happened. Thin it out a bit
so I can understand.'

Her body relaxed as her mind sorted out suitable and simple phrases, easy enough for an adult to understand.

'When you first done it with the box. Why?'

'To measure the voltage.'

'Outside?'

'Of course. You measure voltages outside the circuit.'

'Then the last time you done it?'

'That was to measure current.'

'Inside?'

'Yes, inside. You have to get inside the circuit to measure current.'

'That's like people an' church, ain't it?'

She knew full well that I hadn't got it, so she continued.

'People,' she paused to let this sink in, 'when they go to church,' another lengthy pause, 'measure Mister God from the outside.' She hacked at my shins with her toes in order to stress this point. 'They don't get inside and measure Mister God.'

She waited patiently, waited to see if these ideas had caught fire somewhere.

Out in the night the continental express hurtled its way towards Liverpool Street station and bed, its whistle shrieking out its desire for sleep. Flashing past our bedroom window, it dropped its whistle a couple of semitones, acknowledging my presence, hissing and laughing at my confusion. Sleepy Pullman cars chanted their lullaby – diddle-didum, diddle-di-dee diddle-di-dee, suck it and see, suck it and see. Everything was having a go at me this night. I did suck it and see. At least a couple of brain cells rubbed together and nudged the firefly of my imagination awake. Not enough to really see by, but something was there. I'd been reading Aquinas recently and he'd made no reference to 'making a radio' so I asked him to move over a bit and make room for Anna. I asked a question here and there, and the answer gradually got pieced together.

As a supposed Christian you can stand outside and measure Mister God. The meter doesn't read voltages, it reads 'Loving, Kindness, All-powerful, Omnipotent, etc.' You have a nice lot of labels to stick about the place. So far so good. Now what's the next step? Oh yes, now I open up the Christian circuit and pop me, the meter, inside. Seems simple enough, nothing to it really

– Hey, wait a blessed minute! Who was it that said, 'Be like your heavenly Father'? Quiet that man, I've nearly solved the problem. If I'm inside the Christian circuit, then I'm a part of – *a real part* of Mister God, *a working part* of Mister God.

'You mean I can think I'm a Christian. I can measure God from the outside and say he's all-loving and all-powerful and all that, but really I'm a dead duck?'

'Them's just people's words.'

'Sure, but I'm people.'

'So you ought to know.'

'What?'

'Them's just people's words.'

I pressed on with, 'So if I get into the circuit and measure Mister God that way, then I'm a real Christian?'

She waggled her head. Sideways.

'How come I'm not then?' I asked her.

'You might be like 'Arry boy.'

'He's a jew.'

'Yes. Or like Ali.'

'Here, hold on a bit, he's a Sikh.'

'Yes, but it don't matter, if you measure Mister God from the inside.'

'Slow down a bit. What the heck do I measure then, if I'm on the inside?'

'Nuffink.'

'Nothing? How come?'

"Cos it don't matter. You're like a bit of Mister God. *You* said so.'

'I never did say such a thing.'

'You did, too. You said that the box is a part of it when you measure it from the inside.'

It was true. I had said so.

So far as Anna was concerned one thing was absolutely certain. Mister God had made everything, there was nothing that God hadn't made. When you began to see what it was all about, how things worked, how things were put together, then you were beginning to understand what Mister God was.

Over the last few months it had begun to dawn on me that Anna's real concern had very little to do with properties. Properties had the rather stupid habit of waiting upon circumstances. Water was liquid except, that is, if it was ice or steam. Then the properties were different. The properties of dough were different to the properties of bread. It depended on the circumstances of baking. Not for one moment would Anna have relegated properties to the dustbin. Properties were very useful, but since properties depended on circumstances, the roadway after the pursuit of properties was unending. No, the proper thing to pursue was functions. Being outside Mister God and measuring him gave you properties, seemingly an unending list. The particular choice of properties that you made produced that particular kind of religion that you subscribed to. On the other hand, being inside Mister God gave you the function, and then we were all the same: no different churches, no temples, no mosques, etc., etc. We were all the same.

What's the function, did you say? Oh, the function of Mister God is another one of those simple things. The function of Mister God is to make you like him. Then you can't measure, can you? As Anna said, 'If you are, you don't know, do you? You don't think Mister God knows he's good, do you?' Anna's opinion of Mister God was that he was a perfect gentleman, and no gentleman could possibly swank about being good. If he did, he wouldn't be a gentleman, would he? and that would lead to a contradiction. It stands to reason, doesn't it? I know that daylight brings questions with it, that it's easy to accept these things at night, in bed with a miniature angel by your side, but stay with it. The function of Mister God is to make you like him. The various religions merely measure the properties, or some of them, for you. It doesn't really matter what colour you are, what creed you subscribe to, Mister God shows no preference in his function.

We didn't sleep any more that night, we just chatted about this and that.

'Miss Haynes.'

'What's wrong with Miss Haynes?'

'Do-lally-tap. She's barmy.'

'Can't be, she's a school-ma'am. You can't be a school-ma'am if you're do-lally.'

'She is.'

'What makes you think?'

'She said I can't know everything.'

'Guess she's right.'

'Why?'

'Suppose your noddle's not big enough.'

'That's the outside.'

'Pardon me. I forgot.'

'I can know everything inside.'

'Ah!'

'How many things are there?'

'Squillions.'

'More than numbers?'

'No, more numbers than things.'

'I know all the numbers. Not the names, that's outside, just the numbers, that's the inside.'

'Yes, I guess so.'

'How many squiggle waves on that 'cilloscope?'

'Squillions.'

'You know how to make squillions?'

'Yes.'

'That's inside.'

'Suppose so.'

'You seen them all?'

'No.'

'No, that's the outside.'

Bless the child, I couldn't tell her that she had just framed the question that had for so long bothered me: 'Why can't I know everything?' Because it's obvious that no man can know everything, so why try? – all the same. We went on chatting. As the time trickled on things began to happen to me. Certainties and doubts stacked themselves on top of each other. Questions were formed and discarded. I felt I was right, but I was afraid to let go. I juggled words into sentences, but each sentence made me vulnerable and that wasn't good. If my guess was right, Anna would have to take the responsibility. The church clock down the road clapped out six o'clock. The question was there and I had to know the answer.

'How many things don't you tell me about?'

'I tell you everything.'

'That the truth?'

'No,' she said quietly and with some hesitation.

'Why's that?'

'Some of the things I think about is very – very –'

'Strange?'

'Um. You're not angry, are you?'

'No, I'm not angry a bit.'

'I thought you would be.'

'No. How strange these things?'

She stiffened up beside me, dug her fingers into my arm and defied me to contradict her.

'Like two and five equals four.'

The world came undone at the seams. I'm right. I'M RIGHT. I knew exactly what she was talking about. With as much calm as I could muster, I gave away my secret.

'Or ten?' I asked.

For a moment or two she didn't move. Finally she turned her face to me and very quietly said, 'You too?'

'Yeah,' I replied, 'me too. How did you find yours?'

'Down the cut, the numbers on the barges, in the cut. How d'you find yourn?'

'In a mirror.'

'In a looking-glass?' Her startled surprise lasted for about one second.

'A looking-glass, like water, yes?'

I could almost hear the chains falling off me.

'Did you ever tell anyone?' Anna asked.

'A couple of times.'

'Wot they say?'

'Not to be silly. Not to waste time. Did you ever tell anybody?'

'Once. Miss Haynes.'

'What she say?'

'I was stupid, so I didn't say it any more.'

We giggled together, both free, both now unfettered. We shared the same kind of world. We were warmed by the same kind of fire. We both stood on the same spot, on the same road, going the same way. Our relationship was now clear to me. We were fellow-searchers, companions, like spirits. To hell with the profits, to hell with the gains! Let's go and have a look, let's go and find out. We both needed the same kind of food.

We'd both been told that 'five' meant 'five' and nothing else, but the figure 5 reflected in the water or a mirror was the figure 2.

And this fact of reflection could produce some pretty curious arithmetics, and this is what fascinated us so much. Perhaps they were not of any practical use, but it didn't matter. 'Five' meant what is usually meant by 'five' only by usage and convention. There was nothing at all special about the figure 5; you could allow it to mean anything you liked as long as you stuck to the rules once you had made them, and you could go on inventing rules for ever – well almost. So you see we were wasting our time, but we didn't see it that way; we saw it as an adventure, something that had to be explored.

Anna and I had both seen that maths was more than just working out problems. It was a doorway to magic, mysterious, brain-cracking worlds, worlds where you had to tread carefully, worlds where you made up your own rules, worlds where you had to accept complete responsibility for your actions. But it was exciting and vast beyond understanding.

I wagged my finger at her.

'Five plus two is ten.'

'Sometimes it's two,' she replied.

'Or then maybe it's seven.' Who the heck cares? There's squillions of other worlds to look at. We gasped to a stop.

'Tich,' I said, 'get up. I've got something to show you.'

I grabbed the wing mirrors of the dressing-table and we crept into the kitchen. I lit the gas. It was cold and dark but it didn't matter. Our inner fires were working overtime. I found a large sheet of white cardboard and drew a long thick black line on it. I hinged the two mirrors together and stood them upright like an open book. Between the open mirrors was the thick black line. I peered into the open mirrors and adjusted the angle.

'Look,' I exclaimed, holding my breath.

She looked but didn't speak. I began to close the angle of the mirror very slowly and I heard her gasp. She looked some more and went on looking, and then all hell broke loose. Her boiler burst. I remembered well the feeling when I had first seen it. I got the mirrors flat on the table before it happened. She hit me like an express train, her arms around my neck nearly strangled me, her fingers dug holes in my back, she laughed and cried and bit me. We were a million years past the use of words. There wasn't one that fitted, anywhere near fitted that moment. We were both physically exhausted. Mentally and spiritually we hadn't touched down. We never did.

CHAPTER SIX

Over a cup of tea we made plans. As soon as it was open we'd go to the market and buy a whole stack of mirrors from Woolworth's.

When we got to the market-place the shops were still closed. The stall-holders were assembling their displays under the flaring carbide lamps. The street was criss-crossed with shafts of good-humoured abuse, instructions and speculations as to the course of the day. Feet were stamped as if to kill the creeping insects of the cold. Oil-drum braziers stood on their bricks bringing the tea water to the boil. The coffee-stall breathed its perfume of hot saveloys and coffee over the market-place.

'A cuppa, two o'drip and a cheese-cake, guv,' said the taxi bloke.

'I'll have a cuppa and a couple of bangers,' said his mate.

'What's for you, cock?' It was my turn.

'Two cuppas and four savs.'

I slapped the money on the counter and got back the change, along with a handful of tea from the dripping counter. Anna stood grasping her mug in both hands, nose buried deep. Over the rim of the mug two smiling and blazing eyes sucked in every-thing. She couldn't hold her tea and the saveloys at the same time so I stuck them between the fingers of my left hand, ready when she wanted them. There was a space on the next stall to put my mug down whilst I jiggled out a fag one-handed. I tried to light a match by scraping it with my thumb. I never managed to learn that trick. The nearest I ever got was when the match-head came off and stuck under my thumb-nail. It lit then; it wasn't supposed

to do that, and it hurt. Anna lifted up her foot and I lit up. The tempo was hotting up.

'Mind yer backs please! Mind yer backs!'

Like the bow wave from a passing ship we all washed into the curb and washed back again as a horse and cart sliced its way through the mob, the horse steaming in the morning frost.

'Ernie!' yelled the lady in the leather apron, 'where the 'ell's them ruddy cabbages?' To anyone who cared to listen she added, 'He'll be the death of me, he'll put me in my grave.'

'Fat chance!' said someone.

The sandwich-board man arrived, announcing to all and sundry that 'The End is Nigh', and asked for a cup of tea.

'Blimey, the 'erald angel's here!'

'Here you are, Joe. Have a cup of wet-and-warm with me.'

It was the taxi bloke.

'Fanks, guv,' said the herald angel.

'Wotcha, Joe. Wot's the good news for today?'

'The end is nigh,' moaned old Joe.

'You give me the flippin 'orrors.'

'What was it last week?'

'Prepare to meet thy doom!'

'How the hell do you get all them messages?'

'He gets a telegram from St Peter.'

From the end of the counter a voice like a clap of thunder menaced all the company with:

'Which of you sodden baskits pinched me bangers?'

'They're under yer flippin' elbow.'

"Arry, mind yer language, ther's a nipper here!'

'Arry pushed away from the counter with a fistful of bangers in one hand and a pint-size mug in the other. The mug looked like an eggcup in his hand.

"Ullo, nipper. Wot's your name?' said 'Arry.

'Anna. Wot's yourn?'

"Arry. You on yer own?'

'No. With him,' she nodded at me.

'Wot you doing down the road this time of the morning?'

'We're waiting for Woolly's to open,' explained Anna.

'Wot you buying at Woolwerf's?'

'Some looking-glasses.'

'That's nice.'

'Buying ten of them.'

'Wot you want ten for?'

'So's we can see different worlds,' said Anna.

'Oh,' said 'Arry, none the wiser, 'you're a proper caution, ain't yer?'

Anna smiled.

'Would you like a bar of chocklit?' asked 'Arry.

Anna looked at me and I nodded.

'Please, mister.'

''Arry', corrected 'Arry, wagging a couple of pounds of forefinger.

'Please, 'Arry.'

''Arfer!' yelled 'Arry over his shoulder. 'Chuck us a couple of bars of chocklit.'

'Arfer chucked and 'Arry caught.

''Ere you are, Anna, some chocklit.'

'Thank you,' said Anna.

'Thank you, wot?' 'Arry's voice curled up into a question-mark.

'Thank you, 'Arry.' Unwrapping one of the bars, she offered it, saying, 'Have a bit, 'Arry.'

'Fanks, Anna, I fink I will.'

A couple of tree-trunks stuck out with large hams on the ends. The hams opened and they turned out to be enormous bunches of bananas. He broke off an 'Arry-sized bit of chocolate.

'You like 'orses, Anna?' queried 'Arry.

Anna admitted to liking horses.

'You come along and look at my Nobby,' invited 'Arry.

We went around the corner into a little side street and there was Nobby, a positively giant-sized shire-horse, festooned with horse-brasses, his coat shining almost as brightly as the brasses around his neck. Nobby was feeding from what looked to me like a two-hundredweight coal-sack slung around his neck. At 'Arry's approach Nobby snorted into his bag and we were all covered with showers of chaff and oats. 'Arry opened his mouth and out poured a tornado of laughter and love. Five minutes ago 'Arry had threatened to bash someone's brains in over his bangers, and I reckon he could have managed four or maybe six fully grown men. Now he'd melted into some kind of fairy-story giant for a little girl and a horse. Anna was given a handful of sugar lumps for Nobby.

''E won't hurt yer, Anna. 'E wouldn't hurt a fly, 'e wouldn't.'

'Nor would you, 'Arry,' I thought, 'you big lummox.'

Nobby's lips curled back, exposing a row of what looked like tombstones, then curled themselves over the sugar lumps which disappeared. After a few more minutes of horse talk 'Arry said, "Ere, Anna, you sit on Nobby and talk to 'im and I'll unload this lot. Then I'll drive yer to Woolwerf's in proper style.'

Anna took off and landed on Nobby's back, transported by one of 'Arry's bunches of bananas. The princess was mounted on her charger. 'Arry unloaded. Crates and sacks were shifted like so many bags of feathers. When 'Arry had finished he lifted Anna on to the driving-box and sat beside her, I sat on the tail-board. Anna was given the reins. With a couple of 'gee ups' we were off. I don't suppose that Nobby needed to be told where to go, he knew his route like the back of his hoof. We didn't go through the market-place since the cart was of the same generous proportions as Nobby and 'Arry, like a battleship with wheels on. We stopped at a corner.

'Woolwerf's,' bellowed 'Arry and leapt down like Pavlova herself. 'There y'are, Anna, Woolwerf's,' he declared.

'Thank you, 'Arry,' replied Anna.

'Fank you, Anna,' he grinned.

'See you some time,' he yelled and he and Nobby turned the corner. We often saw 'Arry and his horse Nobby after that.

The lady behind the counter at Woolworth's needed a little convincing that we really wanted ten mirrors, but she handed them over to us and aimed in my direction:

'You must fancy yourself.'

We hurried home with our prize and cleared the kitchen table. I hinged two mirrors together with glue and pieces of cloth, like the covers of a book. Anna brought out the large piece of cardboard with the thick black line drawn on it, and placed it on the table. Our mirror-book was opened up and stood on the cardboard, the hinge furthest away from the marked line, the near edges of the mirrors just cutting the line. I peered into the angle of the mirrors and adjusted them. The marked line and the two reflected lines made an equilateral triangle. Anna peered. I closed the angle slightly, the lines adjusted themselves and a square appeared. Anna stared into the mirror-book.

'A bit more,' she commanded.

I closed the angle a little more and she counted, 'One, two, three, four, five. It's got five sides.'

After a moment or two, 'What's it called?'

'A pentagon,' I answered.

The book closed a little more and I announced the shapes to be a hexagon – a heptagon – an octagon. I ran out of names after a 'decagon' so we merely counted the sides and called them a 'seventeen-agon' or a 'thirty-six-agon'. Anna thought it was a very strange and wonderful book. The more you closed it the more complex were the figures, very strange to say the least. What was even stranger was that the 'book' was just a couple of mirrors. But if you had a separate page for every different 'agon' you were able to see, why then you were going to need millions of pages, no, squillions of pages. This was truly a magic book. Who'd ever heard of a book with squillions of pictures in it and NO PAGES?

As we closed the 'book' more and more, we ran into a snag. The mirror-book was only open about an inch and we couldn't get inside to see what was going on inside the book, so we started from the beginning again. When we got to the umpteen-agon again we couldn't get inside. What to do?

Anna said, 'When we get to a squillion-agon it's going to be a circle.'

But how do we get inside? This little puzzle was solved after some thought and a lot of false trails. We scraped off some of the silvering from the back of one of the mirrors and made a circle of clear glass about the size of a penny. A spy-hole. We could now look inside. It was true, a 'squillion-agon' was going to be a circle. Already it was difficult to decide that what we saw wasn't a circle.

Then another snag cropped up; as we closed up the book we ran out of light to see things by. Anna wanted to know what we would see if the mirror-book was tight closed. That was a tricky problem. How to get light into a tight-shut mirror-book.

'Can't we put a light inside the mirror-book?' asked Anna.

We dismissed matches and candles and finally hit upon the torch. The torch was quickly dismantled and reassembled; wires were soldered to the bulb and to the battery. We put the bulb into the book. It was a bit too big, we still couldn't shut the book completely. The solution to this little problem was almost immediate.

The two mirrors parallel to each other about a half an inch apart would give us a very good approximation. We set it up and draped a cloth over it so that the light couldn't get in around the edges. Anna looked through the spy-hole and gasped:

'There's millions of lights,' she whispered, and with even more surprise, 'Fynn, it's a straight line!'

It had surprised me ten years ago, so I was ready for this. I reached across her and very gently squeezed the two mirrors together along one side, about a fraction of an inch.

She leaped back, looked at me and said, 'Wot you do?'

I explained to her how to squeeze one pair of edges together.

'It makes the biggest circle in the world,' she exclaimed.

As she sat there with her eye fixed on the biggest circle in the world, I squeezed the other two edges together. The biggest circle in the world straightened up and bent the other way.

The mirror-book opened and closed a hundred times a day. A myriad different things were placed in the angle of the mirror. Patterns were formed of unbelievable complexity, enough to startle anyone.

One afternoon something new happened. Anna wrote large capital letters on pieces of card and placed them in the angle of the mirrors, and got inside.

'That's funny.' Her head swivelled to look into the right-hand mirror, then swivelled to look into the left-hand mirror, back again to the right. 'That's very funny,' she said to no one. 'The next one is the wrong way round, but the next one's the right way round.'

Some of the reflected letters were 'back-to-front' while others were still the 'right way round'. She discarded the 'back-to-front' letters and was left with 'A, H, I, M, O, T, U, V, W, X'.

I slid into a chair beside her and casually rifled through the selected letters until I found 'A'. I put the card on the table beside her and bisected the angle of the 'A' with a single mirror. Anna looked and then took the mirror out of my hands and tried it herself. Then she tried the other letters. It absorbed her for about an hour and then she brought it out:

'Fynn, if the half in the looking-glass is the same as the half on the table then the letter don't change. "O" is the funny one because you can halve it in lots of ways.' Anna was coming to grips with the axes of symmetry.

This was a new game to play, these were new wonders to be seen. Some things turned inside out or at least left to right, some things didn't. We made a pocket-size mirror-book with handbag mirrors donated by Millie and Kate, backed it with wood against possible accidents and took it into the street. This little book went everywhere with us. We'd flop down in the road on seeing some unexpected structure in a paving stone and out would come the mirror-book. Beetles were gently introduced into the mirrors, leaves, seeds, tram-tickets. Why, you could spend the whole of your life doing this sort of thing. Coloured bulbs were sandwiched in the mirror-book and switched on, and we peered through the spy-hole. Why, for a couple of bob we could outdo Piccadilly Circus, Blackpool and Southend all combined. It was all very miraculous, not only miraculous but useful because we could see both sides of an object at one and the same time – well, more or less. Anna wondered if we could see all round an object, so we made a cube of mirrors. One side was hinged with a spy-hole and objects were hung in the centre of the cube by a cotton thread. We had to put lights inside as it was too dark to see and, 'Well, I'll be darned!' we could see all the way around.

I never counted how many mirrors we bought and used; it must have been well over a hundred. All the Platonic figures were made out of mirrors, plus a few shapes that Plato never dreamed of. Ours were just that bit different; we got inside ours and saw things that language would be hard put to describe. We discovered a lot of crazy arithmetics that made sense as long as you were prepared to live with these mirror worlds. Admittedly, on this side of the mirror things got a bit tricky, but as long as you remembered you were doing mirror stuff, that was all that mattered.

We learned to draw, write and do our 'sums' on a pad of paper before us. The difficulty lay in the fact that we didn't look at the paper, we looked at the reflection of the paper in a vertical mirror. The tension was at times unbearable, the concentration was absolute, but we mastered it.

One evening it was suggested that the mirror-book was something more – it was a miracle book. Mr Weekley's dictionary told us that 'mirror' came from the Latin *mirari*, 'to wonder at', and that 'miracle' came from the Latin *mirus*, 'wonderful'. We knew that Mister God had made man in his own image, so could it be, was it possible?

'He might have made a big mirror, Fynn!'

'What would he want to do that for?'

'I don't know, but he might have.'

'Could be.'

'Perhaps we're on the other side.'

'How come the other side?'

'Perhaps we're the wrong way round.'

'That's a thought, Tich.'

'That's why we get it all wrong.'

'Yeah, that's why we get it all wrong.'

'Like numbers.'

'Like numbers?'

'Yes, the numbers in the mirror.'

'How's that?'

'Them numbers in the mirror, them numbers is "take-away" numbers not "add" numbers.'

'Don't get you, Tich. What you driving at?'

Anna took a paper and pencil and wrote '0, 1, 2, 3, 4, 5.'

'Them is "add" numbers,' she pronounced. 'If you put a looking-glass on "0" – then the numbers come out "– 5, – 4, – 3, – 2, – 1". They're "take-away" numbers.'

I was following the argument so far. The reflected numbers were 'take-away' numbers.

She continued, 'People are "take-away" people.'

'Hold it.' I put out a hand. 'I don't get this "take-away" stuff.'

She hopped off the chair and staggered back with an armful of books. Settling herself once again on the chair, she thumped the table once or twice. 'That's "0",' she informed me, 'that's "0" and that is the looking-glass.'

'Right, I've got that bit, that's the mirror.' I gave the table a thump. 'So what's next?'

She placed a book on the table.

'That's add one,' she explained, looking hard at me. I nodded. She placed a second book on top of the first.

'That's add two.' I nodded some more.

'That's add three, that's add four.' The pile grew higher and higher. When she was satisfied that I had grasped exactly what she was saying, an arm knocked over all the books and she swept them on to the floor.

'Now.'

We were obviously coming to the difficult bit.

'Where,' she asked, 'is a "take-away-book"?' The question was asked with hand on her hip and head tilted.

'Search me,' I answered. 'I haven't got it.'

Again she thumped the table a couple of times. 'Down there. It's down there.'

'Oh sure,' I replied, 'it's down there.' I had not much idea what 'there' referred to, and said so.

'A "take-away-one-book" is a hole as big as a book, and a "take-away-two-books" is a hole as big as two books. It's not hard,' she said.

It wasn't, not when you got the hang of things, so I plunged in with, 'So a "take-away-eight-books" number is a hole eight books big.'

She continued on her tutorial way.

'If you've got a "take-away-ten-books" hole and if you've got fifteen "add" books, how many books you got?'

I began to tip the fifteen 'add' books down the hole one by one and watched them disappear. I lost ten that way and ended up with five.

'Five,' I announced, 'but what's that got to do with "take-away" people?'

I shrank about four feet under her sympathetic gaze and just managed to stop myself falling down the 'take-away' hole.

'If,' she underlined, 'people are looking-glass people, then they are "take-away" people.'

It's all pretty obvious, so obvious that it would take an idiot not to see it! We all know that Mister God made man in his own image and images are found in mirrors. Mirrors turned you back to front or left to right. Images were 'take-away' things. So putting it all together, Mister God *was* and Mister God *is* on one side of the mirror, Mister God was on the 'add' side. We were on the other side of the mirror so we were on the 'take-away' side. We ought to have known that. When Mum puts the toddler down and backs off a few paces she does so in order to encourage the toddler to walk to her. So did Mister God. Mister God puts you down on the 'take-away' side of the mirror and then asks you to find your way to the 'add' side of the mirror. You see he wants you to be like him.

' "Take-away" people live in holes.'

'Must do,' I admitted. 'What sort of holes?'

'Different holes.'

'Ah well, that accounts for it. How they different?'

'Some big, some little,' she continued, 'all with different names.'

'Different names – such as?'

She walked around the holes, reading off the names as she went, 'Greedy, Wicked, Cruel, Liar, etc., etc.' On our side of the looking-glass the whole place was littered with holes of various depths with people living at the bottom. On Mister God's side were appropriate piles of whatever, ready to fill up the holes if only we'd got the sense to ask for them. The piles also had names like 'Generosity', 'Kindness' and 'Truth'. The more you filled up your hole the nearer to Mister God's side of the mirror you got. If you managed to fill up your hole and still have something left over, why then you were well and truly on the 'add' side. Mister God's side. You'll understand of course that Mister God looks into his mirror and sees us all, but we can't see Mister God. I mean, after all, a mirror-image can't *see* what's looking at it. As Anna said, 'Your face reflection can't *see* you, can it?' Occasionally Mister God sees fit to do something about somebody's hole, he – well – he sort of fills it up for them. It was what we called a 'mirror-cle'!

Mister God was never far from any conversation, and Mister God was certainly getting more and more amazing. The fact that he could listen to, let alone understand, all the different prayers in all the different languages was something to marvel at, but even this paled into insignificance when compared with the stack upon stack of miracles that Anna was finding. Perhaps the most miraculous of all the miracles was that he had given us the capacity to find out and to understand these miracles. Anna reckoned that Mister God was writing a story about his creation. He had got the plot all worked out and knew exactly just where it was going. True, we couldn't help Mister God with this part of his activities, but we could at least turn over the page for him. Anna was turning over the pages.

One day I was stopped by Sunday-school Teacher. Sunday-school Teacher asked me, no, told me, to instruct Anna to behave herself in the class. I asked what it was that Anna had done or had not done and was told: one, that Anna interrupted, two, that Anna contradicted, and three, that Anna used bad language. Anna could, I admit, use a pretty good cuss-word at times and I tried to explain to Sunday-school Teacher that, although Anna sometimes used language badly, she never in fact used the language of badness. My arrow missed the target completely. I could well imagine that Anna had interrupted her and also that she had contradicted her, but she wouldn't tell me the circumstances of this episode. That evening I spoke to Anna on the subject. I told her that I had met Sunday-school Teacher and told her what had been said.

'Not going to no Sunday school no more.'

'Why not?'

"Cos she don't teach you nuffink about Mister God.'

'Perhaps you don't listen properly.'

'I do, and she don't say nuffink.'

'You mean to say you don't learn anything?'

'Sometimes.'

'Oh, that's good. What do you learn?'

'Sunday-school Teacher is frightened.'

'What makes you say that sort of thing; how do you know that she's frightened?'

'Well, she won't let Mister God get bigger.'

'How is it that Sunday-school Teacher won't let Mister God get bigger?'

'Mister God is big?'

'Yeah, Mister God is good and big.'

'And we're little?'

'Right enough, we're little.'

'And there is a big difference?'

'Yeah, and then some.'

'If there wasn't no difference, it wouldn't be worth it, would it?'

This confused me a little. I suppose I must have looked a bit puzzled, so she came again, sideways this time.

'If'n Mister God and me was the same size you couldn't tell, could you?'

'Yes,' I said, 'I see what you mean. If the difference is very big, then it stands to reason that Mister God is big.'

'Sometimes,' she cautioned.

It obviously wasn't as simple as that. In easy stages I was led to accept the fact that the bigger the difference between us and Mister God the more Godlike Mister God became. At such a time when the difference was infinite, then would Mister God be absolute.

'What's all this got to do with Sunday-school Teacher? She certainly knows about the difference.'

'Oh yes,' nodded Anna.

'So what's the problem?'

'When I find out things it makes the difference bigger and Mister God gets bigger.'

'So?'

'Sunday-school Teacher makes the difference bigger but Mister God stays the same size. She's frightened.'

'Hey, hold on a tick. How come she makes the difference bigger and Mister God stays the same size?'

I nearly lost the answer; it was one of those real 'give-away' lines. Tossed off so quietly.

'She just makes the people littler.'

Then she went on:

'Why do we go to church, Fynn?'

'To understand Mister God more.'

'Less.'

'Less what?'

'To understand Mister God less.'

'Wait a blessed minute. You're flipped!'

'No, I'm not.'

'You most certainly are.'

'No. You go to church to make Mister God really really big. When you make Mister God really really *really* big, then you really *really* don't understand Mister God – then you do.'

She was just a little surprised and disappointed to learn that this was over my head, way over my head, but she explained.

When you're little you 'understand' Mister God. He sits up there on his throne, a golden one of course; he has got whiskers and a crown and everyone is singing hymns like mad to him. God is useful and usable. You can ask him for things, he can strike your enemies deader than a doornail and he is pretty good at putting hexes on the bully next door, like warts and things. Mister God is so 'understandable', so useful and so usable, he is like some object, perhaps the most important object of all, but nevertheless an object and absolutely understandable. Later on you 'understand' him to be a bit different but you are still able to grasp what he is. Even though you understand him, he doesn't seem to understand you! He doesn't seem to understand that you simply must have a new bike, so your 'understanding' of him changes a bit more. In whatever way or state you understand Mister God, so you diminish his size. He becomes an understandable entity among other understandable entities. So Mister God keeps on shedding bits all the way through your life until the time comes when you admit freely and honestly that you don't understand Mister God at all. At this point you have let Mister God be his proper size and wham, there he is laughing at you.

CHAPTER SEVEN

Anna got involved with everything and anything; her involvement was on such a deep level that very little ever frightened her. She was ready to meet everything on its own terms. At whatever level the thing existed Anna would be there to meet it. Occasionally she'd run into a situation for which she had no adequate word. She'd invent one, either a brand new one or she'd teach an old one to do a new trick – like the night she told me that 'the light, it frays'.

Of course I should have known that light frayed but I didn't, so I had to go out into the dark street, armed with a torch and a tape-measure. With the aid of a nearby dustbin and the railway wall it was demonstrated to me that light really did fray. The torch glass measured four inches across. The torch was placed on the top of the dustbin and the beam directed on to the railway wall. We measured the patch of light; it was just over three feet across. The dustbin and the torch were moved back a few paces and we measured the patch of light again; it was over four foot six inches across. The light did indeed fray.

'Why, Fynn? Why does it do that?'

So we'd go indoors again and out would come the paper and pencil and I'd explain.

'Can't you make it so it don't fray?'

So we'd talk about reflectors and lenses. It got taken in, digested, stored in its proper place and poised against some unknown eventuality.

The mirror-book had provided Anna with another technique for wringing out interesting facts, the whole business of turning the thing inside out, or left to right or upside down. That some of her 'facts' weren't facts but fantasy didn't matter a jot, since by this time Anna knew exactly and precisely what a fact was.

A fact was the hard outer cover of meaning, and meaning was the soft living stuff inside a fact. Fact and meaning were the driving cogs of living. If the gear of fact drove the gear of meaning then they revolved in opposite directions, but put the gear of fantasy between the two and they both revolved in the same direction. Fantasy was and is important; it leads to heaven knows where, but follow it and see. Sometimes it pays off.

The mirror-book turned things from left to right, so why not turn everything round the other way for a start? Newton had a law, so did Anna. Anna's law was: First turn it inside out, then turn it upside down, then back to front, and then side to side, and then have a jolly good look at it, and – 'Fynn, do you know that "room" spelt backwards is "moor"?' Well, a room is a particular space surrounded by walls, and a moor is a particular space not surrounded by walls, so it makes some kind of sense, doesn't it? And while we are on the subject of rooms: 'Fynn, if you spell "roof" backwards it spells "foor". Can I put an "l" in it and make it spell "floor"?' Well, I don't see why not. 'Fynn, is a rood a window, because it's "door" spelt backwards?' 'Fynn, do you know that "lived" backwards is "devil"?' 'Do you know that "Anna" spelt backwards is "Anna"?' All right, so it's all coincidence, it's not relevant. Perhaps not, but it's fun, and sometimes the most surprising things happen.

Words became for Anna living things. She took them apart and put them together again. She learned what made them tick. She made no great etymological discoveries but she learned words and how to use them. Anna also painted – not very beautiful pictures, I admit, but then she painted under a severe handicap. She'd paint a picture wearing coloured glasses and then laugh at the result. And then, 'Fynn, will you make my red glasses blue for me?' and she'd paint another picture. None of Anna's pictures ever hung on the wall; they were never meant to. They were explorations into looking. It was very rash to deny the possibility that a red rose might be able to see. It might, just might, be able to see through its red petals or its green leaves, and you had to find out what the world might look like, hadn't you?

Being a 'sum-doer' myself, I was very interested in Anna's approach to mathematics. It was love at first sight. Numbers were beautiful things, numbers were funny things, they were without a doubt 'God stuff'. As such, you treated them with reverence. God stuff behaved itself. True, God stuff was sometimes very difficult to grab hold of. Mister God had, it seemed, told the numbers just what they were and just how to behave. Numbers knew exactly where and how they belonged in the scheme of things. Sometimes it suited Mister God to hide his numbers in sums or in mirror-books, and mirror-books, as you know, could get pretty darned complicated at times.

The love-affair with numbers soured a bit and, for a long time, I never knew why. It was Charles who put me on to the track of the explanation. Charles taught at the same school as Miss Haynes, and Miss Haynes taught sums. Anna's attendance at school was reluctant and not too frequent, as I was to discover later. At one of these sums lessons Miss Haynes had focused her attention on Anna.

'If,' said Miss Haynes to Anna, 'you had twelve flowers in a row and you had twelve rows, how many flowers would you have?' Poor Miss Haynes! If only she had asked Anna what twelve times twelve was she would have got her answer, but no, she had to start messing around with flowers and rows and things. Miss Haynes got an answer, not the one she expected, but an answer.

Anna had sniffed. This particular kind of sniff indicated the utmost disapproval.

'If,' replied Anna, 'you grewed flowers like that you shouldn't have no bloody flowers.'

Miss Haynes was made of stern stuff and the impact of this answer left her unmoved. So she tried again.

'You have seven sweeties in one hand and nine sweeties in your other hand. How many sweeties have you got altogether?'

'None,' said Anna. 'I ain't got none in this hand and I ain't got none in this hand, so I ain't got none, and it's wrong to say I have if I ain't.'

Brave, brave Miss Haynes tried again.

'I mean pretend, dear, pretend that you have.'

Being so instructed, Anna pretended and came out with the triumphant answer, 'Fourteen.'

'Oh no, dear,' said brave Miss Haynes, 'you've got sixteen. You see, seven and nine make sixteen.'

'I know that,' said Anna, 'but you said pretend, so I pretended to eat one and I pretended to give one away, so I've got fourteen.'

I've always thought that Anna's next remark was made to ease the look of pain and anguish on Miss Haynes's face.

'I didn't like it, it wasn't nice,' she said, as a sort of self-inflicted punishment.

This sort of attitude to the Mister God stuff of numbers was almost unforgivable and it rocked Anna more than somewhat.

The final blow came in the street one summer evening. Dink was sitting on the door-step doing his homework. Dink was about four-teen and going to the Central School. Dink could score goals from impossible angles and could knock a sixer over the railway wall with one wallop, but Dink and maths were strangers, pretty well.

'Silly bugger,' said Dink.

'Wot's up, Dink?'

'This geezer's having a bath.'

'Ain't Friday, is it?'

'Wot's Friday got to do with it?'

'Barf night.'

'That's got nuffink to do wiv it.'

'What's the geezer doing, Dink?'

'He's got both taps turned on and he ain't got the plug in.'

'Strewth, some mothers do have 'em – and they live.'

We ain't got no taps on our bath. We keep it in the yard and fill it up with a bucket outa the copper.'

'Wot you gotta do, Dink?'

'Find out how long the bath takes to fill.'

'He'll never do it.'

'Never?'

'He'll get his deaf a cold standing around in the nood.'

'He's a twit.'

'Let him barf 'imself. Have a game of footy, Dink. I bags being goal-keeper.'

Anna had been listening to this exchange and it confirmed her worst fears. Sums were an invention of the Devil, they turned you away from the real God stuff of numbers and tied you up in a world of idiots.

It was just past knocking-off time and we had got the worst of the muck off our hands. Cliff and George and I were crossing the yard, heading for the gate, and there she was waiting. I broke into a run at seeing her – wondering. She ran to meet me.

'What's wrong, Tich? What's happened?' I asked.

'Oh Fynn,' she threw her arms around me, 'it's so lovely. I couldn't wait.'

'What's lovely? What is it?'

Anna fished about in her pouch and thrust something into my hands – a sheet of graph paper, numbered in each square.

It looked straightforward enough to me. The number in the top left-hand corner was −2. The numbers progressed across the paper: '−1, 0, 1, 2, 3, 4, 5, 6, 7.' The next line began '8, 9, 10, 11, etc.' Six rows of numbers, ending up with 57 in the bottom right-hand corner of the page. It was a simple arrangement of consecutive numbers. Anna searched my face, waiting for it to light up. It didn't. It just registered puzzlement.

'I'll show you, I'll show you,' she said excitedly.

We knelt there on the pavement, homeward-going workers making a detour around us, with amused smiles on their faces. Anna traced around a large square made up of four smaller squares. The top two squares were numbered '22' and '23', the bottom two '32' and '33'.

'Add those two,' she commanded, pointing to the diagonal numbers, 22 and 33.

'Fifty-five,' I obliged her.

'Now those two.' She pointed at the other pair of diagonal numbers, 23 and 32.

'Fifty-five,' I grinned.

'The same.' She squirmed with delight. 'Ain't it wonderful, Fynn?'

Next she traced a larger square made up of sixteen smaller squares. With two quick strokes of her pencil she divided sixteen into four squares each containing four of the smaller squares.

'And that lot and that lot.' She pointed to the top left group of four squares and the bottom right group of four squares.

'Now these,' she said, indicating the top right group and the bottom left group. The answer was the same.

For the best part of thirty minutes we juggled with groups of squares. It was always the same. The group of numbers on one diagonal was the same as the group of numbers on the other diagonal!

It was obvious when you thought about it – one diagonal was the mirror-image of the other diagonal, so it followed naturally that all the numbers on one diagonal were, in some mysterious way, the mirror-image of all the numbers on the other diagonal!

Good old Mister God! He'd done it again!

Later that evening I was told that she had made scores of these arrangements, putting the '0' wherever her fancy led her. Also she had found some very complicated series and it always worked. Mister God numbers, the real God stuff, was, as you might expect, a never-ending miracle. As for that other stuff, the bath-filling lark that Old Nick used numbers for, well!

Anna's refusal to get involved in this 'Devil stuff' in sum-books was absolute. There was no power on earth, or for that matter in hell, that could make her. I tried to explain that all this 'Devil stuff' was simply a means of demonstrating the laws of what you could and couldn't do with numbers. I needn't have bothered. Anyhow Mister God stuff told you what you could and couldn't do, too. Do you mean to tell me that you'd go to all the trouble to get two men to dig a hole in two hours and then – what do you do? You don't ask the proper question, 'What are you digging the hole for?' No, you bring along another five men to dig the same size hole, just to find out how long it takes. The man in the bath? You can't tell me that you actually know anybody who would turn both the taps on and then deliberately leave the bung out. As for the rows of flowers, well—

Anna never had any difficulty in separating the idea of six in six apples and applying it to six buses. Six was simply 'this amount of that', but even this did not exhaust the content of six. It wasn't until Anna came to grips with shadows that things really got under way. Strange, too, when you consider that a shadow is more or less an absence of something. Anyhow shadows started a chain-reaction and she took off in every direction at once.

To while away the long winter evenings we had a magic lantern, a fairly large number of funny slides that weren't funny and about an equal amount of educational slides that weren't educational – unless of course you were interested in the number of square feet of glass in the Crystal Palace or you wanted to know for some reason the number of blocks of stone used in the construction of the Great Pyramid. What was both funny and educational, although I didn't know it at the time, was a lit-up magic lantern with no slides in it. It was funny because when you put your hand in front of the beam, it cast a shadow on the screen, actually a bed sheet. It was educational because it brought forth three extraordinary ideas. Anna's request, 'Please can I have the lantern on?' always prompted me to ask, 'What do you want to see?' As likely as not her reply would be, 'Nuffink, I just want it on.' I was more than a little concerned for she would sit there and stare at the rectangle of light. For a long time she would just sit and stare, unmoving. I was torn between breaking this hypnotic trance she seemed to be in and waiting to see what it was all about.

This looking at the rectangle of light went on for about a week or so. After what seemed to be a lifetime of agony, she spoke:

'Fynn, hold a matchbox in the light.'

I went forward, matchbox in hand, and held it in the beam of light. The screen filled with the black shadows of hand and matchbox.

After a long and careful scrutiny she exclaimed, 'Now a book.'

I duly produced a book and held it in the beam. Again this breath-holding look. About a dozen or so various objects were placed in the beam before I was bidden to 'turn it out'. Sitting on the table with the gas light full on, I waited for an explanation, but nothing came. My patience cracked wide open and I asked, in as unconcerned a voice as I could manage:

'What you cookin' up, Tich?'

Her face pointed in my direction but her eyes were somewhere else.

'It's funny,' she murmured. 'It's funny.'

Sitting there looking at her, I had the queerest feeling that some inner part of her was slowly, so very slowly, turning on its axis. Her eyes were fixed straight ahead, her head turned with painful slowness to the left. Suddenly her concentration broke and she giggled. I was left with the feeling that I had been reading a 'who-dunnit' with the last page missing.

This whole episode was repeated six or seven times in as many days; in all other ways she was still her exciting, fun-loving self.

For me it was a nail-biting and anxious time. It was on the fifth or maybe sixth repeat that she asked for a sheet of paper and requested that it be pinned on to the screen. This I did. A jug was this day's object and Anna explained that she wanted me to trace around the shadow of the jug with a pencil on the sheet of paper. So there I was, standing with a jug in one hand and a pencil in the other. I couldn't make it, I was about two feet short of the screen. I pointed this fact out to her but she just sat there like some director on a film set, ordering her minions about to achieve the effect she wanted. In response to my plea for help she merely stated, 'Stand it on something.' I just did what I was told. With the help of a small table and a pile of books I managed to set it up and traced the outline of the jug on to a piece of paper.

'Now cut it out,' she commanded.

Feeling that my considerable talents were being wasted on such menial tasks, I told her to do it herself.

'Please,' she said, 'please, Fynn.'

So, with an adequate show of reluctance, I cut it out and handed it to her. With the lantern out and the gas light on she stared at the cut-out, going through the whole rigmarole of screwing her head off in order to – what? Whatever it was seemed to satisfy her for she nodded, got up and placed the cut-out in the pages of the concordance.

The next night produced three more cut-outs and I was still none the wiser. I didn't know it at the time but Anna had solved her problem. Not a sign, however, hinted at the solution. Anna was marshalling her facts and her ideas. Three days passed before she once again asked for the magic langern to be put on. Three days of cunningly worded questions. Three days of enigmatic smiles, like some half-pint Mona Lisa. Finally the stage was set.

'Now!' exclaimed Anna with complete confidence. 'Now!'

The four cut-out figures were taken from the book and placed on the table.

'Fynn, hold this one up for me.'

I held the cut-out in the beam of the light. What did she want a shadow of a shadow for I wondered.

'Not that way! Hold it perpendicular to the sheet.'

'Rightee are,' I replied, holding the paper shadow perpendicular to the sheet.

'Wot you see, Fynn?'

I turned to her. Her eyes were screwed tight-shut, she wasn't looking.

'A straight line.'

'Now the next one.'

I held the next cut-out perpendicular to the screen.

'Wot you see now?'

'A straight line.'

The third and fourth also gave straight lines. Natch! Anna had established the fact that any object, be it mountain or mouse, petunia or King George himself, produced a shadow. Now, if we hold this shadow perpendicular to the screen, then all the shadows of all the objects produced a straight line. There was still more to come.

Anna opened her eyes and looked hard at me.

'Fynn, can you hold a line perpendicular to the screen? In your head I mean. Wot would you see, Fynn? Wot, eh?'

'A spot,' I answered.

'Yes.' Her smile was brighter than the beam from the magic lantern.

'I still don't get what you're on about.'

'That's what a number is.'

I suppose the nicest compliment ever paid to me was Anna's silence. That silence I interpreted as, 'Well, you've got the intelligence to finish it off yourself, so get to it.' I did. Mind you, my mental gymnastics always ended up with: 'Do you mean that ...?'

It did this time; I started off, 'Do you mean to say that ...?'

What she meant to say was this. If a number, say seven, could be used to count things as diverse as banknotes and babies, books and bats, then all these diverse things must have something in common. Some common factor unnoticed and unattended to. What could it be? Things had shadows; having a shadow was a positive indication that something existed. A shadow lost you many of the things that you could not count, like redness and sweetness, and that was good, but it left you with shapes. A shadow had still got too much information attached to it. Since shadows were different, you obviously had to lose some more information. Now since a shadow lost you a lot of useless information, then it was reasonable to suppose that a shadow of a shadow would lose you some more. So it did, if, and only if, you held the shadow perpendicular to the screen, and then all shadows became straight lines. The fact that all these straight lines were of different lengths was something else you didn't want, but the solution to this was easy. Simply make all the straight lines cast shadows and there you are. What all these diverse things had in common, the thing you really counted with, a number, was the shadow of a shadow of a shadow, which was a dot. Every scrap of uncountable information had been lost by this method. This was it. This is what you counted.

Having reduced all the multitude of things to a common essence, the dot, the thing that you really counted, Anna proceeded to unwind things again. With a pencil in one hand, she plonked a dot on a clean sheet of paper.

'Ain't it wonderful, Fynn?' she said, pointing to the dot. 'That might be the shadow of a shadow of a shadow of me or a bus or anything – or it might be you.'

I had a good look at myself. I didn't recognize myself but I got the point.

She unwound a dot to a straight line, from a line to a shape, from a shape to an object, from an object to a – Before she knew where she was, she was climbing like a monkey up the tree of higher and higher dimensions. An object, you see, might after all be the shadow of something more complex, and that something might be the shadow of something even more complex, and so on. The mind boggles at the thought. But there was really nothing to it, so I was told. Once you had managed to reduce everything to a dot, you couldn't reduce it any further. That was the end of the line, but as soon as you started to unwind things again, well, where did you stop? There was no reason why you shouldn't go on for ever. Except, of course, that there was one thing in this universe that was so complex that it couldn't become any more so. Even I guessed that one. None other than Mister God. Anna had reached the ends of an infinite series of dimensions. At one end of the series was a 'dot', at the other Mister God.

Feeding the ducks in the park the next day, I asked her how she had gotten on to the idea of shadows.

'In the Bible,' she announced.

'Where in the Bible?'

'Mister God said he would keep the Jews safe under his shadow.'

'Oh.'

'And then St Peter.'

'Wot about St Peter? Wot he do?'

'Made people better.'

'How'd he do that?'

'He put his shadow on ill people.'

'Oh! Yes. I should have known.'

'An' Old Nick.'

'How did he get in?'

'Wot's his name?'

'Satan.'

'Another one.'

'The Devil?'

'No. Another one.'

Finally I hit on 'Lucifer'.

'Yes. Wot's it mean?'

'Light. I think.'

'How about Jesus?'

'Yeah – how about Jesus?'

'Wot's he say?'

'Lots of things, I suppose.'

'Wot did he call himself?'

'The Good Shepherd?'

'Something else.'

'Er – the Way?'

'Something else.'

'Oh, you mean the Light?'

'Yes. Old Nick and Jesus – both the Light. You know what Jesus said, don't you? "*I* am the Light".' She stressed the word 'I'.

'What did he say it like that for?'

'So's you won't get muddled.'

'How d'you get muddled?'

'Two kinds of light – a pretend one and a real one. Lucifer and Mister God.'

Anna's second idea flowed naturally and easily from the first. Shadows were indeed seen to be of the utmost importance in the proper understanding of Mister God and consequently in the proper understanding of Mister God's creation. First we have Mister God and we know that he is Light. Then we have an object and we know this is Mister God's creation. And finally we have the screen on which shadows are formed. The screen is that object that loses us all the redundant information which enables us to do things like sums and geometry and all that.

Now you don't think that Mister God wasted all this miraculous stuff just on simple sums and simple geometry, do you? Oh no. First of all you can place the screen at an angle to the beam of light or you can move the source of light about. The shadows distort but you can still talk about them in a reasonable way, you can still do sums. Then of course you can distort the screen in all sorts of interesting ways and still you can talk about the shadows in a logical way. Also you can put the light inside the object and cast the shadow on to a screen and that is really very interesting. If you make a shadow of a shadow on a screen, then distort the screen, why a distance like an inch might collapse into nothingness or maybe stretch to I don't know how far. Once you start distorting the screen, well there's no knowing what kind of sums you might be able to do. That's what Anna called real God stuff. But you can do none of these tricks with a shadow of a shadow. That's such a tiny little dot that it won't distort at all, no matter what you do with it.

Anna's final shadow revelation was delivered one wet and windy winter's night – a night that I haven't quite come to terms with in thirty years. I was sitting comfortably and warm by the fire reading. Anna was fiddling about with paper and pencil when it all started.

'Wot you reading, Fynn?'

'All about space and time and stuff like that. You wouldn't be interested.'

'Wot's it say?'

'Lots of things about space and time' – and then I made my mistake – 'and light.'

'Oh!' She stopped writing. 'What about light?'

I started to get itchy under the collar; after all, light and shadow were Anna's province.

'Well, a fellow called Einstein has figured out that nothing can go faster than light.'

'Oh,' said Anna and went on writing. Suddenly she flung over her shoulder, 'That's wrong!'

'So it's wrong, is it? Why didn't you stop me?'

The joke misfired.

'Didn't know wot you were reading,' she replied.

'All right, then, tell me what goes faster than light.'

'Shadows.'

'Can't do,' I countered, 'because the light and the shadow get there at the same time.'

'Why?'

'Because it's the light that makes the shadow.' I was beginning to get a bit muddled: 'Look a shadow is where there isn't any light. You can't have a shadow getting there before the light does.'

She digested this for about five minutes; I had gone back to my book.

'Shadows go faster. I can show you.'

'This I've got to see, start demonstrating.'

She hopped off the chair and put on her outdoor coat and mac-intosh and picked up the large torch.

'Where we off to?'

'Down the cemetery.'

'It's pouring with rain and it's perishing dark.'

She waved the torch at me, 'Can't show you the shadow if'n it's light, can I?'

Outside it was as black as pitch and the rain wasn't waiting to fall down. It was just solid water.

'What are we going to the cemetery for?'

''Cos of the long wall.'

As the cemetery road led to nowhere in particular, and as the road was bounded on the one side by a railway fence and on the other side by the high cemetery wall, the road wasn't very well lit, and nobody used it very much – I hoped. Reaching the mid-point of the wall, we stopped.

'What now?' I questioned.

'You stand here,' and I was stood in the road, about thirty feet from the wall.

'I'm going up there,' she continued, 'and I'll shine the light on you. You watch your shadow on the wall.'

With that explanation she trotted off into the dark. Suddenly the torch light flipped on, fingering about in the darkness until it found me.

'Ready?' came the yell out of the darkness.

'Yes,' I yelled back.

'See your shadow?'

'No.'

'I'll come nearer. Say when.'

The torch bobbed nearer, transfixing me in the middle of the beam.

'Righty ho,' I yelled as I made out my dim shadow away down the far end of the wall.

'Now watch your shadow.'

She walked a path parallel to the cemetery wall about two feet further away from it than I was. I watched my shadow, staring into the darkness. It zoomed towards me at a fair rate of knots, certainly much faster than Anna was walking. It slowed down as it passed me on the wall and then speeded up again. Anna was walking backwards with the light still on me.

Suddenly she was by my side again.

'See it?' she questioned.

'Yeah, I saw it.'

'Goes fast, don't it?'

'Sure does. How did you work that one out?'

'The cars. The lights on the cars.'

I agreed that my shadow was moving faster than she was walking, but certainly not faster than light, and I said so. I got no answer. By the light of the torch I could see that she was miles away. The outside experiment now finished, she was busy setting up some internal experiment.

I grabbed her hand, saying, 'Come on, Tich, let's go to Ma B's for a cuppa tea and a bite to eat.'

On the way we met Sally.

'You daft?' she said. 'What are you doing taking the kid out on a night like this?'

'Not taking,' I answered, 'being took.'

'Oh,' said Sally, 'one of them?'

'Yes. Come and have a cuppa at Ma B's.'

'Suits me,' replied Sally.

I'd just about finished my pork pie when Anna's internal experiment came to an end.

'The sun,' she said, 'it's like the lights on the cars.'

After a few more moments' thought she stabbed in my direction with her unused fork. 'You,' she said, 'you are like the earth – the wall is – the wall is – squillions of miles away, but it's only a pretend wall.' She returned with a bump and noticed Sally for the first time.

'Hello, Sal,' she smiled.

'Hi, Tich,' replied Sally. 'What gives?'

Anna transfixed me with her eyes. 'The sun makes a shadow of the earth on the wall – the pretend wall.'

'Well,' I replied rather doubtfully, 'I'm not so sure of that.'

'Well it can,' she smiled, 'in your head it can. If the earth goes round the sun, and the shadow goes on the wall which is –'

'– a squillion miles away.' I finished off the question for her.

'How fast,' she grinned, 'how fast does the shadow go on the wall?' She jabbed her fork into her meat pie and circled it around

her head like the earth going around the sun. Her head tilted to one side, and with a big grin she dared me to give an answer.

But I wasn't going to. I wasn't going to say squillions of miles a second, at least, not until I had thought about it a bit longer.

I knew I was right, that nothing could go faster than light. I believed it completely. I was certain that Mr Einstein hadn't missed it.

Looking back over the years, I realize just where I went wrong. Not with the sums I mean, but with Anna's education. You see, I didn't teach Anna the Right and Proper way to do things. Oh sure, I showed her ways to do things, funny ways, quick ways, hard ways, and all sorts of ways, but not THE RIGHT WAY. In the first place I wasn't at all sure myself what the RIGHT way was; so naturally Anna had to find out ways for herself. That's what made it all so difficult for me.

CHAPTER EIGHT

I suppose that the most frequently used words in Anna's writings and speaking were 'Mister God'. Running them a close second were the words that she called the 'whuh' words. 'Whuh' words were those words that began with 'wh', and these, so far as Anna was concerned, were question words. 'What', 'which', 'where', 'why', 'who', all question words, the well-behaved question words. There was however a rebel question word; it was 'how'. 'How' was undoubtedly a question word, and according to Anna should have been spelt 'whow', or more exactly 'who'. But we'd already got a 'who', so it was obvious to her that somebody must have taken the 'w' from the front of the word and simply stuck it on the end. 'How' was a more or less well-behaved word: it did at least contain the letters 'w' and 'h' which indicated that a question was coming up.

Question words were odd in many ways. Perhaps the strangest thing about a 'whuh' question word was the fact that if you substituted the letter 't' in place of the letter 'w' in a question word you were face to face with an answer word – well for the most part. Answer words were words that indicated something, they pointed at something. You didn't point with your finger, you pointed with your tongue. Any word that began with a 'th' was a tongue-pointing word. 'What is a tram?' could be answered by 'That is a tram.' 'Where is the book?' is answered by 'There is the book.' 'When' and 'then' were also a couple of question and answer words. The problems of 'which' and 'thich', 'why' and 'thy', and 'who' and 'tho' were obviously problems that could be cleared up, given a little time. Anna was satisfied that 'whuh' words were, and were meant to be, question words in the same way that 'thuh' words, like 'that', 'the', 'those', 'there', etc., were, and were meant to be, answer words.

With regards to language itself, Anna was convinced that it could, by and large, be divided into two parts: the question part of the language and the answer part of the language. Of the two the question part of the language was the most important. The answer part had a certain satisfaction, but was nowhere near as important as the question part. Questions were a sort of inner itch, an urge to go forwards. Questions, that is real questions, had this about them, they were risky things to play about with, but they were exciting. You never quite knew where you were going to land.

This was the problem with places like school and church; they seemed to be more concerned with the answer part of the language than with the question part of the language. The problems that places like school and church raised were absolutely tremendous because of the kind of 'answers' they gave you. Certainly you could make up the question from the answer given to you, but the trouble was that so often this kind of question had no real place to land – you just kept on falling for ever and ever. No, the mark of a real question was that it landed somewhere. As Anna said, 'You can ask the question, "Do you like skudding?"' It certainly looks like a question, it certainly sounds like a question. 'But it don't land nowhere.' If you supposed that it was a real question, if you supposed that it really landed somewhere, why, you could go on asking questions about it all your life and still get nowhere.

Anna was certain that heaven was, certain that angels and cherubs and things like that were real and she knew more or less what they were like, at least she knew what they were not like. For one thing, they weren't like those pictures of angels with nice feathery wings. It wasn't the wings that bothered her one bit, it was the fact that they looked like people that bothered Anna. The possibility that an angel could, let alone would want to, blow a trumpet filled her with the deepest dismay. The idea that, come the resurrection day, Anna would still have the same number of legs, still have eyes and ears, still be generally constructed after the same present pattern, was to her an idea too monstrous to contemplate. Why was it that grown-ups insisted on talking about where heaven was? The whole question of where heaven was was neither here nor there, it was immaterial, it was non-sense. And why, oh why, were angels and cherubs and things like that, and goodness me, even Mister God himself, represented as human people? Oh no, the question of where heaven was was one of those non-questions, it had nowhere to land, and therefore was no question fit to be asked.

As Anna saw it, the question of heaven was not concerned with 'where' but it was concerned with the perfection of the senses. Language was hard put to it when trying to describe or explain the concept of heaven, but then language depended upon the senses and it therefore followed that the grasp of heaven was also dependent on the senses. These pictures, these statues, these stories about angels, simply shouted aloud the fact that the perpetrators of these monstrosities had no idea what they were on about. They merely showed quite clearly that angels and such-like were simply men and women with wings on. They were bur-dened with the same kind of senses as we were and as such were no fit creatures for heaven. No, whatever the description of heav-en was, and that was really most unimportant, it didn't describe a place but the inhabitants. Any place could be heaven where the senses were perfect. Mister God's senses were perfect. Well, it stands to reason, to be able to see us over impossibly immense distances, to hear us, and to know our thoughts were not unrea-sonable characteristics of Mister God, or for that matter the angels either, but to represent them in stories, paintings or sculp-tures with ordinary ears, ordinary eyes and ordinary shapes was childish in the extreme. If the heavenly hosts had to be painted, then they ought to be represented in such a way as to show the perfection of their senses, and since language depended upon the senses, the perfection of their language too.

The strange insistence of Sunday-school Teacher Miss Haynes and the Rev. Castle on using the words 'seeing' and 'knowing' in such a clumsy way was a very sore point with Anna. The Rev. Castle talked about 'seeing' Mister God, about meeting him 'face to face', in a sermon one Sunday morning. He never knew how close he was to disaster. Anna grasped my hand tightly, shook her head violently and turned to face me. All her efforts were directed to damping down her inner fires, which would have consumed the Rev. Castle had they been let loose.

When it comes to fires, Old Nick had nothing on Anna. She could make the fires of hell look like glowing embers.

In a whisper that echoed around the church, Anna said, 'Wot the 'ell he gonna do if Mister God ain't got no face? Wot'll he do if he ain't got no eyes, wot then, Fynn, eh?'

The Rev. Castle faltered for a second and pressed on, dragging with him the heads and eyes of the congregation.

Anna mouthed the words, 'Wot then?'

'Search me,' I whispered back.

She pulled at my arm and signalled me to come closer. Her lips plugged into my ear. 'Mister God ain't got no face,' she hissed.

I turned my face to her, and my raised eyebrows asked the question, 'How come?'

Plugging in again, she said, "Cos he don't have to turn round to see everybody, that's why.' She settled back in her pew, nodding her head at her own certainty and folded her arms with a full stop.

On our way home from church I asked her what she had meant by 'he don't have to turn round'.

'Well,' she said, 'I've got an "infront" and I've got a "behind" so I have to turn round to see what's behind me. Mister God don't.'

'What's he do then?' I asked.

'Mister God's only got an "infront", he ain't got no "behind".'

'Oh,' I nodded, 'I see.'

The idea of Mister God having no 'behind' struck me as deliciously funny and I tried hard to suppress the giggles. I didn't manage it. I exploded.

Anna was a bit puzzled at my outburst. 'Wot you laughing for?' she asked.

'Just the idea of Mister God having no behind,' I chortled.

Her eyes narrowed for a moment or two and then she grinned. The grin fanned her eyes into flame and she lit up like a Roman candle. 'He ain't got one of them too!' Her laughter ran along the road, erecting little barricades as it went. The all too obvious and self-satisfied Christian worshippers bumped into the laughter and frowned.

'Mister God ain't got no bum,' sang Anna to the tune of 'Onward Christian Soldiers'.

The frowns turned to scandalized looks of horror. 'Disgusting!' said the Sunday Suit, 'Little savage!' squeaked the Sunday Boots, 'A limb of Satan!' said the Albert Watch dangling from the waistcoat, but Anna went on, laughing with Mister God.

On our homeward journey Anna practised her newly discovered game with me. In the same manner that she launched her spiritual being at Mister God, so she launched her physical being at me. 'Mister God ain't got no bum' wasn't a joke, she wasn't being naughty or just a silly child. It was just an eruption of her spirit. With these remarks she hurled herself at Mister God and he caught her. Anna knew that he would, knew that there was no risk involved. There was really no other way, it just had to be done. This was her way of being saved.

Her game with me was similar. She would stand some distance off, run towards me and launch herself at me. The run towards me was deliberate and active; the moment after her launch she was completely passive and limp. She made no effort to help me catch her, no effort towards her own safety. Being safe meant not doing these things at all, being saved meant trust in another.

Being safe was easy. You simply accepted Mister God as a superman who hadn't shaved for about six months or so, that angels looked like men and women with wings on, that cherubs looked like fat little babies with wings that couldn't support a sparrow, let alone a couple of stone or more of chubby infant. No, being saved was for Anna only possible in that act of creative violence to the images of being safe.

Every minute of every day Anna lived, she totally accepted her life, and in accepting life, accepted death. Death was a fairly frequent topic of conversation with Anna – never morbid or anxious, simply something that would happen at some time or other, and it was better to have some grasp of it before it happened than to wait until the moment of death and then get panicky about it. For Anna, death was the gateway to possibilities. It was Mum who provided Anna with the solution to the problem of death. Like Anna, Mum had this lovely gift of asking questions that landed somewhere.

'What,' she asked us one Sunday afternoon, 'was God's greatest creative act?'

Although I didn't go along with Genesis, I answered, 'When he created mankind.'

I was wrong, according to Mum, so I had another shot. I was still wrong. I ran through the six days of creation and drew nothing but blank looks. There was nothing more that I could think of. It wasn't until I had run out of ideas that I became aware of the exchange between Mum and Anna. So often with Mum that smile happened. It was her Christmas-tree smile, she lit up, she twinkled, and there was no other place to look. She sort of gathered everything around her. Anna was watching her intently, chin cupped in hands. There they sat, looking at each other, Mum with her wonderful smile and Anna with her intense look. The insulation of the six foot or so that separated them was beginning to give way. Anna drilled away at it with her blue eyes whilst Mum melted it with her smile. Suddenly it happened. Anna slowly placed her hands on the table and pushed herself upright. The gap had been bridged. Anna's matching smile had to wait whilst astonishment shaped her face. She gasped, 'It was the seventh day, course it was, the seventh day.'

I looked from one to the other and cleared my throat to capture their attention.

'I don't get it,' I said. 'God worked all his miracles in six days and then shut down for a bit of a rest. What's so exciting about that?'

Anna got off her chair and came and sat on my lap. This I knew. This was her approach to the unseeing and unknowing infant – me.

'Why did Mister God rest on the seventh day?' she began.

'I suppose he was a bit flaked out after six days' hard work,' I answered.

'He didn't rest because he was tired though.'

'Oh – didn't he? It makes me tired just to think about it all.'

'Course he didn't. He wasn't tired.'

'Wasn't he?'

'No – he made rest.'

'Oh. He did that, did he?'

'Yes, that's the biggest miracle. Rest is. What do you think it was like before Mister God started on the first day?'

'A perishing big muddle, I guess,' I replied.

'Yes, and you can't rest when everything is in a big muddle, can you?'

'I suppose not. So what then?'

'Well, when he started to make all the things, it got a bit less muddly.'

'Makes sense,' I nodded.

'When he was finished making all the things, Mister God had undone all the muddle. Then you can rest, so that's why rest is the very, very biggest miracle of all. Don't you see?'

Put like that, I did see, and I liked what I saw. It made sense. Sometimes, though, I found that I kicked against being the infant at the bottom of the class, and this feeling often caused me to put a dig in whenever I got the chance.

'I know what he did with all that muddle,' I exclaimed, feeling rather pleased with myself.

'Wot?' asked Anna.

'He stuffed it in people's brainboxes.'

I had meant it as a bombshell, but it didn't go off; instead two heads nodded in agreement and pleasure that I had grasped the point so quickly. I did a sharp about-face and accepted their agreeing nods as if I was entirely entitled to them. It left me with a problem. How could I ask the question 'Why did he stuff the muddle in people's brainboxes?' in such a way as not to find myself at the bottom of the class again!

'It's a funny thing, this muddle,' I began.

'It ain't,' said Anna. 'You have to have a muddle in your head before you really know what rest is.'

'Oh yes. Yes. I suppose that must be the reason.'

'Being dead is a rest,' she went on. 'Being dead, you can look back and get it all straight before you go on.'

Being dead was nothing to get fussed about. Dying could be a bit of a problem, but not if you had really lived. Dying needed a certain amount of preparation and the only preparation for dying was real living, the kind of preparation old Granny Harding had made during her lifetime. We had sat, Anna and I, holding Granny Harding's hands when she died. Granny Harding was glad to die; not because life had been too hard for her, but because she had been glad to live. She was glad that rest was near, not because she had been overworked but because she wanted to order, wanted to arrange, ninety-three years of beautiful living, she wanted to play it all over again. 'It's like turning inside out, me dears,' she had said. Granny Harding died smiling, died in the middle of a description of Epping Forest on an early summer's morning. She died happily because she had lived happily. Old Granny went to church for the second time in her life.

It was three weeks to the day that we all went to another funeral. About a couple of dozen or more of us went to Skipper's funeral – six or so of the older ones and about twenty or so of assorted sizes. 'She won't make old bones,' they had said, and they were right. Skipper was a natural practical joker, always ready for a laugh. She would have laughed a lot more but it made her cough and she had been coughing a lot lately. Skipper was just coming up to fifteen when she died. Flaxen-haired, blue-eyed, with skin about as transparent as tissue-paper, Skipper funned and punned her way through her fifteen years. Why, it hadn't been all that many weeks ago that we'd all been talking about dying.

It was Bunty who opened the conversation with: 'How do you die?'

Someone answered with, 'It's easy, you just stop.'

Skipper had flipped back with, 'Sure, it's easy. Dead easy.'

We all groaned.

The funeral service was a solemn occasion, far too solemn for such as Skipper. The Rev. Castle went on about the innocence of youth and someone had to stifle a giggle. Lifting his eyes upwards, he told us that Skipper was now in heaven. Amen. Little faces all turned upwards and little mouths opened wide in appreciation, except for young Dora. She looked downwards. She got a good nudge and someone said in one of those thunderclap whispers, 'Up – up there.'

Dora's head went up to the roof of the church, overbalanced and toppled back with a thud. 'I dropped me sweets on the floor,' she complained.

The Rev. Castle droned on his easy way, painting his word-picture of Skipper. It wasn't our Skipper he was talking about, at least none of us recognized her. It's a good job that the dead don't talk back. I can just imagine what Skipper would have said: "Oo the bleedin' 'ell he talking about? Silly old sod!' Fortunately the Rev. Castle didn't hear and brought the proceedings to a close. We trooped off to the cemetery to pay our last respects. The kids chucked various items into the grave and walked away. We all stood a few yards off and waited for Buzz, who stayed a little longer. It had been that way with Skipper and Buzz. We made tracks for the cemetery gates, passing a twelve-foot angel laying a marble bunch of flowers on a grave.

'D'you reckon Skipper's got wings now?' somebody started up.

'Suppose so,' came an answer.

'Don't fancy wings meself.'

'Why's that?'

'How can you get yer shirt off?'

'Don't be daft, angels don't have no shirts.'

'Wot then?'

'It's a nightie.'

'I ain't gonna wear no nightie, it's cissy.'

Life had started up again.

'Maggie,' someone yelled, 'where's 'eaven?'

'Somewheres,' replied Maggie.

'It's up there.'

'Better not be.'

'Why's that?'

'If it was, betcha Skipper'd widdle on yer head.'

'Oo, you are 'orrible.'

'Buzz, you gonna get married now Skipper's dead?'

'Silly cow,' said Buzz, 'what's she wanna die for?'

'Better'n coughing yer guts up for years.'

'Suppose so – still.'

'Maggie, is there a different heaven for the Protties and the R.C.s and the Jews and all them?'

'No, only one.'

'What's all the different churches and synnigogs for then?'

'I don't know.'

'Old Nick done that. Just like Old Nick, he mucks everyfing up.'

'D'you reckon Skipper's gone to Old Nick?'

'She'd better not. Old Nick would chuck her out in a couple of days.'

'Poor Old Nick. Yer gotta laugh.'

'Can't stand that, can Old Nick.'

'Stand wot?'

'Laughing. It drives him up the wall.'

'What you think Skipper is doing now?'

'Singing hymns, I suppose.'

'Don't fancy that lark, singing hymns all the time.' This was Mat. Looking upwards, he began to yell and in a moment was joined by all the other kids:

> *'Sam, Sam, the dirty old man,*
> *Washed his face in a frying-pan,*
> *Combed his hair with a leg of a chair,*
> *Sam, Sam, the dirty old man.'*

'Betcha Skipper'll teach all them angels that one.'

'Yeah, and "There was an old man of Lancashire who—" '

'Not that one, stoopid, it's dirty.'

'Cors it ain't. Betcha God laughs.'

'Bet he don't.'

'Wot's he make us with arses for, if we can't say it?'

'It's dirty, that's all.'

'Why's everybody make God out to be miserable for? I wish I was God, I'd laugh.'

'Yeah, and what about Jesus?'

'Wot about Jesus?'

'All them pictures make him look like a pansy.'

'Bet he didn't look like that.'

'His old man was a chippy.'

'So was Jesus.'

'If'n you sawed up bloody great lumps of wood all day you'd have bloody big muscles.'

'Yeah. I bet he was all right.'

'Course he was. He had a bloomin' good booze-up an' all.'

'Where's it say that?'

'The Bible. He turned the water into wine.'

'Good job my old man can't do that.'

'Your old man can't do nuffink.'

'Why can't I say "arse"?'

"'Cos you can't.'

'Jesus had one.'

'He didn't say "arse".'

'How do you know?'

'Bet he said "bum".'

'He didn't, he talked Yiddish.'

'You're daft.'

'Like that nit at Sunday school, says the rain was the angels crying. Wot the 'ell they got to cry about?'

'Twits like you asking silly questions.'

'You reckon God gets fed up?'

'What for?'

'All them prayers and questions.'

'If I was God, I'd make people laugh.'

'If you was God, you wouldn't have to make 'em.'

'If I was God, I'd bash 'em on the head wiv a funderbolt.'

'I got a good idea.'

'Annuvver miracle!'

'No, straight up. What about starting another Church?'

'Stone the perishing crows, ain't we got enough?'

'No. I mean no prayers, and no hymns. We'll all tell funny jokes about Old Nick. That'll make him curl up.'

'Yeah, a laughing Church.'

'Hey, that's good that is. A laughing Church.'

And so it went on. Hour after hour, day after day, year after year. Like summer lightning the conversation flickered and flared, lighting up the dark places, forging a philosophy, a theology, a way of life, something to live with. It was this that Anna was so greedy for. It may not sound very much but it was the ore from which the gold came. One thing was certain. Skipper was dead, and as she would have said, 'Ah well, that's life!' Being dead was a fact of life. Life hereafter was a fact of being dead.

That night, after Skipper's funeral, I was wakened by a cry of despair from behind the curtains. I went to Anna and I cradled her in my arms. A nightmare was my first thought, or perhaps grief for Skipper. I rocked her gently in my arms and made those kinds of noises that 'made it all right again'. I was holding her tightly for comfort but she fought her way out of my arms and stood on the bed. I was a bit scared and lost at this turn of events and didn't quite know what to do. I lit the gas. Something seemed to go bad inside me. Anna was standing on the bed, her eyes wild and wide, tears streaming down her cheeks, both hands pressed over her mouth as if to stifle a scream. It seemed as if all the familiar objects in the room suddenly raced away to infinity and the world dissolved into formlessness.

I tried to say something, but nothing came. It was one of those senseless moments; my mind was racing around in circles but my body wasn't in gear. I tried to do something, but my body was frozen. What really frightened me was that Anna didn't see me, I wasn't there for her, I couldn't help her. I cried; I don't know if I cried for her or for myself. Whatever the reason, the miseries took over. Suddenly out of my tear-filled void I heard Anna's voice.

'Please, please, Mister God, teach me how to ask real questions. Oh please, Mister God, help me to ask real questions.'

For a moment of eternity I saw Anna as a flame and shuddered as I grasped the uniqueness of being me. How I managed that moment I shall never know for my strength was not equal to that moment. In some strange and mysterious way I 'saw' for the first time.

Suddenly there was a hand on my face, soft and gentle. A hand wiping away my tears and a voice saying, 'Fynn, Fynn.' The room began to reassemble again, things were once more.

'Fynn, wot you crying for?' asked Anna.

I don't know why, perhaps it was just plain fear, but I began to swear, coldly and efficiently. Every muscle in my body ached and trembled. Anna's lips were on mine, her arm about my neck:

'Don't swear, Fynn, it's all right, it's all right.'

I was trying to make some sort of sense out of that awful and beautiful moment, trying to get back to normality again; it was like climbing down an unending ladder.

Anna was talking again, 'I'm glad you came, Fynn,' she whispered. 'I love you, Fynn.'

I wanted to say 'Me, too,' but nothing happened.

In some curious way I seemed to be facing two ways at once. I wanted to be back among the familiar objects that I knew so well and at the same time I wanted to experience that moment again. From the middle of my fog of confusion I realized that I was being led back to bed, utterly exhausted. I lay there, trying to make some sense of it all, trying to find some starting-point from which I could begin to ask questions. But the words didn't seem to fit together in any reasonable pattern. It was a cup of tea in my hand that started the world turning again.

'Drink it, Fynn, drink it all up.'

Anna was sitting on the bed wearing my old blue sweater over her pyjamas. She had made the tea, hot and sweet, one for each of us. I heard the scrape of a match on the matchbox and Anna's splutter as she lit a fag for me and stuck it between my lips. I got myself up on my elbow.

'What happened, Fynn?' asked Anna.

'God knows,' I said. 'Were you asleep?'

'Been awake for a long time.'

'I thought you were having a nightmare,' I muttered.

'No,' she smiled, 'I was saying my prayers.'

'The way you was crying – I thought –'

'That why you cried?'

'I dunno, suppose so. It sort of got kind of empty all of a sudden. It was funny. I thought I was lookin' at myself for a moment. Painful.'

She didn't answer for a moment, and then very quietly she said, 'Yes, I know.'

I was too tired to prop myself up any longer and suddenly I found myself with my head resting on Anna's arm. It didn't seem right, it ought to have been the other way around, but it wasn't and I realized that I liked it, it was what I wanted. We stayed like that for a long time, but there were questions I wanted to ask her.

'Tich,' I said, 'what were you asking God about real questions for?'

'Oh, it's just sad, that's all.'

'What's sad?'

'People is.'

'I see. What's sad about people?'

'People ought to get more wise when they grow older. Bossy and Patch do, but people don't.'

'Don't you think so?' I asked.

'No. People's boxes get littler and littler.'

'Boxes? I don't understand that.'

'Questions are in boxes,' she explained, 'and the answers they get only fit the size of the box.'

'That's difficult; go on a bit.'

'It's hard to say. It's like – it's like the answers are the same size as the box. It's like them dimensions.'

'Oh?'

'If you ask a question in two dimensions, then the answer is in two dimensions too. It's like a box. You can't get out.'

'I think I see what you mean.'

'The questions get to the edge and then stop. It's like a prison.'

'I expect we're all in some sort of prison.'

She shook her head. 'No, Mister God wouldn't do that.'

'I suppose not. What's the answer then?'

'Let Mister God be. He lets us be.'

'Don't we?'

'No. We put Mister God into little boxes.'

'Surely we don't do that?'

'Yes, all the time. Because we don't really love him. We got to let Mister God be free. That's what love is.'

Anna searched for Mister God and her desire was for a better understanding of him. Anna's search for Mister God was serious but gay, earnest but light-hearted, reverent but impudent, and single-minded and multi-tracked. That one and two made three was for Anna a sign that God existed. Not that she doubted God's existence for a moment, but it was for some time a sign that he did exist. By the same token a bus or a flower was also a sign that he existed. How she came by this vision of the pearl of great price I do not know. Certainly it was with her before I met her. It was just my luck that I happened to be with her when she was doing her 'working out'. To listen to her was exhilarating, like flying on one's own; to watch her was to be startled into seeing. Evidence for Mister God? Why, there was nowhere you could look where there wasn't evidence for Mister God; it was everywhere. Everything was evidence of Mister God and it was at this point that things tended to get out of hand.

The evidence could be arranged in too many ways. People who accepted one sort of arrangement were called by one particular name. Arrange the evidence in a new way and you were called by a different name. Anna reckoned that the number of possible arrangements of the available evidence might easily run into 'squillions' of names. The problem was further complicated by the fact of synagogues, mosques, temples, churches, and all the other different places of worship, and scientific laboratories were not excluded from the list. By any reasonable standards of thinking and behaviour nobody could, with their hand on their heart, honestly say that these other people were not worshipping and loving God, even if they did call him by some other name like 'Truth'. She could not and would not say that Ali's God was a lesser kind of God than the Mister God that she knew so well, nor was she able to say that her Mister God was greater or more important than Kathie's God. It didn't make sense to talk about different Gods; that kind of talk inevitably leads to madness. No, for Anna it was all or nothing, there could be only one Mister God. This being so, then the different places of worship, the different kinds of names given to those worshippers, the different kinds of ritual performed by these worshippers could be due to one thing, and to one thing only, the different arrangements of the evidence for Mister God.

Anna solved this problem to her own satisfaction, or better still resolved it, on the piano. I've played the piano for as long as I can remember, but I can't read a note of music. I can listen to music and make a reasonable copy of it by ear, but if I attempt to play the same piece of music by reading the score, I turn it into a dirge. Those little black dots throw me into a flat spin. Whatever I've managed on the piano stems from the popular sheet-music of pre-war, the little frets with their constellation of dots which showed you how to finger the ukelele – or was it the guitar? – and those cryptic symbols underneath the lines of music such as 'Am7' or the chord of A minor seventh. This was the kind of music that I learnt, limited perhaps, but it did have one great advantage. Given a suitable handful of notes, you could call it a 'this' chord or a 'that' chord, or perhaps any one of half a dozen names, it all depended on something else.

This then was the method I used to teach Anna something about the piano. Soon she was romping through major chords, relative minor chords, minor sevenths, diminished sevenths and inversions. She knew their names and how to call them, more than that, she knew that the name given to a sprinkling of notes depended on where you were and what you were doing. Of course the question of why a group of notes was called 'a chord' had to be gone into. My Weekley's dictionary was called into service. We were informed that 'chord' and 'accord' were more or less one and the same word. One more flip through the dictionary to find out how the word 'accord' was used and we ended up with the word 'consent' and there we stopped.

It wasn't many hours later that day when I was confronted with the open-eyed, open-mouthed look of astonishment on Anna's face. She suddenly stopped playing hop-scotch with the rest of the kids and walked slowly towards me.

'Fynn,' her voice was a squeak of amazement, 'Fynn, we're all playing the same chord.'

'I'm not surprised,' I said. 'What are we talking about?'

'Fynn, it's all them different names for Churches.'

'So what's that got to do with chords?' I asked.

'We're all playing the same chord to Mister God but with different names.'

It was this kind of thing that was so exciting about talking to Anna. She had this capacity for taking a statement of fact in one subject, teasing it until she discovered its pattern, then looking around for a similar pattern in another subject. Anna had a high regard for facts, but the importance of a fact did not lie in its uniqueness but in its ability to do service in diverse subjects. Had Anna ever been given a convincing argument in favour of atheism she'd have teased it about until she had got a firm hold of the pattern, viewed it from all sides and then shown you that the whole argument was a necessary ingredient in the existence of God. The chord of atheism might be a discord but then discords were in Anna's estimation 'thrilly', but definitely 'thrilly'.

'Fynn, them names of them chords,' she began.

'What about them?' I asked.

'The home note can't be Mister God because then we couldn't call them different names. They would all be the same name,' she said.

'I guess you're right at that. What is the home note then?'

'It's me or you or Ali. Fynn, it's everybody. That's why it's all different names. That's why it's all different Churches. That's what it is.'

It makes sense, doesn't it? We're all playing the same chord but it seems we don't know it. You call your chord a C major while I call the same notes A minor seventh. I call myself a Christian, what do you call yourself? I reckon Mister God must be pretty good at music, he knows all the names of the chords. Perhaps he doesn't mind what you call it, as long as you play it.

CHAPTER NINE

Maybe it was the fact that Anna and I had met at night that made the night-time so magic for us. Perhaps it was because the night-time could be, and so often was, so surprising. The multitudes of sights and sounds of the daytime got down to manageable size at night. Things and sounds became separate at night, they didn't get muddled up with everything else, and things happened in the dark that couldn't possibly happen in the daylight. It's not impossible to have a conversation with a lamp-post at night; do the same thing in the daylight and they would take you off in a padded van.

'The sun is nice,' said Anna, 'but it lights things up so much that you can't see very far.'

I agreed that sometimes the sun was so dazzling that on occasions one was quite blinded. That wasn't what she meant.

'Your soul don't go very far in the daylight 'cos it stops where you can see.'

'That supposed to make sense?' I asked.

'The night-time is better. It stretches your soul right out to the stars. And that,' she pronounced, 'is a very long way. In the night-time you don't have to stop going out. It's like your ears. In the daytime it's so noisy you can't hear. In the night-time you can. The night-time stretches you.'

I wasn't going to argue with that one. The night-time was the time for stretching, and we often stretched ourselves.

Mum never batted an eyelid over our night-time rambles. Mum knew that stretching was important and Mum had been a past master at the art of stretching. Given half a chance she'd have been with us. 'Have a nice time,' she'd say, 'and don't get too lost.' She didn't mean in the streets of London Town, she meant up among the stars. You didn't have to explain to Mum about getting lost among the stars. Mum reckoned that 'getting lost' and 'finding your way' were just different sides of the same coin. You couldn't have the one without the other.

Mum was something of a genius, certainly she was a mum in a million. 'Why don't you go out,' she used to say, 'it's raining hard?', or, 'it's blowing a gale?' Whatever mischief the weather was up to Mum suggested that we go out, just for fun, just to see what it was all about. Outside in the streets windows were being flung open and other mums would be yelling for their various Freds and Berts, Bettys and Sadies to 'come in outa that rain! You'll be soaked to the skin'. Come storm or tempest, rain or snow, daytime or night-time, we'd always be encouraged to 'go out and try it'. Mum never protected us from God's works, as she called them. Mum protected us, for a while, from ourselves. She'd light up the big copper so that there was a good supply of hot water when we got home. She did it for years, until she figured we'd got enough sense to do it for ourselves, then she stopped.

Staying out all night was for Mum something not to be missed.

Most 'night-time people' were pretty wonderful people. Most 'night-time people' liked to talk. Those who thought we were mad or just plain stupid were in the minority. True, there were those who didn't hesitate to tell me exactly what they thought of me. 'Fancy taking a child out at a time like this, you must be stark raving mad.' 'You ought to be home and in bed, you wouldn't get up to any mischief there.' The assumption on the part of these people was that the night-time was for mischief, for foul deeds, for 'getting up to no good'. All God-fearing people went to their beds at night. The night was for the 'nasties', for 'beasties that go bump in the night', and for Old Nick. Perhaps we were lucky; in all the times that we roamed the streets at night we never ever bumped into a 'nasty' or a 'beasty' or even Old Nick, only nice people. At first we tried to explain that we wanted to be out, that we liked it, but this only confirmed some people in their suspicion that we were mad, so we gave up any attempt at an explanation and simply went out.

Parting from a little group of 'night-time people' on one of our walks, Anna remarked, 'It's funny, Fynn, ain't it? All the night-time people have got names.'

It was true too. You'd bump into a group of 'night-time people' round a fire and before you could say 'How's your father?' you'd be introduced all round. 'That's Lil, she's a bit funny in the 'ead, but she's all right.' 'That's Old Flintlighter.' His real name was Robert Somebody-or-other but everybody called him 'Old Flintlighter'.

Perhaps it was because the 'night-time people' had more time to talk to each other, or perhaps they were not over-involved in 'making it good' – whatever the reason, the 'night-time people' talked and talked and shared and shared.

It was on one such night that the bottle was passed. It went from hand to hand round the circle. On each pass, the mouth of the bottle was wiped with a dirty sleeve before a good swig was taken. It was my turn; I did a quick wipe and took a big swig. I wish I hadn't. My inside turned a somersault and everything dried up. Coughing and spluttering, with tears streaming down my eyes, I passed it along to the next man. It tasted like well-seasoned varnish laced with TNT. One mouthful was an experience, two was a punishment, and three was certain slow death.

'That yer first time, cock?' said Old Flintlighter.

'Yes,' I gasped, 'and me last.'

'It gets better as you go on,' said Lil.

'What the hell do you call it?' I was getting my breath back.

'That's Red Biddy, that's what it's called,' said Old Flintlighter.

'It keeps the cold out when it gets a bit parky.'

'It tastes like petrol to me,' I said.

Old Lil cackled. 'Ain't that the truth,' she said. 'Yer gets the taste for it after a bit.'

Anna wanted a taste, so I poured a drop on the corner of my handkerchief, half expecting it to burst into flames at any moment. She sucked at the corner of the handkerchief and made a face.

'Ugh,' she spat, 'it's horrible.'

They all laughed.

It struck me as odd that this ritual of wiping the mouth of the bottle still went on; perhaps it was a left-over from the more palmy days. Certainly no germ could get within a foot of it without curling up.

After that experience we never drank anything else but tea or cocoa. We'd sit on old oil drums or wooden boxes and drink tea from battered old tin mugs, cooking our bangers on the ends of sticks and talking.

Convict Bill, from down under, told of his adventures before the mast. Convict Bill had had so many extraordinary adventures he must have had at least four man-sized adventures per day. What did it matter if they were not true? What did it matter if they were all adventures of the imagination? It was pure genius, pure poetry. It was true, the stars stretched a person out, the stars broke open this prison of a box and let the imagination roam.

Anna, on her oil-drum throne, was always and everywhere the centre of attention, her face radiant in the fire's glow as she listened to the adventures of the 'night-time people'. Her contributions to these occasions varied – a little dance, a song or a story.

On one such night Anna began a story. Old Flintlighter picked her up and stood her on a packing-case. There she stood with the eyes of a couple of dozen 'night-time people' fixed on her. She told the story of a king who was about to have someone's head chopped off but had a sudden change of heart when he saw the smile of a little child. All the heads nodded in unison and Convict Bill said, 'Ah! It's pretty powerful stuff, a smile is. Why, it reminds me of the time ...', and he was launched on some new and fantastic adventure.

It was a chilly April night when we first met Old Woody. Old Woody commanded great respect from the 'night-time people', obviously well-educated, well-mannered and utterly content with his life. Old Woody was tall and as straight as a pole. Hawk-nosed, bearded, and with eyes that focused somewhere near infinity. His voice was like roasted chestnuts, warm and brown. When Old Woody smiled it just touched the corners of his mouth. But it wasn't there that you looked for his smile, it was in his eyes. Those eyes just sort of wrapped you up, those eyes were full up with good things, and when he smiled, why, they just poured out all over you.

As we stepped into the light of the fire Old Woody looked up and sized us up for a minute or two. Nobody spoke. His eyes

passed from my face to Anna's, and there they stuck. With a smile
he held out his hand to Anna and she went across to him and
held it. For a long, long moment they stared at each other, showering each other with good things, and smiling fit to bust. They
were two of a kind, they didn't need to use language. The
exchange was immediate and complete. Standing Anna in front of
him, he looked her over once more.

'You're a bit young for this, aren't you, little one?'

Anna held her silence, testing and probing Old Woody. He did-
n't demand an answer, he wasn't anxious, he was prepared to
wait.

He passed the test, so he got his answer, 'I'm old enough to
live, mister,' said Anna quietly.

Old Woody smiled, shifted a wooden box beside him and pat-
ted it. Anna sat down.

I was left standing, so I rummaged around until I found a suitable box to sit on and joined the circle. The silence had been held
for three minutes or more. Old Woody was busy stuffing his pipe
and testing it to see if it was drawing properly. Satisfied that all was
as it should be, he got up, went over to the fire and lit up. He put
his hand on Anna's head before he sat down and said something
that I couldn't catch. They both laughed. Old Woody took a long
and satisfying pull at his pipe.

'Do you like poetry?' he asked.

Anna nodded. Old Woody settled the glowing tobacco in his
pipe with his thumb.

'Do you,' he said, sucking away, 'do you know what poetry is?'

'Yes,' replied Anna. 'It's sort of like sewing.'

'I see,' Old Woody nodded, 'and what do you mean by sewing?'

Anna juggled the words around in her mind. 'Well, it's making
something from different bits that is different from all the bits.'

'Um,' said Old Woody, 'I think that is rather a good definition of
poetry.'

'Mister,' said Anna, 'can I ask you a question?'

'Of course,' Old Woody nodded.

'Why don't you live in a house?'

Old Woody looked at his pipe and rubbed his thumb on his
beard. 'I don't think there is a real answer to that question, not
put like that. Can you ask it in another way?'

Anna thought for a moment, then said, 'Mister, why do you like living in the dark?'

'Living in the dark?' smiled Old Woody. 'I can answer that very easily, but can you understand my answer, I wonder?'

'If it's an answer, I can,' responded Anna.

'Yes, of course. If it is an answer, you can. That's true, only if it's an answer.' He paused, and then, 'Do you like the darkness?'

Anna nodded. 'It stretches you out big. It makes the box big.'

He gave a little chuckle. 'Indeed, indeed,' he said. 'My reason for preferring the darkness is that in the dark you have to describe yourself. In the daylight other people describe you. Do you understand that?'

Anna smiled, and Old Woody reached out a gnarled old hand and gently closed Anna's eyes, held both her hands and settled some inner aspect of himself. This particular little spot in London

Town looked by daylight a shambles; at this moment, in the light of the fire, it was pure magic.

Old Woody's firm and strong voice spoke to his God, to Anna, and to all mankind:

> *'In faith, I do not love thee with mine eyes,*
> *For they in thee a thousand errors note;*
> *But 'tis my heart that loves what they despise.'*

His nut-brown chuckle broke the spell. 'Do you know that one? It's one of Shakespeare's sonnets. They,' he said, and his arms swept out to embrace the world, 'will tell you and encourage you to develop your brain and your five senses. But that's only the half of it, that's only being half a human. The other half is to develop the heart and the wits.' He ticked them off on one old gnarled hand with the end of his pipe. 'There's common wit, there's imagination, there's fantasy, there's estimation, and there's memory.' Old Woody's face turned upwards, his spirit danced and was warmed out among the stars whilst his body remained with us and was warmed by the old tin-can brazier. 'Never let anyone rob you of your right to be complete. The daylight is for the brain and the senses, the darkness is for the heart and the wits – Never, never be afraid. Your brain may fail you one day, but your heart won't.' He returned like a comet, leaving behind a shining trail of love.

He stood up and stretched himself, looked around at all the faces, and his gaze stopped at Anna. 'I know you, young lady, I know you well.' He pulled his coat closer round his old shoulders, moved out of the circle of light, and stopped and smiled once more at Anna. He held out his arm to her and spoke:

> *'Thus doth she, when from individual states*
> *She doth abstract the universal kinds,*
> *Which then reclothed in divers names and fates,*
> *Steal access thro' our senses to our minds.'*

Then he was gone. No, not gone, for some part of him, perhaps the biggest part of him, remained and remains even to this day. We stayed looking into the fire for ten minutes or so. We asked no questions, for there were no answers. We didn't even say goodbye to the 'night-people' as we left. I wondered if we had left as much behind us at our going.

We walked on slowly through the streets of London, each afloat on our own thoughts. One of the council's motorized road-sweepers made clean the mess of the day. It came towards us, spraying the roadway and the pavement as it came, its large cylindrical brushes clearing up the streets of London for the day-light people. We did a *pas de deux* to the right as its spray hissed on to the pavement and one to the left as it passed us.

Anna switched on her klaxon-horn laugh and spun like a top with joy. Pointing after the receding sweeper, she said, 'Fairies, they're like fairies.'

'Some fairies,' I chuckled.

'Like what you read to me – about Puck.'

The mood and joy of the night caught hold of me. I ran and leapt on to a nearby pillar-box and stood up and declaimed the lines of Puck to the night:

> *I am sent with broom before,*
> *To sweep the dust behind the door.'*

Titania pirouetted and circled the pillar-box in fairy dance. A policeman advanced in the distance, and pointing a finger at him, I yelled, 'How now, spirit! whither wander you?' His 'What do you think you're up to?' was almost lost in our laughter. I jumped off the pillar-box and grabbed Anna by the hand and we raced after the disappearing road-sweeper. We dashed through its fountains of spray and waited ahead of it, breathless with running and laughter.

'Look! it's Moth and Mustardseed,' I gasped out.

'No, it's not, it's Peaseblossom and Cobweb,' she squeaked.

Our feet and legs were drenched as the sweeper passed. It went on for a few more yards and then stopped; the spray was turned off. The cab door opened and Mustardseed stepped to the ground. The sight of a six-foot, twenty-stone, overall-clad Mustardseed was too much – we clung to each other, helpless with laughter. Mustardseed moved towards us from one direction while the policeman, with measured tread, approached from behind us. We fled howling down a side street and stopped at some safe distance. The policeman and Mustardseed, now joined by Moth, were looking down the street after us. What they were talking about who knows? but my guess was that it was something to do with the madness of the young. I grabbed Anna's hand again and we ran. We didn't stop running until we came to the Embankment. We climbed on to the parapet and opened our sandwiches and munched them whilst we watched the night traffic on the Thames pass by.

After finishing the sandwiches I lit a fag. Anna climbed down and began a lonely game of hop-scotch on the pavement. She got about thirty yards away, turned, ran back and stood in front of me.

'Hello, Fynn!' She twirled around and parachuted her skirt.

'Hello, Anna.' I inclined my head and threw out a gracious hand. She was off again, hopping away for all she was worth, chanting a 'One, two, three' song. She stopped and performed a little dance of pure joy. She ran back, her finger drawing a wavy line on the wall. She stopped again about five yards short of me, turned again and drew another wavy line with the fingers of her other hand on the wall.

Twenty or thirty times she covered that twenty-yard length of wall. Long and slow waves, short and fast waves. Sometimes she walked as she drew her wavy lines, sometimes she went backwards and then forwards as fast as her legs would carry her. The wall showed no signs of her activity, bore no witness to her thoughts, it remained a blank, but then Anna was writing on her inner blackboard.

At the end of her run she stopped, the lamplight glinting on her hair. She shook her head violently and a cloud of copper sparks rose up and settled. She began to walk, head down, heel to toe along the cracks of the paving-stones, her course unplanned and uncharted, led only by the chance intersection of the paving-stone cracks. I doubt if she was even aware of what she was doing. This activity absorbed about one per cent of her attention. The other ninety-nine per cent had got turned around and was looking inside at something. It's funny how you learn to read the signs. This was the impending revelation prelude, that is if it 'got worked out'. I put my packet of fags and matches beside me. It was possible

I wouldn't have another chance for an hour or so if I had read the signs right.

Her walk finished, she drifted over to the wall, leant against it and remained perfectly still for a minute or two. With about as much attention as she had walked the cracks of the pavement she shuffled her feet forwards about a yard or so. She made an angle with the wall, supported only by her heels and the back of her head. I nearly yelled, but I didn't. It wouldn't have made much difference if I had; there wasn't much of her outside. She couldn't have heard me where she was.

She didn't walk back, she didn't hop, jump, skip or run back, she rolled back. For thirty or more yards she rolled, balanced between head and heels. Over and over and over she rolled, ending up with her head buried on my legs, and there she stayed.

Her voice, muffled by my trousers, said, 'I'm dizzy.'

'Ain't that the truth,' I replied.

'The wall's hard,' came her muffled voice.

'So's your head.'

I got a sharp 'don't-be-funny' bite on my leg.

'Oi! that hurts,' I reminded her.

'So does my head.'

'It's your own fault. You shouldn't be so daft. What was all that in aid of?'

'I was thinking.'

'That was thinking?' I asked. 'Please God I never learn to think.'

'Do you want to know what I was thinking about, Fynn?'

She looked up at me.

'If I've got a choice,' I answered, 'no, I don't.'

She knew that I was teasing her and her smile told me that I didn't have a choice anyway.

'It can't be light.' Anna gave that sentence a finality that was irrefutable.

'So, fine,' I said. 'If it can't be light, what is it?'

'Mister God can't be light.' The words flew like stone chippings as Anna hacked away with her mental chisels.

I could imagine Mister God edging forwards on his golden throne and peering down through the clouds, a little anxious to know what kind of a mould he was being forced into now. I had the itch to look upwards and say, 'Relax, Mister God. Just relax, you're in safe hands.' I reckon Mister God must get a bit fed up now and again considering all the various shapes we'd pressed on him over the last umpteen thousand years, and I don't suppose we've come to the end of it yet, not by a long chalk.

'He can't be light, can he? Can he, Fynn?'

'Search me, Tich. Search me.'

'Well he can't be, 'cos what about them little waves we can't see and the big waves we can't see? What about them?'

'See what you mean. I reckon things would look a whole lot different if we could see by those waves.'

'I think that the light's inside us. That's what I think.'

'Could be. Could be you're right,' I said.

'I think it's so's we can *see* how to see,' she nodded her head, 'that's what I think.'

Upstairs Mister God – if you'll pardon the image – slapped his leg and turned to his angel hosts and said, 'How about that! How about it?'

'Yes,' continued Anna, 'the Mister God Light inside us is so's we can see the Mister God Light outside us, and – and, Fynn,' she jumped up and down with excitement as she rounded it all off, 'the Mister God Light outside us is so's we can see the Mister God Light inside us.'

She played the whole melody over again to herself in silence. With a grin that would have put the Cheshire cat to shame, she said, 'That's nice, Fynn. Ain't it nice?'

I agreed that it was nice, very nice, but I was beginning to think that I had had just about enough for one night. I was glutted and needed a little time to digest the night's happenings, but not Anna, she had just got into her stride.

'Fynn, can I have the chalks?'

It was time to come up for air and I rummaged about in my pockets for the tin.

Going out with Anna fell naturally into three categories. There was 'oozing' along, like we were doing this night. The demands of 'oozing' were simply met. Two smallish tins containing coloured chalks, string, bits of coloured wool, 'lastic bands, a small bottle or two, paper, pencil, pins and a few other knick-knacks, odds and ends, and suchlike.

Category two was 'going for a walk'. This was a bit more complicated. Over and above the two tins just for 'oozing', 'going for a walk' demanded such things as collapsible fishing-net, jam-jars, boxes of various sizes, tins, bags, etc., etc. Ideally we should have had a five-ton truck following us, carrying everything necessary for 'going for a walk'. If Mother Nature had been a little kinder to all the bugs, beetles, caterpillars, frog spawn and what have you that Anna brought back from 'going for a walk', I reckon that London would have ground to a halt. We'd have been up to our eyes in frogs and bugs.

The last category was 'going for a walk with a fixed purpose in mind'. This was a daunting experience, such as would give you nightmares for the rest of your life. To satisfy every contingency in 'going for a walk with a fixed purpose in mind' would take about three – better make it half a dozen – pantechnicons. Little items, like maybe an oil-rig or two, air-compressors, a hundred-foot ladder, a diving bell, a crane or two, little things like that. It's far too painful to talk about. After the three times we 'went for a walk with a fixed purpose in mind' I couldn't stand upright for a week.

Carrying chalks about, then, came as naturally as breathing. They went everywhere with me. Carrying about these chalks produced a sort of Walter Mittyish fantasy game. I'd be at the opera, or maybe the proms, and the performance would stop. Someone would step forward and say, 'Has any gentleman in the audience got a piece of chalk?' I'd get up and say, 'Yes, I've got some. What colour would you like?' Applause! Applause! Nobody ever asked me, except Anna that is, but Anna never used the chalks as a prop for fantasy, she used them to explain the fantastic.

I passed her the chalks. She knelt down on the pavement and drew a large red circle.

'Pretend that's me,' she said.

Outside the circle she liberally sprinkled a number of dots. About the same number of dots were sprinkled inside the circle. She beckoned me off my perch on the wall. I went and knelt beside her. Looking around, she pointed to a tree.

'That,' she said, 'is that there,' and she pointed to a dot outside the circle and marked it with a cross. Then, pointing to a dot inside the circle, she said, 'That is that dot outside the circle, and that is the tree,' and with her finger on the 'tree dot' inside the circle, she continued with, 'And that's the tree inside me.'

'I seem to have been here before,' I murmured.

'And that,' she exclaimed in triumph, laying her finger on a dot inside the circle, 'is a – is a – a flying elephant. But where is it outside? Where is it, Fynn?'

'There ain't no such beastie, so it can't be outside,' I explained.

'Well then, how did it get into my head?' She sat back on her heels and stared at me.

'How anything gets into your head beats me, but a flying elephant is pure imagination, it's not factual.'

'Ain't my imagination a fact, Fynn?' she quizzed me with a tilt of her head.

'Sure, of course your imagination is a fact, but what comes out of it isn't necessarily a fact.' I was beginning to wriggle a bit.

'Well then, how did it get in there' – she thumped the inside of the circle – 'if it ain't out there?' she went on with a few more thumps. 'Where did it come from?'

I was thankful that I wasn't given the opportunity to answer that one. She was in full flight. She got up and walked around the diagram of her universe.

'There's a lot of things out there that ain't in here.'

She leaped from the edge of the universe into the circle of herself and knelt down.

'Fynn, did you like my painting?'

'I liked it fine,' I said. 'I thought it was pretty darn good.'

'Where,' she said with her hands on her hips, 'was it?'

I pointed to a dot outside the circle. 'There, I suppose.'

She scrabbled backwards until she was clear of the diagram and pointing a finger to the centre of the circle. Her finger stabbed out her sentence. 'There, that's where I painted it – inside me.'

She remained silent for a long moment, then, sweeping her hands over the diagram, she said in a puzzled voice, 'Sometimes I don't know if I am locked out or locked in.'

Touching the inner dots and then the outer dots, she continued, 'It's funny, sometimes you look inside and find something outside and sometimes you look outside and find something inside. It's very funny.'

As we knelt considering the south-east sector of Anna's universe a pair of shining size-twelve boots appeared in the north-west section and a voice said, 'Well, well, if it isn't Master Puck and the Lady Titania.'

'Blimey, it's Oberon,' I muttered, looking up and seeing the policeman.

'Haven't you got a home to go to? And what do you think you're up to, drawing pictures on the pavement?'

'We've got a home to go to,' I admitted.

'That ain't a picture, mister,' said Anna, still hunkered down on the pavement.

'What's it supposed to be then?' asked the policeman.

"It's really Mister God. That's me, that's inside me and that's outside me, but it's all Mister God.'

'Well now,' said the policeman, 'it's still drawing on the pavement and that's not allowed.'

Anna reached out and pushed a pair of size twelves out of her universe. The policeman looked down at Anna.

'You've just flattened a couple of billion stars,' I told him.

The policeman may have represented law and order but Anna was concerned with higher laws and higher orders.

'That's you, mister,' Anna was undeterred and went on, 'and that's you inside me. Ain't it, Fynn?'

'Sure. Sure is, constable, that's you right enough,' I agreed.

'Only you don't look like that really. You look like this.' She shuffled a few feet to one side and drew another large circle and filled it with dots.

'That's me inside you,' she said, pointing to a dot, 'but that dot is really that circle. That's me.'

The policeman was leaning forward looking at Anna's universe. 'Ah!' he said knowingly. He looked at me and raised his eyebrows. I shrugged my shoulders. After a 'hum' or two he pointed his size twelves at one of the outside dots.

'Know what that is, Titania?'

'Wot?' said Anna.

'That's the Sarge. He'll be along in a few minutes and if this pavement isn't cleaned by then, you'll be in one of these.' His foot described a large circle. 'Know what that is? That's a police-station.' His broad smile softened his gruff voice.

Anna took my offered handkerchief and erased the universe from the pavement of Westminster embankment. Standing up, she flapped the chalk-dust from my handkerchief and handed it to me.

'Mister,' she said, 'do you always work here?'

'Most times,' the policeman replied.

'Mister,' Anna took his hand and pulled him to the wall, 'mister, is the Thames the water, or the hole it goes in?'

The policeman looked at her for a moment and then replied, 'The water, of course. You don't have a river without water.'

'Oh,' said Anna, 'that's funny, that is, 'cos when it rains it ain't the Thames but when it runs into the hole it is the Thames. Why is that, mister? Why?'

The policeman looked at me. 'Is she having me on?'

'You're being let off lightly,' I said. 'I get it all day long.'

The policeman had had enough. 'Hop it, you two, hop it or I'll – Oh yes. One last word of warning. You'd better go home that way,' he pointed with his finger. 'Er – Peaseblossom and Cobweb,' his grin was difficult to control, 'will be along here in no time. If you're still around, you might get your Bottom smacked – Get it?' he chuckled, pleased with himself.

'Comics,' I muttered, 'the whole world's full of comics.'

I grabbed Anna's hand and led her away. 'Nice work, Tich, nice work. A good bit of thinking, all that Thames stuff.'

'Oh,' murmured Anna, 'but when do you, Fynn?' When do you start calling it the Thames and when do you stop calling it the Thames? Do you have a mark? Do you, Fynn?'

Old Woody was right. The daylight schooled the senses and the night-time developed the wits, stretched the imagination, sharpened fantasy, hammered home the memory and altered the whole scale of values.

I began to realize why most people went to sleep in the night-time – it was easier. A whole lot easier.

CHAPTER TEN

I t looked pretty certain that the war would come. Already the gas-masks were making rude noises in the streets. The men with the Anderson shelters were dumping corrugated-iron sheets in back-gardens. Notices about gas attacks, sirens, shelters and what to do 'if', were multiplying like the spots of some disease. The decay of war was spreading everywhere. The walls against which the kids played their ball-games had become the notice-boards of war. The rules of 'four sticks' chalked up on the wall had been covered over with the regulations for the blackout. We were being instructed in the rules of a new game. On very rare occasions an instruction said something other than had been intended: 'All expectant mothers must show their pink forms.' It would have been nice to think that it had been done deliberately, but it hadn't.

The infection of war was spreading through the kids. Balls were no longer things to bounce, balls had become bombs. Cricket-bats were pressed into service as machine-guns. Kids with out-stretched arms gyrated through imaginary skies with a 'rat-a-tat-tat', shooting down enemy planes or shooting up enemy soldiers. A shriek of 'wheeeeee, booooom' and a dozen kids died in feigned agony. 'Bang, you're dead!'

Anna held tightly to my hand and pressed herself close to me. It wasn't the kind of game that she could play, the acting and the pretending belonged to something real and it was this reality that Anna saw so clearly. She pulled at my hand and we went indoors and out into the garden. It wasn't much better there, for over the housetops a barrage-balloon made mock of the skies. She turned a full circle looking at these intruders in the sky. She looked me full in the face as her hand stretched out for mine. A frown flickered over her face.

'Why, Fynn? Why?' she asked, searching my face for an answer.

I could give her no answers. Kneeling down, she gently touched the few wild flowers that grew in the back-yard. Bossy arrived and rubbed his battered old head on her leg. Patch, lying full length, eyed her with concern. It must have been the best part of an hour that I stood there watching her touch and explore these few square yards of garden. Delicately and reverently her fingers moved from beetle to flower, from pebble to caterpillar. I was waiting for her to cry, expecting her at any moment to run to my arms, but she didn't. I wasn't at all sure what was going on in her mind. All I knew was that the hurt was deep, perhaps too deep for my comfort.

Some time ago I had started to light up a fag, but I hadn't got very far. It was still unlit between my lips when I heard her say, so very quietly, 'I'm sorry.' She wasn't talking to me, she wasn't talking to Mister God. She was talking to the flowers, to the earth, to Bossy and to Patch and to the little bugs and beetles. Humanity asking the rest of the world for forgiveness.

I was intruding here so I went into the kitchen and swore. It struck me as curious that since knowing Anna I was swearing much more frequently. It ought to have been the other way around, but it wasn't. I grabbed the unlit fag out of my mouth. It had stuck to my lips and it felt as if I had pulled half the skin from my lips. It made me swear some more, but it didn't make me feel any better.

I don't know how long I sat there. It seemed for ever. It was the horror of my own imagination that drove me into the garden again. My imagination had somehow provided me with a machine-gun and I was busy killing off those who had caused Anna so much hurt. Confused and bewildered at my own violent thoughts, I went out into the back-yard half afraid that in some mysterious way she had divined them.

She was sitting on the garden wall with Bossy on her lap. She grinned as I approached her, not one of those full-blooded grins but full enough for me to slam the door on my own violence.

I went back into the kitchen and put on the kettle. Soon we were both sitting on the wall drinking our cocoa. My mind was racing away with questions I wanted to ask but I managed not to. I wanted to be assured that she was all right, but I wasn't given that assurance. I knew that she wasn't all right. I knew that the horror of the impending war had struck deep down inside her. No, she wasn't all right, but she was managing very well. For Anna, this war creeping up on us was a deep sorrow of the soul. It was me that was anxious.

Later that evening, when Anna was ready for bed, I suggested she could come into bed with me if she wanted to, to give her comfort, to give her protection, of course. Lord, how easy it is to fool yourself, how easy to cover up your own maggots of fear, by pretending they belong to someone else. I knew full well that I was concerned for her, that I was aware of her distress and that I was ready to do anything to comfort her. It was only in the middle of the night that I realized how much I needed her assurance that she was all right, how much her sheer sanity protected me. For all her few years, I saw her then as I see her now, the sanest, the most uncluttered and the most direct of beings. Her ability to ignore the excesses of information, dismiss the useless frill and uncover the heart of things was truly magical.

'Fynn, I love you.' When Anna said that every word was shattered by the fullness of meaning she packed into it. Her 'I' was a totality. Whatever this 'I' was for Anna was packed tight with being. Like the light that didn't fray, Anna's 'I' didn't fray either; it was pure and all of one piece. Her use of the word 'love' was not sentimental or mushy, it was impelling and full of courage and encouragement. For Anna, 'love' meant the recognition of perfectibility in another. Anna 'saw' a person in every part. Anna 'saw' a 'you'. Now that is something to experience, to be seen as a 'you', clearly and definitely, with no parts hidden. Wonderful and frightening. I'd always understood that it was Mister God who saw you so clearly and in your entirety, but then all Anna's efforts were directed to being like Mister God, so perhaps the trick is catching if only you try hard enough.

By and large I thought I could understand Anna's attitude to Mister God but on one aspect I got stuck completely. Perhaps it was hidden in 'Thou didst hide these things from the wise and understanding and didst reveal them unto babes.' How she managed it I truly don't know, but in some manner she had scaled the walls of God's majesty, his awe-inspiring nature, and was on the other side. Mister God was a 'sweetie'. Mister God was fun, Mister God was lovable. Mister God was for Anna pretty straightforward, not presenting her with any real problem in the understanding of his nature. The fact that he could, and often did, put a large spanner in the works was neither here nor there. He was perfectly free to do so and obviously it was for some good purpose, even though we were not able to see or understand that purpose.

Anna saw, recognized, admitted to, and submitted to, all those attributes of God so often discussed. Mister God was the author of all things, the creator of all things, omnipotent, omniscient, and at the very heart of all things – except. It was this exception that Anna saw as the key to the whole thing. This exception was funny, exciting, and made Mister God the 'sweetie' he was.

What puzzled Anna was that nobody had seen it before – at least, if they had seen it, nobody seemed willing to talk about it. It was very odd since it was for Anna so strange a thing that only Mister God could have thought about it. All the other qualities of Mister God, those qualities so often talked about in church and school, were magnificent, tremendous and, let's face it, a little frightening. Then he had gone and done this thing. It made him lovable, funny, giggly.

You could, if you wished, deny that Mister God existed, but then any denial didn't alter the fact that Mister God was. No, Mister God was, he *was* the king-pin, the centre, the very heart of things, and this is where it got funny. You see, we had to recognize that he was all these things and that meant that we were at our own centre, not God. God is our centre and yet it is we who acknowledge that he is the centre. That makes us somehow internal to Mister God. This is the curious nature of Mister God, that even while he is at the centre of all things he waits outside us and knocks to come in. It is we who open the door. Mister God doesn't break it down and come in, no, he knocks and waits.

Now it takes a real super kind of God to work that one out, but that's just what he's done. As Anna said, 'That's very funny, that is. It makes me very important, don't it? Fancy Mister God taking second place!' Anna never got involved in the problem of 'free will'. I suppose she was too young, but she had got to the heart of the matter: Mister God took second place, ain't that something!

It was after ten o'clock on a Sunday morning. Anna had been up for a long time. She was shaking me awake with one hand and holding a cup of tea with the other. My one opened eye registered on the teetering cup and saucer in her left hand. It was more than possible that the cup would end up in bed with me if she shook much harder. I moved across the bed to give me more room for any emergency manoeuvre.

'Desist, infant,' I implored.

'Cuppa tea, Fynn,' she plonked down on the bed. The cup gave a last frantic twirl around the saucer and settled down. After scraping the bottom of the cup on the saucer edge she handed it to me. The amount of tea left at the bottom of the cup might have been enough to drown a fly or two, or at least certainly inconvenience them. I lifted the cup to drain what was there and was smitten on the nose by half a dozen lumps of undissolved sugar. I made a face at her.

'That is tea?' I questioned.

'Drink wot's in the saucer then. I'll hold it for you.'

I'm never at my best first thing in the morning and need both my arms to prop myself up. I sat on the edge of the bed and braced myself, closed my eyes and opened my mouth. The saucer rattled against my back teeth as she thrust it in and tipped it up. I got about a third of the tea inside me and the rest outside. Anna giggled.

'A drink I need, a wash I can wait for. Away to the kitchen and start brewing.'

I pointed to the door. She went.

'Fynn's awake,' she yelled. 'He wants some more tea. He spilt that lot down his pyjamas.'

'May you be forgiven,' I muttered as I took off my pyjama jacket and mopped my chest with the dry bit.

You didn't have to wait long for tea in our house. Tea was for us what serum is for a casualty ward, ever present. Tea with saffron was good for something or other, fevers I believe. Tea with peppermint was good for flatulence. Tea woke you up and tea sent you to sleep. Tea without sugar was refreshing, tea with sugar was energizing, tea with a lot of sugar was good for shock.

For me, waking up was a shock so the first cup of tea of the day was nice and sweet.

Anna arrived back in a couple of shakes with more tea.

'Will you make me two paddle-wheels this morning?' she asked.

'Could be,' I answered. 'Where you paddling off to?'

'Nowhere. I want to do an experiment,' she replied.

'What size paddle-wheels and what are they in aid of?' I questioned.

'Little ones like this,' and her hands measured about three inches apart. 'And it's for finding out about Mister God.'

Requests like that I took in my stride these days. After all, if it was possible to read sermons in stones and things, why not in paddle-wheels?

'And can I have the big bath, and some hosepipe, and a tin with a hole in it? I might want something else but I don't know yet.'

While I made the paddle-wheels Anna assembled her experiment. The paddle-wheels were mounted on axles. A large cylindrical tin had a half-inch hole drilled in its side near the bottom of the tin. One of the paddle-wheels was soldered inside the tin across the newly drilled hole. After about an hour of hectic activity I was called into the yard to see the Mister God experiment in action.

A hose from the tap was filling the large bath. The tin with its paddle-wheel sat in the middle of the bath, weighted down with stones. As the water poured in through the hole, the paddle-wheel was turning. More hosepipe was doing service as a syphon, taking the water out of the tin, falling on to and spinning the second paddle-wheel and ending up going down the drain. I walked around the experiment and raised my eyebrows.

'Do you like it, Fynn?' asked Anna.

'I like it. But what is it?' I asked.

'That's you,' she said, pointing to the tin with its paddle-wheel.

'Bound to be. What am I doing?'

'The water is Mister God.'

'Gotcha.'

'The water comes out of the tap into the bath.'

'I'm still with you.'

'It goes into the tin, that's you, through the hole and makes you work,' she said, pointing to the spinning wheel, 'like a heart!'

'Ah!'

'When you work, it comes out of this tube,' she pointed to the syphon, 'and that makes the other wheel work.'

'What about the drain?'

'Well,' she hesitated, 'if I had a little pump like Mister God's heart I could pump it all back into the bath. Then I wouldn't need the tap. It would just go round and round.'

So there you are then. How to make a model of Mister God, with a couple of paddle-wheels. No home should be without one. I sat on the wall and smoked a fag while I watched Mister God and me spinning paddle-wheels.

'Ain't it good, Fynn?'

'Sure is good. We'd better take it to church on Sunday. It might give somebody some ideas.'

'Oh no, we couldn't do that. That would be bad.'

'How's that?' I asked.

'Well, it isn't Mister God, but it's a little bit like him.'

'So what? If it works for you and it works for me, that's fine. It might work for someone else.'

'It works because me and you is full up.'

'And what might that mean?'

'Well, if you are full up, you can use anything to see Mister God. You can't if you're not full up.'

'Why's that? Give me a for instance.'

She never hesitated.

'The cross! If you're full up, you don't need it 'cos the cross is inside you. If you're not full up, you have the cross outside you and then you make it a magic thing.'

She tugged at my arm and our eyes met. She spoke quietly and slowly: 'If you're not full up inside you, then you can make anything a magic thing, and then it becomes an outside bit of you.'

'Is it that bad?'

She nodded. 'If you do that, then you can't do what Mister God wants you to do.'

'Oh! What's he want me to do then?'

'Love everybody like you love yourself, and you've got to be full up with you to love yourself properly first.'

'Like most of a person is outside,' I said.

She smiled. 'Fynn, there ain't no different churches in heaven 'cos everybody in heaven is inside themselves.'

Then she went on:

'It's the outside bits that make all the different churches and synagogues and temples and things like that. Fynn, Mister God said "I am", and that's what he wants us all to say – that's the hard bit.'

My head went up and down in bewildered agreement.

'"I am" … that's the hard bit.' 'I am.' Really get around to saying that and you're home, really mean it and you're full up, you're all inside. You don't have to want things outside you to fill up the gaps inside you. You don't leave bits of you hanging around on objects in shop-windows, in catalogues or on advertising hoardings. Wherever you go you take your whole self with you, you don't leave bits lying around to get stamped on, you're all of a piece, you're what Mister God wants you to be. An 'I am', like he is. Hell's bells! All this time I had thought that going to church was in order to look for God, for praising him. It didn't dawn on me what Mister God was doing. All this time he had been working overtime trying to knock a bit of sense into my noddle, trying to turn an 'It is' into an 'I am'. I got the message. That was the Sunday I really signed on.

I was beginning to get the hang of this 'I am' stuff. Considering how important it was to Mister God, I was finding it not too impossible to cope with. The tricky bit was looking inside yourself to see what bits of the works were missing. Once you'd overcome that hurdle the rest was fairly simple. My first real peek inside myself caused me to slam the door in a hurry. 'That's me in there!' Holy cow, I looked more like an overgrown Gruyère cheese, full of holes. Anna's remark that 'You're full up, Fynn', I now saw as an encouraging statement rather than a factual one.

After getting over the shock, I opened the door a crack and took another peek. It wasn't long before I was able to identify one of the holes. It was shaped like a motor-bike. What's more, I recognized that hole. It was an exact fit of the motor-bike in the shop-window down the High Street.

After some practice it became more and more easy to identify the holes: A rather super microscope, one of these new-fangled television things, and a clock that told you the time in Bombay, Moscow, New York, London, and a few other places, all at the same time. There were bits of me all over the place, leaving identical holes inside me. I was, to say the least, spread out a bit. Somewhere down the line it had all gone wrong. I was certain that I hadn't started out with these holes. It was those damned banners that kept on cropping up: 'Get on', 'Get ahead', 'A motor-bike makes you someone', 'A car is even better', 'Two cars, and, brother, you've hit the jackpot.' I had fallen for it, hook, line and sinker. The banners were inside me and they were rooted in pretty fertile soil. The more banners inside me, the more bits of me were outside me. 'Most of a person is outside.' You can say that again.

There was no overnight miracle, no sudden flash of revelation. It crept up on me unannounced, and I'm still trying to work on it. Like a child learning a new word, I found myself struggling with 'I want to be me', 'I do want, I really do want to be ME'. It wasn't so difficult to open the doors these days. I now knew where I was. The motor-bike hole was still there, but it seemed to be flickering a bit, like some faulty electric light bulb. Then one day it went out. The hole was no longer there, a good-sized bit of me had come home. I was on my way at last. A couple of peeks inside me and I realized that I was beginning to fill up. The world was 'an all right place' in spite of the war.

CHAPTER ELEVEN

I t was a beautiful sunny day. The street was full of kid noises. Laughter drowned the sounds of marching feet, when suddenly the world fell to pieces.

One scream killed the laughter. It was Jackie's. I turned around in time to catch her in my arms as she hurled herself at me. Her face was a white mask of horror.

'Fynn! Oh Christ! It's Anna. She's dead! She's dead!'

Her scarlet finger-nails dug into my chest and the ice-cold water of fear flooded over me. I ran down the street. Anna was lying across the railings, her fingers clinging to the top of a wall. I lifted her off and cradled her in my arms. A flicker of pain narrowed her eyes.

'I slipped outa the tree,' she murmured.

'All right, Tich, hold on. I've got you.'

Suddenly I felt terribly sick. Out of the corner of my eyes I had seen something, something that in a curiously distorted way was even more terrifying than this injured child in my arms. Her fall had broken off the top part of one of the railings. A broken iron stump. A few years ago nobody could see that, now it was clear for all to see. This iron stump, these crystal mountains, were now red with shame and horror at its part in this dreadful thing.

I carried Anna home and put her to bed. The doctor came and dressed her wounds and left me with her. I held her hands and searched her face. The pain flickered across her eyes but was chased away by a grin that slowly blossomed over her face. The grin won; the pain was hidden somewhere inside her. Thank God, she was going to be all right. Thank God.

'Fynn, is the Princess all right?' Anna whispered.

'She's fine,' I answered. I didn't know if she was all right or not.

'She was stuck up the tree and couldn't get down – I slipped,' said Anna.

'She's all right.'

'She was very frightened. She's only a baby kitten.'

'She's fine, she's all right. You rest. I'll stay with you. Don't be frightened,' I said to Anna.

'Ain't frightened, Fynn. I ain't frightened.'

'Go to sleep, Tich. Have a little sleep, I've got you.'

Her eyes closed and she slept. It was going to be all right. I knew it deep down inside. For two days this feeling that it was going to be all right grew and took over my fears. Her grin and her excited conversations about Mister God made me doubly sure. The knots inside me were coming undone. I was looking out of the window when she called me.

'Fynn!'

'Here, Tich. What d'you want?' I crossed to her.

'Fynn, it is like turning inside out!' There was a look of amazement on her face.

An ice-cold hand gripped my heart and squeezed hard. I remembered Granny Harding.

'Tich,' my voice was too loud, 'Tich, look at me!'

Her eyes flickered and her smile spread. I hurried to the window and flung it up. Cory was there.

'Get the doctor quickly,' I said.

She nodded, turned on her heels and ran. Suddenly I knew what was going to happen. I went back to Anna. It wasn't time for crying, it was never time for crying. The cold dread in my heart had frozen the tears within me. I held Anna's hand. My head pounded with the idea that 'whatever you shall ask in my name ...' I asked. I pleaded.

'Fynn,' she whispered, and the smile lit up her face, 'Fynn, I love you.'

'I love you too, Tich.'

'Fynn, I bet Mister God lets me get into heaven for this.'

'You betcha. I bet he's waiting for you.'

I wanted to say more, a whole lot more, but she wasn't listening any more, just smiling.

The days burnt up like giant candles, and time melted, ran, and congealed into useless and hideous lumps.

Two days after the funeral I found Anna's seed pouch. It gave me something to do. I went to the cemetery and stayed for a little while. It just made things worse, that much more empty. If only I had been nearer at the time—If only I had known what she was doing, if only – if only – I tipped the seeds on the fresh-turned earth and hurled the pouch from me in misery.

I wanted to hate God, wanted him out of my system, but he wouldn't go. I found God more real, more strangely real than ever before. Hate wouldn't come, but I despised him. God was an idiot, a cretin, a moron. He could have saved Anna, but he didn't; he just let this most stupid of all things happen. This child, this beautiful child, had been cut off – cut off and not yet eight. Just when she was—Hell!

The war years took me out of the East End. The war dragged its bloody boots over the face of the world until the madness was over. Thousands of other children had died, thousands more were maimed and homeless. The madness of war became the madness of victory. Victory? I got good and drunk on VJ night. It was a good way out.

I had been given a bundle of books some time previously, but I hadn't bothered to undo them. There didn't seem much point. It was one of those idle moments; I didn't know what to do with myself. Those years had made my eyes tired with looking and my ears ache with listening. Some sign, some vision, just for a moment. I picked up the books. They didn't seem all that interesting. Nothing seemed very interesting. I flipped through the pages. It wasn't until my eyes fell upon the name of Coleridge that I stopped the pages of the book slipping through my fingers. For me Coleridge is at the top of the heap. I began to read:

'I adopt with full faith the theory of Aristotle that poetry as poetry is essentially ideal, that it avoids and excludes all accident, that is ...'

I turned back a few pages and began to read again. Out of the pages of that book Old Woody appeared.

'The process by which the poetic imagination works is illustrated by Coleridge from the following lines of Sir John Davies:

*"Thus doth she, when from individual states
She doth abstract the universal kinds,
Which then reclothed in divers names and fates,
Steal access thro' our senses to our minds." '*

The smoky fires of the 'night-time people' came drifting through my imagination: Old Woody, Convict Bill, Old Lil, Anna and me. A few lines further on my eye caught one word, 'violence'.

'The young poet,' says Goethe, 'must do some sort of violence to himself to get out of the mere general idea. No doubt this is difficult, but it is the very art of living.'

It slowly began to make sense, the bits began to fall into place. Something was happening and it made me cry; for the first time in a long, long time I cried. I went out into the night and stayed out. The clouds seemed to be rolling back. It kept nagging at the back of my mind. Anna's life hadn't been cut short; far from it, it had been full, completely fulfilled.

The next day I headed back to the cemetery. It took me a long time to find Anna's grave. It was tucked away at the back of the cemetery. I knew that it had no headstone, just a simple wooden cross with the name on it, 'Anna.' I found it after about an hour.

I had gone there with this feeling of peace inside me, as if the book had been closed, as if the story had been one of triumph, but I hadn't expected this. I stopped and gasped. This was it. The little cross leaned drunkenly, its paint peeling off, and there was the name ANNA.

I wanted to laugh, but you don't laugh in a cemetery, do you? Not only did I want to laugh, I had to laugh. It wouldn't stay bottled up. I laughed till the tears ran down my face. I pulled up the little cross and threw it into a thicket.

'OK, Mister God,' I laughed, 'I'm convinced. Good old Mister God. You might be a bit slow at times, but you certainly make it all right in the end.'

Anna's grave was a brilliant red carpet of poppies. Lupins stood guard in the background. A couple of trees whispered to each other whilst a family of little mice scurried backwards and forwards through the uncut grass. Anna was truly home. She didn't need a marker. You couldn't better this with a squillion tons of marble. I stayed for a little while and said goodbye to her for the first time in five years.

As I made my way back to the main gates I passed by hordes of little marble cherubs, angels and pearly gates. I stopped in front of the twelve-foot angel, still trying to lay down its bunch of marble flowers after God knows how many years.

'Hi, chum,' I said, saluting the angel, 'you'll never make it, you know.'

I swung on the iron gates as I yelled back into the cemetery.

'The answer is "In my middle".'

A finger of thrill went down my spine and I thought I heard her voice saying, 'What's that the answer to, Fynn?'

'That's easy. The question is "Where's Anna?".'

I had found her again – found her in my middle.

I felt sure that somewhere Anna and Mister God were laughing.

WHEN I SHALL DIE
by
ANNA

When I shall die,
I shall do it myself.
Nobody shall do it for me.
When I am redy,
I shall say,
'Fin, stand me up',
and I shall look
and lagh merry.
If I fall down,
I shall be dead.

ANNA'S BOOK

Contents

FOREWORD

In *Mister God, This is Anna* Fynn told the story of his friendship with this extraordinary child, and of her relationship with 'Mister God' and the world around her.

Anna's story, with its timeless truths, lives on in the minds and hearts of countless readers. But after her death, little was left of Anna herself – except the abiding memory of her presence, and a few treasured fragments of her writing. In *Anna's Book* Fynn shares these with us.

Anna's spelling and punctuation were, like herself, uniquely original and exuberant. In a few places we have altered these slightly, for the sake of clarity, but in no way do these alterations detract from the flavour of Anna's language.

The Publishers

INTRODUCTION

I told the story of Anna in *Mister God, This is Anna*. This is how it was. Anna and I found each other in one of these pea soup, foggy nights in November. I can't remember the precise date, it was probably in 1935. I used to wander around the docklands of East London night after night. It was a nice quiet thinking place, and often I needed to think.

It wasn't at all unusual to find a child roaming the streets at that hour – in the 1930s it was just like that. When I had taken her home, and after she had washed the dirt from her face and hands, I really saw her – a very pretty little red-haired child, but as she later told me, 'that's on the outside'. It took me a very long time to know her on the inside, as she demanded to be known.

The relentless pursuit of beauty engaged the few short years of Anna's life. It was at first a little strange to be told that a picture smelt good, but I soon got used to that. Anything that delighted all your senses at once was, for Anna, God! And the microscope was a special way of seeing him.

So it was that Anna found God in the strangest of places – tram tickets, grass, mathematics and even the dirt on her hands, and then somebody told you to wash it off!

Whatever satisfied Anna's idea of beauty had to be preserved, written down by anyone who was prepared to do so, and saved in one of her numerous shoe boxes. Every so often these boxes were placed on the kitchen table and the contents sorted out.

Where she got the idea of beauty I do not know. In those years the East End of London was, for most people, a grimy, dirty place, but for Anna it was just beautiful. Anna spent most of her efforts in turning the ugly into the beautiful. This often meant inventing a whole new situation into which the ugly facts could be transformed.

It was beauty that really drew Anna and me together. I can't remember a time in my life when I haven't been totally absorbed with the subject of mathematics. In fact, I'd rather 'do' mathematics than eat or sleep. Old John D., who taught me mathematics for seven years, once defined it as 'the pursuit of pure beauty'. Although I liked that as a definition, it wasn't until Anna had been with us for about two years that I really grasped what that meant. Anna and I were sitting at the kitchen table whilst I was working out the reciprocal of seventeen, which is another way of saying one divided by seventeen, which in the nature of things gave me another number, which was what I was after.

A little while later it occurred to Anna to ask what happens if you divide one by the number you've found? We worked it out the hard way. The answer was seventeen!! So often we sat at the kitchen table, Anna sitting on her curled up legs, chin cupped in her hands, whilst we 'worked out things'.

One evening, after we had been doing things on pieces of paper, she suddenly announced 'It is just beautiful ideas'. I don't accept that entirely, but I do accept G. G. Hardy when he says 'there is no permanent place in the world for ugly mathematics'.

Although I was considerably older than Anna, this pursuit of pure beauty made us companions in our explorations.

Her life was a continuous quest for knowledge and understanding as well as for beauty. Any thing or person that could answer her question would be stored in boxes or asked to 'write it down big'. This request to 'write it down big' did mean that her collection of writings were often spelt in various ways – not always right – but that didn't really matter. Often what had been written on her bits of paper were the kinds of things that grown ups would say. Adults' words on the lips of a six year old child were a bit puzzling at times, but Anna worked on the basis of 'if it says the right thing in the right way, use it, if not scrap it'.

During the years that Anna lived with me and my Mum and our changing household she wrestled with words and sentences to fit her ideas. It took me some time to realize that although we lived in the same world we saw it in different ways. Everything was for Anna a means of understanding 'what it was all about'. Grown ups had called her jackdaw, or parrot, little monkey, sprite – she was certainly all of these things but, more than these, she was a child.

Chapter One

NOT GOING TO CHURCH AND WHAT MISTER GOD IS LIKE

A lthough Anna went to church and Sunday School she was often more than a little irritated by this experience. It did n't seem to matter to her that God was meant to be the Creator, all powerful and loving, etc. Anna saw God as something other than this. God wasn't good because he loved or was just. God was good because he was beautiful. The very nature of God was pure beauty.

It was at first a bit of an ordeal taking Anna to Church, for it was the chess board flooring that grasped her, more than any preacher's words. As she once told me 'it makes you tingle all over', and whatever made you tingle all over was very close to God.

What bothered Anna so much about going to Church was the fact that so many people seemed to be looking for miracles. For Anna everything was a miracle and the greatest miracle was that she was living in it.

I dont like to go to cherch very much and I do not go becase I do not think Mister God is in cherch and if I was Mister God I would not go.

Peple in cherch are miserable becase peple sin misrable songs and misrable prers and peple make Mister God a very big bully and he is not becase he is not a big bully becase he is funy and luving and kind and strong. When you look to Fin it is like wen

you lok to Mister God but Fin is like a very baby
God and Mister God is hunderd time bigger, so you
can tell how nice Mister God is.

Anna divided numbers up into People Numbers and God
Numbers. People Numbers were fairly easy to understand and
fairly easy to work out. On the other hand, God Numbers were
even easier to understand, but sometimes impossible to work out.

Anna seldom played with what would be recognized as the usual toys these days. The exceptions to this were her rag doll, her paints and my old train set. This consisted of one engine, one coal-tender and eight trucks. She played with them for about a week and then put them back into the box.

It was at this point that God Numbers started to appear. Anna asked, 'How many different ways can I join together the engine, the coal-tender and the eight trucks?' I told her how to arrive at the answer. It turned out to be somewhat bigger than she anticipated and so she thought the final answer went into the realm of God Numbers. It was 3,628,800 and this was merely the result of finding out how many different ways ten articles could be arranged in a straight line. It didn't take her very long to realize that there would be a lot of questions with People Numbers that were going to land you up to your neck in God Numbers.

Peple say Mister God is like a king but fancy King Gorge coming down our street, I bet he do not know were our stret is is and I bet he do not know me. But Mister God know, Mister God know our stret and Fin and Mily and Twink and Pilet and all the darling flotkins. And I bet Mister God know the mark on my face even.

Anna had many friends in the neighbouring streets. Two of them were a little girl about four years old, Pilet, who was often called 'Pill' and her baby brother William, who was always known as 'Twink'. All the children were known as 'flotkins'. The poor of the East End were often referred to as 'the flotsam of society'. Anna's friends Henriques and Niels called the kids 'die Kinder' and the two words became 'flotkins'.

Because of the poverty in the East End at that time it was rare that any child had a new toy; most of the time it was a question of pretending that cardboard boxes could be anything you wished them to be. Many of the younger children joined in these games of 'let's pretend'.

One of the things that I had made was a device for blowing bubbles. With this I could produce a constant stream of fairly large soap bubbles – these the children would chase and burst with their hands, cricket bats, rolled up newspapers, etc. Twink's special instrument was a wire fly swat. Although these games could and did last as long as an hour or two, some of the children saw in these bubbles all the colours of the rainbow and realized the beauty of them. Some, Anna in particular, saw reflections. It was my efforts to explain to Anna just how these reflections came about that made me buy a garden globe for her. This garden globe was about eighteen inches in diameter, made of silvered glass. She soon realized that the images at the edge of the globe were, to use her own words, 'squashed up'. What was never and could never be seen as a reflection in this global mirror was the bit behind the globe. It was for Anna an indication that it was here that Mister God lived.

Anna put together the idea of the garden globe, soap bubbles, glass Christmas tree decorations and finally highly polished ball bearings, which did exactly the same kind of thing, as everything could be reflected in a small ball bearing – that is, except the bit where Mister God lived. It was clear to Anna that everything that God had made could be reflected in a ball bearing. Being such a tiny thing it could easily be put in your pocket or even your ear, couldn't it?

I did not go to cherch on Sunday becase I did not want to go and Fin tuk me on a trane to a big forist. It is a wondfull forist and Fin cudle me and tell sum wondfull story about Mister God and it was better than Sunday school. In cherch people make Mister God big and big and big and Mister God get so big that you dont know, but Fin make Mister God so little, he get in your eye.

This would have been Epping Forest.

In the forist I see sum rabit and sum bager and a lot of bird and sum deer and a ded one too, but I did

not see no peple becase they was in the boozer and
wen I saw the ded deer it make me cry a bit and Fin
say it is sily to cry for ded thing but I can cry for
peple in the boozer. Fin say to tuch the ded deer
and I tuch the ded deer and it Puft like face powdr
all up my nos. Wen it gos all to powdr it gos into dirt
and then the gras gros in it and then the shep eat the
gras and then I eat the shep and so I eat the ded
deer and because Mister God make it all, I eat
Mister God all time like the people do in cherch. But
mine is better becase I do it all the time. Not only
sometimes like they do in cherch but every time.

One of Anna's problems was the fact that things had a habit of
changing shapes, from frog spawn to frogs, from caterpillars to
butterflies; dead rabbits she had seen in Epping Forest certainly changed their shapes. Even in the house near to us with
the green painted woodwork, the house that Anna called the
'green house' was slowly changing its appearance and shape.

It seemed to Anna that everything needed its shape to live in.
I could, of course, have tried to explain the word 'decay' but
I didn't. Anna concluded that when a thing changed its shape
it was because it had something else to do for Mister God. For
Anna, death was just one of those things that happened. Death
was that point in life when you began to change shape. Anna
and I had sat by Old Granny Harding as she died; changing
shape sometimes took a long time, a very long time. Even if
Anna never knew what shape Granny Harding changed into,
who would argue with her? Not me. After all, if Mister God
wanted it, it must be good.

I asked Fin where do the shape (of the deer) go to?
And Fin say about the green hous and Fin say

becase no one is in it to look after the shape, it start
to fall down becase mows and rat go in and they
want their shape and they make hols and the shape
go to another shape. So wen the deer gos out of its
shape, som more thing go in for another shape. And
it do too! becase we see a ded rabit shape that was
full up of worms and betels and spidres to make
another shape and every shape is Mister God shape,
but Mister God has not got a propre shape. Mister
God is like a pensil, but not like a pensil you can see,
but like a pensil you can not see, so you not see what
shape it is, but it can draw all the shapes ther is and

this is like Mister God. When you grow up you get a bit funy becase you want Mister God to have a propre shape like an old man and wiskers and wrinkels on his face but Mister God do not look like that.

When Twink play tranes, he have a big wood box. Sumtime the box is like a trane and somtime lik a house and sumtime like a ship and sumtime like a car and sumtime you put sum thing in it and sumtime you do not, but you take sumthing out. And the box is like Mister God. Sumtime it luk like sumthing and sumtime is luk like another thing. If you say Mister God is green then Mister God cannot be red, but he is. If you say Mister God is big, how can you say Mister God is litle, but he is. And if you say Mister God is fat, you can not say Mister God is thin, ha! ha! ha! but he is too so! How can you say of Mister God, becase you can not. But I can becase I have a sekrit book Fin give to me. It is a pictur book all about snow flak and every snowflak is not the same. If you look at a snowflak shape it is not the same as another snowflak shape, so it has not got a propre snowflak shape. But you can only call it snow and you can not call it a shape and you see THAT IS LIKE MISTER GOD. You can not call Mister God a thing and you can not call Mister God a shape and you can only call Mister God Mister God.

Chapter Two

MY DARLING MUMMY

As Anna began to grapple with her ideas and those very important things she had asked people to write down for her, she began to weave them into little stories. Everything had to be looked at and questions had to be asked. Her questions flowed like a flood tide around and over everything. All this activity made me glow with some pride.

While she sorted through her store of ideas and pieces of paper contained in her numerous shoe boxes, I had to admit to myself that there was indeed something a little strange about Anna. She had no strange powers, no special senses, no special abilities or anything like that. Now, about half a century after her death, I can see that she had the strangest of all qualities. She could WAIT. Wait for the right moment, wait until, for her, everything was just right.

I'm fairly certain that Anna had never been seriously abused. Badly neglected, yes. But, Anna still kept hold of her idea of the perfect mother.

Anna's 'Darling Mummy' was no real person, but something like putting together the jigsaw of the many stories she wrote about her ideas. Her waiting was like cooking – the mixture of the various bits came out as a different dish.

Before I go to sleep I think about Mummy and this is what I think. Did you ever see stars on a frost nigt? They look very clos and it is like they are tide to you with string and yor feet dont tuch the ground and you have not got any wate and when I luk in

Mummy eye it is like I have not got no wate and if
Mummy dont hold me tite I shall go up in the air like
a bird.

Did you ever bump into a spidre web when you
didnt no and did you ever go asleep on the cul gras
and did you ever have a hot drink when you was
cold and tired and did you ever strok a duk's

tummy? Well, when Mummy kiss you, it is like that. Sumtime Mummy lips is delekat like a spidre web. Sumtime cul lik gras and sweet. Somtime hot and berning like soop and somtime soft lik a duk tummy very smooth. And when you kiss you have to put yor lips toogethre and so Mummy breeths on you and it smel like all the flowrs in the world and you can tell becase that is wot luv smell like so you can tell how luvly Mummy is.

If you see a funy thing you larf out lowd, but if you have a spesial sekrit insid you, you dont. But you have a spesial smile. And this is like a flower bud that is just going to open, you cant see it but you no it is so butefull inside. And Mummy smile is like that, but you cant see all the flowrs in the world at the sam time. So then Mummy dont smile all her secret smile at the sam time and I am very pashent because Mummy has got milions and milions of sekrit smiles and I luv her so much.

Sumtime Mummy ly down and clos her eye and she luklike Mary, who I saw in a cherch in a candel lite, but I dont remembr were. But Mummy luk so luvly and cuddly it make me trembul with joy. Dont you think that Mummy is the most butefull one in all the world? Ah but I am going to tell you sum more. I told Neels how luvly Mummy is and Neels told Mister Henriks and I here Neels say if Mummy butey corsed combustion then the hole world wuld go into flams. Neels say it is a complemant. But Neels dont now sumtims. Mummy make me berst in flams. And I ask Neels what is the most big numbre I could say for luving Mummy becase I am not very gud with sums and Neels say if I rite down 'infinity' that is the most big. But it dont luk very big but milions and milions of them wold be, but I luv Mummy so much and I will rite sum more.

Mummy is not like no one els becas she dont have to speak if she dont want to. And somtime it is nice when she dont speak and somtime it is nice when she do speak. Becas when she dont speak, Mummy smile and this is very good. Mummy has got a speshul smile and you dont no where it is going to start. Somtime it start from her toes and somtime from her finger and somtime from her tummy and then it pop out of her eye and out of her mouth and this is very nice becas you now it is coming and you wate for it to cume. So it

cum like a pressant wich is a big surprise. And wat is nice about Mummy is watever she do is like a pressant. And wen you think about Mummy this is good too. When you think about peple you can think bad thing and narsty thing like hurt and pane and sick, but when you think about Mummy, you cant. And you can only think nice thing that are happy like Mister God. And warm. And how nice to be me, becas if I was not me I would not know, would I?

Oh dear, ther is so many things I wish I culd say, but I do not know how to say becas how can you say about love with a pensel and a paper becas you can not reely. But you can try, cant not you, so I will try.

Love is a very funy thing becas you cant see it and you cant here it and you cant tuch it when it belongs to you. So how do you know you have got it? Well I will tell you. When Neels say to me pretend you have for sweets in one hand and six sweets in another hand, how many have you got? So I say I have not got none, becas I have not and if I say I have got some, it is a lie and this is bad to do. Wen someone say I love you Anna, how do I know if it is true?

Chapter Three

THE VERY VERY FIRST

T he Bible at home was one of those huge brass-bound books. It was from this that Anna read or was read to. Seated at the table she worked her way through some of the passages of the Bible. At School and at Church she was told which passages to read; at home she was free to read whatever she wanted to. This meant that she was often puzzled as to the meaning and I had to do my best to help her understand. Trying to understand that Adam knew Eve was not the same as Anna knew Fynn, or that God asked Adam, 'Who told thee that thou wast naked?' and caused her many problems.

The more she read the more puzzled she became. Often she was presented with passages that simply did not make sense to her, passages that seemed to contradict other passages. Like Luke 2:23 – 'Every male that openeth the womb shall be called holy to the Lord.' And Luke 23:29 – 'Blessed are the barren and the wombs that never bare.'

It seemed to Anna that the Bible was sometimes a bit muddled and that it asked more questions than it answered, but whatever its shortcomings, it was beautiful and since for her beauty was all important, there was no reason why she should not add her own idea of beauty to it.

Perhaps the most exciting thing about Anna was how she always managed to put together to her own satisfaction various ideas that in the normal course of education would have been frowned on. On one occasion she glued together shadows, mathematics, God and sundry ideas, to my delight and her satisfaction. It happened like this –

One evening I had been explaining to Anna how to tell the time from a sundial. Early next morning I took her to see the sundial in the local churchyard. I pointed to the part that cast the shadow and said this is called the 'Gnomon'. As usual, I had to write this word down on a piece of paper. Later that day the word Gnomon had to be looked up in the dictionary. The definition read 'That part of a parallelogram left over when a similar parallelogram is taken from its corner.'

This idea was passed over for about a year until it became another idea to work on. What excited her was the fact that it came from a Greek word meaning 'Indicator'.

As she carefully wrote this down on her piece of paper, her eye caught the next word 'Gnosis' – knowledge of spiritual mysteries.

This bit of information made Anna search for all the words that started with the letters GN, which you must admit is an odd combination. All these words were carefully written down – gnarled, gnash, gnat, gnathic, gnaw, gneiss, gnome, gnomic, gnomon, gnosis, gnu.

Anna felt that these strange words which all started with GN ought, because of their very strange beginnings, to have something in common. And then – on the same page, was the word GOD. I did try to explain to her, but it was no use, she had found her clue, the GN words now made sense.

Serendipity is the faculty of making happy and unexpected discoveries by chance.

On one evening we were scribbling numbers and ideas on pieces of paper. I was trying to explain to Anna the mysteries of the binary system by asking the question what is the fewest number of weights and what is the value of the weights that would enable you to weigh anything up to 1,000 lbs in steps of 1lb; after a little while she grasped the idea of how to 'do it':

1, 2, 4, 8, 16, 32, 64, 128, 256, 512.

It was then quite clear to her that these 10 weights could weigh up to 1,023 lbs. This was certainly one of those beautiful things that had to be written down and treasured.

All this was nice and organized, but things are not always quite like you work them out. The greengrocer in the market didn't do things quite like that. Anna took me to the market place to show

me this new miracle. On our workings out we had put the article to be weighed in the left pan and the weights in the right pan, but the man in the market place wasn't doing this, for he seemed to put weights in either pan. It certainly looked as if the man was cheating, so we went back to working it out again. In the first case we only put the weights in the right-hand pan, and in the second case you could put the weights in the right-hand pan or maybe the left hand or sometimes even both, and the numbers we had found for the first case certainly didn't work in the second case, so I had to explain how to work out these other weights, and they turned out to be 1, 3, 9, 27, 81, 243, 729.

This is a story about the very very first. Mister God is very very old, but a long time ago he was yung and before that he was only a baby and before that he was not even born and their was not a world and their was not a star and there was not anything.

But there was Mister God's Mummy and Daddy. But you could not see them. And you could not see them because they were so big.

If you have a very little thing, you have to go very clos befor you can see it and if you go far away, you cant. If you have a montain wich is big you cant see the top if you are clos, but you can if you go far away and this is like Mister God's Mummy and Daddy. You cant go far away from them, so you cant see them. If you go too far away, you can see them but you get very lonly, so you cant. So you have to stay very clos and you know they are there but you cant see them, so that is why they had a little baby.

Well, you see, when the little baby GOD was getting redy to be born he was in his mummy woom, that is were all the babys is made. It is very dark in there. When the baby GOD was born, then he must have some light and when his Mummy and Daddy had a party to selebrate with all the angles, they put lots and lots of light in the sky and made it look pritty and this is stars. The Mummy and Daddy are very polite and teech the little baby GOD to be polite too and to say 'If you please' and 'No thank you' and thing like that. The little GOD have all the thing he want. A gold spoon and a gold plate and a gold chair and everything and then he want a ball to play with, so his Mummy tuk a lot of dirt and spit on it and roll it into a ball and this is the world, so you can see how big the little baby GOD is.

All the thing was very pritty. And because the little GOD was very polite and kind he want to share all the thing, so he told his Mummy and his Mummy say I cant make you a little brother and sister because it take such a lot of time. And the little GOD said 'Oh dere what shall I do'? And the Mummy say 'I have got a good idea' and she tuk off the table a looking glas and say 'What can you see?' So the little GOD look and say I can see my face, it is a reflekshun. And Mummy say 'Can you play with yor reflekshun?' and the little GOD say 'How can I share all the pritty thing with my reflekshun? That is greedy'. And it is too!

Then the Mummy say 'Do you know where you come from?' and the little GOD say 'Yes, I come from yor woom' and the Mummy smile a big smile and say, 'Yes, but first you come from a pictur in my hart and the picktur in the hart come true if you love them enogh. What is the picktur in yor hart little one?' And the little GOD say 'Ther is a picktur of people and animal and I want to share all this pritty things and you and Daddy and all the angels with the animals and people'.

In the night time all the picktur come true becase the little God love them so much. And all the people and animals come out of the little God's hart. And you know your hart is not very big, so you can see for milions of people and animals to cum out, they must be very tiny and so they were. Well, at the very first everybody was happy and the little GOD teech the people to talk and play musik and make things and everybody was happy because all the people could see him.

But when the little God grow up, he got so big that nobody could see him and all the people tuk the pritty things and say 'This is mine'. Of corse, they wasnt but that is what they said and then they got greedy and greedy and then start to hit each other and throw stomes and make boms. Because the little GOD grow up and got so big that they culdn't see him and they neerly forgot him.

So a lot of people make a statoor of GOD small enogh
to see and then another lot of people make another statoor of GOD and then they fite to see what statoor is best. And they make boms and guns and a lot of peple is hurt and it is very silly because Mister God is much bigger than statoors.

Well, Mister God luvs peple very much, so he says 'I know what, people cant see me because I am too big, so I will send my little baby boy who is the rite sise'. So he send his little baby boy who is called Jether to a lady called Mary to luk arfter and Mister God say 'That is all rite now, Jether is just the rite sise'. And you would think that was the end, would not you? Arfter all the trubble Mister God tuk, woodnt you? But It wasn't, Oh no!

Anna very rarely used the name Jesus; she preferred the name Jether, which she found in the Concordance. This is the next name in the list of proper names in the Concordance. Its meaning is 'He that excels or remains; or that examines, searches: or a line or string.'

It was the idea of 'line or string' that so attracted Anna. We had often spent hours lying on the deck of a deep water sailing vessel, listening to Niels's explanation of what all the ropes and gear were for. The fact that every rope had a place and a purpose, and that Englishmen, Frenchmen and Germans, every nationality, understood where the rope for a certain sail was to be found, was sufficient for Anna to rename Jesus as Jether. Kurt, a German sailor, told Anna she was 'wider sinn', that is to say, 'against the sense'.

When Jether was a man, he started to tell all the peple about Mister God, but a lot of peple didnt want to here because first Mister God was too big and then he was too little and peple are eccasperating. They dont know what they want. And Jether keep on telling the people 'You have got to becum little Or you wont know'. And they want to be big alredy, And you cant, becase Fansy being born full sise! Then a lot of people cort Jether and put nales in him and stuck him on a tree and stuck sords in him and then he was ded. All because he wasnt big enogh. Some of the people nearly know him, but not qite and like the statoors of Mister God they was rong. So they had another fite and this time a worse fite called a war and this time with tank and aroplane and peple keep on fiteing because they dont know what sise they are and they are silly, becase

208

Mister God and Jether and Vrach and all the angels
are so luving. So I will tell you sum story about them.

Vrach was Anna's own spelling of the Hebrew word *Ruach*, meaning spirit or breath, which was used in the Old Testament but
linked with the Holy Spirit of the New Testament. I was surprised
these words – Vrach, Jether – were so important to her, but felt
that she had to find her way, in her own words, in her relationship with Mister God.

If you dont know what Mister God and Jether and
Vrach look like I will tell you. Now I will tell you
about Mister God first. He dont luk like me and you.
He has not go no arms and legs and no face and no
body like me and you so you will know he luk
diffrent but he luk very luvley all the sam.
    If you go for a walk you see a lot of things and
you think a lot of things in yore hed. Well one of the
things you think of is going home. So then you think
it is a long way away and all the thinks is insid you
and yore home is outsid you. So when you go home,
all you think cum out of you and yor home go insid
you, you see. Wen I am not with Mummy I have a lot
of think in my hed, I think I wish I culd hold Mummy
hand and I wish I culd kiss Mummy and I wish I culd
tuch Mummy, but it all stay in my hed. But when I go
home, it all come out of my hed, becase I do it. And
when I do, Mummy go insid me and I go insid
Mummy. If I dont go insid Mummy, how can I luk at
me because I luk the wrong way. So when I luv
Mummy then I go insid her and luk out out of her eye
and see me and see how much Mummy luv me and
this is very nice and thriling.

If someone luv you they let you cum insid. But if they dont luv you, they dont. Well Mister GOD is like that to. He let you com insid and see yourself, but you got to let MISTER GOD cum in too, becase he want to luk out to see himself. You see, MISTER GOD dont like no reflekshun and if he dont luk out of peples eye, how do he know what peple think of him? and this is the only way MISTER GOD can see himself. If you luk in a luking glas and see yor face reflekshun and then wink yore rite eye, the reflekshun wink the othre one, but if you see your reflekshun wink its rite eye then you know it is not a reflekshun, but you.

Chapter Four

THE STORY OF FIN

This is a story of Fin. Some people do not know how Fin is and I am sad for that because Fin is the best person in all of the world. Fin is very big and very strong but he is very delikat and very gentle. And he can frow me rigte up in the air like a bal and catsh me too. He is like a butefall flowre made from stone.

Fin say if you live in a howse and you let the window get sploshd and dirty and if you look out of the window it look like the world is dirty, but it is not. If you look inside it look dirty too but it is not dirty becase the window is dirty. Well I will say sum more of Fin becase Fin say all of the peple have two windows. First all peple have got eye window and then a hart window. The eye window is to look out and seen thing from and the hart window is to see inside to see you. Fin say wen you cry it is for to wash the window so you can see better.

One day I ask Fin for som sweet and Fin say no and I was sad and I cry som ters and I cry some ters to wash my eye window becas my eye window was all dirty, dirty with greedy for sweets. And Fin did not say nothing and Fin piket me up and put me to a luking glas to see my face reflecshun and it was all funy like rain on a hows window. And I culd not see

proper and then I stop the cry and see Fin face
reflecshun and it was all smilig. And so I smile too
and then I see my eye sparklin becas I can see
good. And then I see that Fin say no, becas he have
got no mony, becas he give it all to Missis Barkr to
buy som penuts to sell to get som mony to buy som
food and I did not see good, becase I have got a
dirty eye window and it was all splosht with greedy
dirty.

Mrs Barker was a little old lady who sold peanuts outside the cinemas called the Coliseum and the Palladium in the Mile End Road. One day I found her without any stock – so we took a tram towards Aldgate and bought about £3 worth of peanuts, which we brought back to her.

Everybody has got a eye window and a hart window.
Fin teech me how to clean my eye window and my hart
window. And if you know Fin then you have got a very
speshal Fin window. And this is very nice to have. If you
take some dirt to Fin he say about it and make it lik
dimons and if you take to Fin a tram tiket he make it like
a butefall piktur. Fin is very very speshal and very very
butefall but you have to be little inside or you can not
see propre.

Anna and I explored dirt under the microscope, where anything
seemed to be transformed. The tram tickets were of different
colours and collected from the streets very easily, so they could
be used to make patterns, or folded into complicated paper chains
and even turned into Christmas decorations.

One day Fin was very sad becase Danny was kild
with a big stiker (knife). So in the nighte I crep in
bed with Fin. Fin go to slep and I then see the ters
on his face becase we have a stret lighte in the stret
to see with. I cry a bit too becase I was sad for
Danny.

There is on thing abot Fin. A lot of time he is not
full up with his self but is full up of some othre
people. Som time he is just full up of his self. I like
this time best of all becase I do not want to see no
thing els and I am full up of laghin. I ask Fin can I
have a nothre name and Fin say yes I can have two
names. One is Mowse, becase Fin say I crep in his
hart and make a nest ther. And the nothre name is
Joy becase I make him hapy and I am very glad for
that becase that is very very holy.

Somtime I think that Fin is an angel. If you want to
know the diffrence from a person and an angel I will

tell you. An angel is easy to get inside of, and a person is not. Every bit of an angel is inside and every bit of a person is not and most of a person is outside.

One person who is very special is dere Fin. It is like loking at the very very inside of love. All the thing are nice to do with Fin and some of the thing are very nice and special.

One of the nice things is to go for a walk with Fin in the simitery (cemetery). Only Fin do not call it a simitery. Fin call it an orchard, becase Mister God come to pick up the sols when they are redy like aples. I like going to the orchard with Fin becase there is no one ther, only ded one and Mister God and sols. Fin say no on go to the orchard becase people are afrade to be ded, but I am not afrade becase the orchard is very butefall and ther is million of flowre and it is sily to be a frade to be ded in all them flowre. When we go to the orchard Fin tell the name and how old and wen they was ded and ther are a lot of little children ded in the orchard. Only they are not ther no more, but they are in heven. When Fin tells the name, I say hello Susan this Anna and Fin talking and then I say how butefall the orchard is and thing like that and then we say a little prer and say will you give all our lov to Mister God and to Jether and to Vrach and to all the angel and to all the peple. What I am sory for is Judas and Pontas Pirot and all the peple that put Jether on the cross. And one day I cry in the orchard for them and Fin cudle me and then say we rite all the names of them on som paper and put it in a tin and put in the holy ground and leeve it to Mister God. Fin say every peple have got a bit of Judas inside and a bit

of Pontos pilot inside and every peple put a nother
nale in Jether.

Fin say one thing to remmber and this is it. If it is
good to do, then do it, if it is not good to do, then
do not do it. And so I say how do I know if it is
good and Fin say it is easy. Do not git stuck inside
of you, com out and go inside of peple and
animles and flowres an trees and see if you like it
and if you do like it, then it is good and if you do
not like it, then it is bad. If you pertend to be a cat
and you kik it, it hert, so it is bad. If you stroke it, it
is nice, so it is good. Fin say if you lok at a howse
on the outside it is a howse, but if you look at a
howse on the inside, it is not a howse but it is a
home. And that is like peple. If you lok at one on
the outside it is a person, but if you lok at one in the
inside then it has got a reel name. And so has
everything got a reel name. Even flee and spidre.
And Fin say somtime this is hard to lern, to see

inside a thing. Somtime you can not tell becase a church look like a mewseum and lik a flic hows and you can not tell from the outside, but you can only tell from the inside and that is wat to be alive is.

Oh Oh Oh I do love Fin very much and I ask Mister God evernighte if I can marry Fin and have a hows and som baby too. If I am six and Fin is tweny then I can mary Fin when I am tweny and Fin is tirthy fore. I ask Jacky and Sally and Corry if they marry Fin first can I too and they say yes.

For nerly everybody down our stret say up the top (of the street) is bad, but it is not becase Fin say it is not bad. Nerly everbody say they are very wicked and they are not wicked becase Fin say we must not say that. Only Mister God can say that and Mister God is very good.

At the top corner of the street was a house that was a lot bigger than the rest. In this house lived Milly, Sally, Corey, and a few other young ladies. The fact that these young ladies were for the most part prostitutes was the reason why it was commonly called the 'dirty house'. Anna had a vague idea of what it meant but that was no reason why she couldn't be friends with the girls. In fact, she thought that Milly, who was usually known as the Venus de Mile End, was the most beautiful girl in the world and I would never have argued with that. The care and protection that these girls gave to Anna could not have been sweeter. I had known them for a number of years, and I knew them as very good friends. Given other circumstances they would have been different, but with poor homes, little education, and even less money, prostitution was the only way they knew how to make money. I have known these young ladies save over £200 to send little Maria to have her leg corrected after the ravages of rickets. It was more than I could have done.

Many times Anna and I have sat with them and so often the talk turned to the subject of religion and God. The passing years have made me realize that they were among the few people who could admit to themselves that they were sinners, but then they had families to keep and it was the only way they knew how.

Anna's friendship with these young prostitutes taught her a lot – perhaps a bit too much, who knows. I do know that they were very careful in what they said when Anna was around, but things slip out occasionally and Anna, like most children, would often repeat what she had heard the older people say without knowing what was meant by it.

What was puzzling for me was the fact that some of the girl's customers did regard themselves as good solid citizens, to say nothing of good churchgoers, but that was my problem, not Anna's. For her the girls were just nice to be with. What puzzled Anna was how such nice people could be called 'dirty'. Anna would have none of it, neither would I. Milly taught Anna how to make bead belts, necklaces and bracelets. All the adults for streets around knew what the girls did, but it was only Anna and her friends and me who knew what they could do. They were a bit special to those of us who knew them and definitely not dirty.

One of the thing that make me very sad is this. I wuld like all the big girls up the top to have real propre sweet love. Fin culd do it so gentle and sweet and culd make the big girls so hapy and holy and it wuld be so lovly.

Fin go up the top to see them and Fin mummy say I can go too and Fin mummy rote this on some paper and say to put it in my book. If they are blind, give them your hand, if they are in the dark, give them a candel. And then she laft out loud and say a candel calld Anna.

Chapter Five

ONCE UPON A TIME

Whenever Anna was confronted by the latest miracle or had one of those important children's questions to ask, she wrote it into a little story. This could be very confusing, since you could not ask a question of an oak tree that was meant for a beech tree, neither could you ask a black cat exactly the same question you could ask a ginger cat. Her little stories were nearly always about some aspect of a thing or person.

This habit of writing about some aspect of a thing or a person meant that there could be as many as ten or more little stories about dogs or whatever, which had to be put together before any one could understand her more complete picture of dogs, or whatever she was writing about.

Anna's 'Once upon a Time' was the result of many, many little stories that were finally put together after a long time. This putting together was a very solitary and intense activity which could totally absorb her for many days. Nothing was allowed to intrude into this part of Anna's life. It took me some while to realize how important this 'putting together time' was for her.

Since those days I have heard Anna's 'putting together time' called by many names, but I still think 'Talking with God' is the best I've found so far!

When I wok up in the morning it was stil neerly dark and it was just becuming ligte and I thort this is not a nice day. So I pull the sheets over my hed and just my nos wos out and then I here sumthing. It was going drip, drip, drip. And then I was very sad becase I thort it sownd like all the angels criing. But then I here it more drip, drip, drip, so then I no it was rain that was making the noise.

When I luk out of the window I see the sun was all like blood and all the miss was everwere and it was very cold to get out of bed and as I stud at the window I fel my tows get cold and I think of my bed wich is warm so I go bake to bed were it is nise and warm. Then I put my nos under the shets and I lissen to the bird sing in the tree and wunder why bird sing wen the day is so bad.

So then I thort I would like Mummy to make me warm and I thort I wold like to kis Mummy, but it was so cold I did not want to go out of my bed. And I thort soon Mummy will cum out of bed and cum to kiss me, so I wate and think of Mummy to cum to put her arms rownd me and to kiss me and I think how nice it is. So all my tows kirl and so do I like a bal so I wate.

Then I here a funy thing and it go swiss, swiss, swiss. It is like the wind but it is not the wind. Then a

sonbem cum in the windo and hit me in the face, so I
jump out of bed and see a sunbem rite up from the
clowds and on the sunbem was a man. The man was
showting Were is lazy Anna? were is lazy Anna?
and all the bird and all the rabit and all the bear say
it too and I wonder becase I am Anna, but I am not
lazy and then the man slid down the sonbem rite in
my room and say, There is lazy Anna! Then I see the
man is Mister Vrach, so I say I am not lazy and you
must not say that becase we are friends. You are
lazy say Vrach. You must com with me. And then I
say, I wate for Mummy so I cant come. Yes you will
com and Vrach pickt me up and went all up the
sunbem again. Wen we got to the top of the sunbem
Vrach say, This is a lazy werld for lazy children and

you are lazy and wen you are not lazy I will take
you home again. And then he went away.

It was very cold and I was very lonly, so I sit
down becas I was sad. And then I here a lot of
peple talking but it was not peple, so I luk, but it
was not there, and then I know the talking is in the
grownd and in the air. So I put my eer on
the grownd and lissen and I here it say It is
very cold today so I wont grow today. So then I say
Who is talking in the grownd? And it say Who is
that? and I say It is Anna. Who is talking in the
grownd? And it say I am a little flowre seed. Why
dont you want to grow today? Becase it is too cold
and I am warm in my bed, so I will grow two times
as much the nex day. But it will be cold the next
day too. Then I will stay in bed again, say the little
seed. But if all the seeds stay in bed there will not
be any spring and a little seed cant grow two times
as much in one day. But he did say noting becase
he gon to sleep agan and I thort the seeds are sily
and lazy.

Then I went to walk but all the things was stil and
lazy. The tree wuld not grow and the leeves would
not open and the bird would not sing and it was a
very sad werld.

Them I cum to a river that was not going, so I say
River why are you not going? and the river say
Becase I am lazy. And soon I cum to a waterfal, but
the water do not fall, but stay in the air and I say
Waterfal, why do you not fall? and the waterfal say
Becase I am lazy. But you must fall, say Anna,
becase a waterfal must larf and play and go gugle
gugle gugle and if you dont then how can you be a

waterfal? O, says the waterfal, I did not think of that and he start to cry and sum little drips of water fall down and mak a little pule and so I cry. O plese mister waterfal, dont cry becase waterfal is hapy thing, not sad thing. So then he stop and say, O Anna if you culd mak me larf then I wuld be a reel waterfal agan. So I thort very hard and said Mister Waterful I will tell you a funy story. Say wen you are redy. And the Waterfal say I am redy. So I begin.

Once upon a time and the Waterful go Gug gug gug gugel gugel gugel and start to fall down and start to larf so much I am splosht with all the water and the waterfal say Ha! Ha! Ha! Ho! Ho! Ho! Anna! that is a very funy story! But I do not know what it is to larf at becase I have not start the story yet. So I say I have not start the story yet. But the waterful larf mor and more. Then a little bear com out of a hole and say Mister Waterful Wat do you larf about? and the waterful say Ho! Ho! Ho! little bear Anna has told me a very funny story. And the little bare say Wat is the funy story? tell it to me, so I can larf too. So the Waterful say, Anna say Once upon a time. Then the little bare larf and larf and larf til he fall over and roll on the grownd and say Ho! Ho! Ho! Anna say Once upon a time! Then a little bird start to larf and then a little rabit start to larf and the little flowr seeds com out of the grownd to see why all things was larfin for. And then all the trees and flowrs larf and larf and say, Anna say Once upon a time! and all the forest tingl with larfin, but I do not know why.

So I sit on the gras. I am a maze. Then a lot of angels cum dancing and singing in the Forest and all the Forest was a-wak and was not lazy any mor, so I

get up and say to the angel Eccuse me, if you plese, why is all thing larfin? So the angel say Becase you tell a funy story. But I did not start it even. I only say Once upon a time. Then the angles say That is what is funy, you see, Anna. You can not be twise upon a time. Then the angle dans away, but I stil do not think it is funy. So I sit down agan and I think and think and think and then I know. Of cors you can not be twice upon a time becos you can not do two thing at a time.

So I get up and ran and call Mister Vrach I am not lazy no mor. And then ther was a swiss, swiss, swiss and Mister Vrach say Ho! Ho! Ho! Anna you are not lazy no more. Wat did you lern? and so I say I lern I was lazy becase I wanted to kiss Mummy but I was too lazy to get from my bed becase it was cold but wate for Mummy to come to me. Then Mister Vrach say Becase you have lern very good I will give you a pressant Anna. Wot wuld you like? So I say Mister Vrach will you take me back to the very beginning? So Mister Vrach take me to the top of the sonbem and smile a very big smile and kiss me and then puss me very hard down the sonbem and I was going fast and fast and fast and I was most brethles and then ther was a bump and I was in my bed agan.

Then I open my eye and it was just becuming ligte and I hear drip, drip, drip and then a sonbem com in the winder so I ran to the winder and see a man on the sonbem and he wave to me and all the little bird sing and then my tows get very cold, becas it is very cold, but I am very warm inside and I want to kiss Mummy very much and I do not care how cold it is. So I ran to Mummy room and jump to bed with Mummy and kiss her very much becase I am full up of love and Mummy hug me very tite and I am very happy and then Mummy say, Anna it will be a very nice day and I say Yes Mummy! and larf becase it neerly was not.

Chapter Six
THE TREE

I saw a lovly tree today
So lovly that it made me pray
The lefs was all harts and lovly gren
The most lovly tree that you have ever seen
It made my hart sing and my hed go hummy
So I tuk some off to gift to Mummy
And wen I did it make her smile
And I think that is very werth while
And do you know that Mister God
Made a big smile and gift his hed a nod

ANNA AND THE BLACK KNIGHT

Growing up in our little street meant only one thing – getting to the top of the railway wall. A red brick wall nearly ten feet high. Getting to the top of that wall was one thing all the boys wanted to do. It was then that you were grown up. Grown up enough to get a job and earn some money. Grown up enough to stay out late and have a girl friend of your own. It was almost like some sort of ceremony, attempting that wall. Everybody watched you and groaned in sympathy when you failed, which was most likely, and cheered on those very few occasions when somebody managed to get to the top and sit astride the wall. There were a number of ways to get to the top, like swinging from the lamp post to the top. It was not more than four or five feet away.

You could also climb out of Norman's top window. Anybody could do that. Of course, you could always 'borrow' a ladder from the builder's yard but that wasn't growing up, that was just plain cheating. Our kind of growing up was something entirely different. It was simple really. Run as fast as you could for about sixty yards or so, jump as high as you could and hope that your speed and that last mad scramble would take you to the top. As there was nothing to hold on to until you reached the top the inevitable happened – you crashed to the ground! It was easy to see who had tried the wall that day – a bloody nose, a fresh bandage, a torn trouser. Such little things were reminders for all to see.

Getting to the top of that wall was one thing I was determined to do. I don't know how many times I had failed. I never kept count, but it was on such an occasion when I had landed with a crash from that wall that it happened. I know that my nose was bleeding a bit, so I sniffed. Bleeding noses didn't matter at all, as Mum so often said, it lets out the mad blood. Lying on my back I was aware of two people looking down at me. I had no idea who the lady was, but there was no mistake about the man. It was Old John D. Hodge himself.

I had heard a lot about Old John D. He was one of the Senior Masters at the posh school, but I had never seen him. Many people had described him to me and I didn't like him. Not one bit. He was slightly hunch-backed with a club-foot and a hare-lip which he kept covered with a large bushy beard. That sounded bad enough to me, but I was told that he also carried around with him a length of bunsen burner tubing, which he used instead of a cane and which he had no hesitation in using when things didn't go to his liking, which from the sounds of things was often. The tubing was called the 'persuader' by everybody. He was the stuff that nightmares were made of.

Looking down at me looking up at the sky, he laughed at me. He didn't realize how important this wall was. Nobody laughed at that. It was much too important to laugh at ... I was going to have another try at it, and so I did, but the result was just the same. I failed and, as usual, ended up a heap on the floor.

'Only heroes never say "No". Neither do fools.' He was still there and smiling down at me. No, I didn't like him. Not one little bit. I bet he couldn't climb that wall either. I was a bit fed up with that silent and quizzical look he gave me when I failed with the wall, and that slow shake of his head annoyed me. 'Only heroes never say "No". Neither do fools.' I just wished he would go away and leave me alone.

* * *

I was very surprised when the postman handed me that letter one morning. The one that said I had passed my examinations with good marks. I had got that scholarship and a small grant of money which was so important to me, and I could go to one of the posh schools. I didn't think that was going to happen. It was the Maths paper that was the problem. The first nineteen questions were so easy that I never bothered with them, but the last question was the one that interested me most of all, so I tried it. I didn't get very far with it. An hour's work left me a few pages of notes and lots of scribble, but no answer to the problem. I was a little comforted to be told some months later that nobody had ever attempted to answer that question before.

So there I was. All polished and dressed up in my nice new school uniform just off to catch the bus.

'Mum,' I said, 'what is the point of going to school to learn some more?'

'You've got to learn more,' she replied, 'to protect your self from what you already know,' which is one of those sayings that takes you months to understand, but Mum always did have a way of turning things upside down. She had this odd way of putting things that left me standing on my head.

* * *

So it was that we all sat waiting for something to happen. I had managed to get the corner seat at the back of the classroom and soon we heard someone limping along the passage. We all held our breath as the door opened. There he stood, exactly as I had been told: Old John D. Hodge – our form-master!

'I will talk,' he began, 'and you will listen. Is that understood?'

We nodded.

'I will teach and you will learn. Right?'

Again we nodded.

'If any of you don't want to learn there is always another way of going about it,' and he hit the desk with the 'persuader'.

'Who arranged the order for you to sit in?'

For the next few minutes we were all changing places until he was satisfied. I suddenly found myself at the front of the class. Somebody was detailed to hand out exercise books and we were told to write our name, form and address of the school on the cover of the exercise books and, like so many other pupils must have done, mine ended up with:

London
England
Europe
World
Solar system
Universe

I was sorry that I had done that when he began to walk around the room looking at our efforts. I did try to cover it up with my hand. And then his hand was under my chin as he tilted my head back.

'Well, well, young man, you certainly know where you are. I wonder, are you as certain where you are going. Are you?'

'No, sir,' I replied. Perhaps it was at that moment that something happened. Suddenly I was looking into the bluest eyes I had ever seen. I tried to turn away but he held my head tight.

'You're the one that likes to climb things, aren't you?'

'Yes, sir.'

'Ah, I think I can give you plenty of things to climb. Plenty! I can promise you that!'

* * *

The little street where I lived was a real rag-tag and bobtail of a place. Most of my friends lived here. The triplets were amongst our best friends and whenever the kids were playing in the street,

it was pretty certain that if Bombom the black goddess wasn't looking after them, then I was.

The triplets were Millie's younger sisters. Their real names were Billie, Leslie and Josephine, but nobody ever called them that. We all called them Ready, Willing and Able. Something had happened to them. They were strange. I suppose modern medicine would be able to give whatever had happened to them a name. In those days some people simply called them daft or soft in the head. Perhaps now we might be more kindly and call them mentally handicapped. But if three kids could be truly called angels, it was Ready, Willing and Able. Without a husband their mother struggled hard to bring up five kids. The little street was always very protective, and it was no rare sight to see one or other of the women bearing down on number 12 with some steaming left-overs from their own meals. None of the other kids were beyond snitching the odd cabbage, potatoes or, if they were lucky, an apple or two from the Market. PC Laithwaite was quite aware of these acts of pilfering and, under May's leadership, many of the stall holders in the market place were always studiously looking somewhere else when the raiders were about. So all in all they didn't do too badly. After all, the alternative was the Workhouse and nobody in their right mind would wish that on anybody, not even their worst enemy. Things like money for the rentman, the coalman and the gas meter made things more diffi-cult to deal with. Money was in very short supply down our street. On very rare occasions somebody had a few bob to spare and we all knew where that had to go.

So far as Millie was concerned there was only one thing to do and she did it. She joined the big house at the top of the street with the other girls. We all knew why Millie was 'on the game' as it was called, but to begin with we had no idea why the rest of them were at it and certainly nobody was going to condemn them.

Danny and I had more fights over those girls than we ever did for our own pleasure. We were like a couple of knights even though our armour was fairly rusty, but woe betide anybody who said anything about the girls.

One of us would say, 'it's my turn, you thumped the last one'. Wallop. 'That's another one who won't say that again.' When PC Laithwaite called on us with some complaint made at the local by some man who didn't understand what the situation was, all he asked was, 'How many times did you hit him?'

'Once, of course, why? With this, of course,' said Danny, hold-ing up his fist. 'What else?'

'Nothing, I suppose. Just wondered. Well, don't do it again then.'

'Won't,' said Danny, 'it's Fynn's turn next.'

Both of us had spent a night in the lock-up. Not that we were really locked up, because Danny had spent his time playing Twenty One with the sergeant. I spent mine reading *The Police Manual* and drinking tea. We were both home in time for break-fast. This fact about Millie and the girls up at the top was some-thing that neither John nor Arabella – the spinster sister who lived with him – knew about and none of us was going to tell them. Eventually it was PC Laithwaite who told them. I'm sorry to say that they understood much better than the Rev. Castle did. Maybe he was just too concentrated on souls, but he needn't have worried because Danny and I had fixed them up with a place to pray in, and even though the Vicar had said an altar was out of the question. Well, the flowers were 'by courtesy' of the local park.

* * *

I don't know when, or how, I came to like John D. I never thought I would, but it wasn't all that long before I found it a real pleasure to be with him. It could have been – possibly – that as my father had died so long ago old John was coming to be important to me. Whatever the reason might be, it always gave me great pleasure being with him, even though he always seemed to be having a dig at me in one way or another. I know that I had never met anyone like him before. He could hardly utter a sentence without being sarcastic, but his dry manner of giving a lesson was something that excited me. I just liked listening to him. Even the dreaded 'persuader' didn't bother me. It didn't hurt all that much, and after a minute or two it was as if nothing had happened at all.

I was just about to make my way home from school when he called me over to his car and first introduced me to his sister Arabella.

'One of your friends has just changed the tyre for my sister,' he said.

'I wonder who that was,' I began to say.

'His name was Danny Sullivan.'

'Good old Danny! He's my fighting mate.'

'So,' he continued, 'you are the one they call Fynn, are you? I've heard about you. I understand you have other things you like doing. Other than fighting and climbing impossible walls.'

I nodded.

'And may one ask what else young Fynn likes doing?'

'Mathematics mostly. I guess I like that most of all.'

'The art of the mind.'

'What?' I asked. 'I don't understand that.'

'The art of the mind,' he said once again. 'Mathematics.'

That idea was a new one on me.

'Have you many books on the subject?' he asked me.

'Not many,' I said, 'they are all falling to bits and I reckon they are a bit out of date now.'

'Maybe. If you would care to come to my study after school is over, I'll see if I can find anything for you. We mustn't let our finest brains suffer from lack of books, must we?' The sarcastic old so and so!

'Who knows,' he went on, 'we may even manage to kindle some spark in that head of yours, but please keep it away from walls until I am able to see if there is anything inside! I doubt it. I doubt it very much, but it is just possible!'

The next day after school had ended I went to his study. Away from the classroom he was a different person altogether. He was still dry, sarcastic as ever and never missed any opportunity to trip me up, but he asked me many questions. He handed me a bundle of books.

'Here you are, young Fynn, see what you make of these. I don't suppose you'll make much of them, but you never know. What will you do, young Fynn, if you don't understand them?'

'Try to work it out, I suppose. I don't know yet.'

'You could always come and ask me if you get stuck. Come after school. I'm always ready to help you out. We really can't afford to let the spark go out now, can we? That's if we ever manage to kindle it.'

I smiled and he turned his back on me.

John had had a very bad time of it in the 1914–1918 War and would rarely speak of it. What with that experience and the deformities that he had been born with, he had become slightly sour. The very mention of the word 'God' or 'religion' often provoked an outburst of scorn and anger. He was that strangest of mixtures of outspoken bitterness and almost total generosity. I really had to be so careful with him and choose my words with great care.

It was one of his great pleasures to be called a rationalist and, after World War I, Arabella and he had joined a new group called The New Liberation Society. From the little that I knew of it, I knew it was not for me. Even though in those days I did like a tight argument it appeared to me that the rationalists were carrying things a bit too far.

The whole of John's personal life was so strictly regimented and his possessions so carefully ordered that no room was left for any kind of spontaneous gesture. If a thing could not be calculated it more or less did not exist for him, so much of a rationalist was he.

On the other hand, he could be very kind. He was more than willing to help those of his students who found it hard to grasp the point, and his willingness to help old comrades who had suffered in the war knew no bounds. On those occasions he was all gentleness and concern. He was an odd mixture, and the mix made it difficult for some people to understand him.

* * *

It must have been late summer or so when I had gone to see Old John to ask him for help. I was completely stuck with a problem. Although I had tried all the various ways that looked possible, I was just unable to resolve it. He looked at the problem for a moment or two, pointed out my mistake and left me to it. Of course, it was such a silly mistake to have made. The resolution of it was so simple that I could have kicked myself. He edged his way through the door from the kitchen, bearing a tray of coffee and some buns.

'Solved it, young Fynn?'

I nodded. 'I feel a right fool. How did I ever come to make that mistake?'

'It's one of the hazards of mathematics, Fynn!' He laughed. 'It so often turns out to be the simple thing. I've done it often myself.'

It gave me a lot of comfort to hear that. He handed me a cup of coffee and asked, 'Well, young Fynn, your sentence is almost up. Any idea what you are going to do with yourself?'

It was true. I was of an age when earning a living was necessary. I had one or two ideas, but I hadn't made up my mind.

'Well, what might my young genius do?'

'Not really sure yet, John,' I replied. 'Just don't know. All I am certain of is that I can't give up mathematics or physics.'

'Glad to hear you say that, young Fynn. You're always welcome here, you know that. But what about earning your keep, eh? An accountant? A teacher? There's plenty of room in this world for anyone able to add two and two together.'

'I know that, John, but I don't think that I want to do that sort of thing.'

'Why is that?' he asked.

'I know it sounds a bit daft, John, but I enjoy it too much! I suppose I just don't want to lose the fun and magic of it.'

His laughter at that filled the room. 'Oh, Fynn, oh Fynn, I've always known that to be a fact. You are reasonably good at it, you know, even if occasionally you do some silly things. That makes you doubly welcome here. Have you no idea what you might do then?'

This was the question I dreaded most of all, but the time had come to answer it.

'John ... well ... I ... I, er ... think I would like to go into the Church.'

I waited for the explosion, but it never came. He merely said 'Oh,' and his voice dropped a couple of octaves. Still there was no explosion, no tirade against religion. Just a simple, 'Why, Fynn? Why? Can you tell me?'

'It's just important, John, that's all, I can't give you any more reason than that.'

'Important, certainly,' he replied. 'Important to know where we are, and why too, if that's a proper question. I'm really not certain of that.'

His calmness had left me totally puzzled. 'John, I thought that you would ...'

'I would blow my top ...'

I nodded.

'You know, Fynn,' he said with a smile, 'I wasn't born without faith. I had to work very hard for my lack of it. I wouldn't want to stop you becoming a priest, if that is what you really want. All I must ask of you is that you think hard and long before you make up your mind.'

Perhaps I had made some movement, some indication that I was about to ask a question. He laid his hand on mine.

'No questions, young Fynn, not now. Perhaps one day when you visit me, and I am sure that there will be many days, many, many visits, I might even tell you all, but not now. There is one thing, however, that bothers me most of all, which you might like to ponder over before you take the plunge. Will you please fetch my Bible from my study? It's on the small table by the lamp. Don't look so surprised, Fynn. I really do have a Bible, and what is more I have even read it. In fact, more than once, mainly in the hope that I might have missed something, but I fear I haven't.'

I fetched the Bible and put it on the chair beside him and waited. His next words were such a surprise that I had to laugh.

'Do you drink beer, Fynn?'

'Well, I have once or twice, not much though.'

'Perhaps a small glass won't hurt a young man who is soon to go into the world. It's my own brew and I'm really rather proud of it.' He handed me a glass of beer.

'Before you drink perhaps you will read me verses 19 and 20 of the second chapter of Genesis.'

'And out of the ground the Lord God formed every beast of the field and every fowl of the air, and brought them unto Adam to see what he would call them and whatsoever Adam called every living thing that was the name thereof. And Adam ...'

'Enough, enough,' John broke in. 'Now you may drink.'

I took a swig.

'Well, what do you think of that?'

'Think of what?'

'The beer first, of course, and if you have any comments, the verses next.'

'The beer is good, John.'

'Good, Fynn? Good? Why, the only word to describe that beer is sublime. Take another draught and then tell me what you think about those verses.'

'I can't see anything wrong with them, John. They look all right to me. If they are true, it's wonderful. What are you on about?'

'I'm not on about anything. If, as we are told, God is all powerful, omnipotent, et cetera, et cetera, then why, oh why am I required to be amazed, pleased or full of wonder at the things he is supposed to have made? I'm not. What does puzzle me, however, is why then did he do such a stupid thing as to ask Adam to name them? Damn it, Fynn. I mean Babel and all that nonsense. What with that and the supposed flood, he does seem to me to spend a lot of time undoing his own creations. If only Adam had had the good sense to give everything a number rather than a name, it would have saved us all a lot of heartache. Ah well, my young friend, after too many years of trying to teach mathematics, I have come to the conclusion that it's the "numb" in numbers that causes the blockage. That is partly the reason why I am always so happy to have taught you and will always be so glad to see you. You are just a tiny bit different from my other pupils. Not much, mind you, but enough!'

I wanted to say something that would justify my difference, but nothing came.

'For goodness sake, Fynn, don't look so dumbfounded. Finish off your drink and indulge me occasionally in my hobby-horses. My problem is really quite simple. I cannot believe. It's as simple as that. If I could, I would, but even now I have not said what I wanted to say. Anno Domini, I suppose. What I am trying to say to you is, whatever else mathematics might be, it is certainly a language and that's important. Now, my young friend, it's about time you were off. Let me know what you decide to do and please come again and often.'

I was really quite confused by all this. He had never been as open with me before and I felt that I would like to stay with him, except that it wouldn't have been much use because I was perhaps even more uncertain about things myself. The idea that mathematics was a language was new to me and it gave me much to think about, for if it was true that you could talk about God in any language and if mathematics was a language, then ... except that I couldn't see how that might work.

* * *

I never did become a priest. I just wasn't sure enough for that. I became involved in the blending of oils and all sorts of lubricants. I suppose it was interesting enough. At least I was earning a wage, but except for adding a few numbers now and again and the occasional need to find seven per cent of a barrel of oil containing forty-seven gallons, my knowledge of maths was rarely used. It wasn't much used in conversation either. If I said that a particular problem and its solution was very beautiful, I found I had produced one of the best conversation-stoppers.

Fortunately, mathematics does have one great advantage. You don't need much to do it with – paper and pencil, perhaps, but often not even that. In fact, nothing but the room and time in which to think. So my roaming around the docklands of London at night were times of great contentment. I might meet the odd cat or two, perhaps a seaman overfilled with beer, trying to find his ship, or those ladies who called me 'Dearie', but whether it

was cats, tarts or drunks, the well-aimed answer 'Pi R squared to you' or perhaps, 'the square root of minus 1' was a sure-fire way of clearing a space!

Occasionally I met the dockland tapper or PC Laithwaite. Then one particular night when my head was full of numbers, Old John, God, language problems and all the odd bits and pieces of puzzlement, out of the fog a small girl suddenly appeared.

There was not much I could see of her in the fog even by a gas lamp. She was not very tall. She told me she had 'runned away' and she carried an old rag doll, a box of paints and she was hungry. She made a large hole in my bag of saveloys and she liked fizzy drinks, particularly the ones with a marble in the neck.

A couple of necessary fags to regain my composure and I learned that her name was Anna, that she was going to live with me and that she loved me as I loved her. I never was one to get into an argument that I had no hope of winning, so I simply accepted all that she had told me.

As time went by I did try to find out more about her background, but nobody had missed her, or if they had, they did not want her back. So she came home with me and stayed until she died a few years later. Later that night a hot bath revealed a mop of fiery red hair and a number of bruises. As a hot bath revealed her own special beauty, so warm love laid bare her devotion to Mister God, her endless chatter and her enormous appetite for trying to find out about things, as I have described in *Mister God This is Anna*. I did try to keep Anna and John apart, but since I talked about them so much, it was inevitable that they would meet, and it made me nervous. Like keeping the positive and negative poles of a battery apart. If you do that, nothing happens. But then if you join the poles of a battery to various things, you might get anything from light to a blown fuse. Whatever it was that did happen between them I was always in the middle of it!

* * *

And so I was talking to John about taking Anna to church. 'Church,' he exploded, 'utter piffle!' After his calm comments about my possibly becoming a priest, this outburst astonished me. But John liked to be perverse at times.

'Religion is nothing more than a bloody fortress of chaos,' he went on. 'Haven't you yet learned that people will protect their wrong beliefs with greater ferocity than they ever will their right beliefs. I really cannot see how anybody can believe anything that cannot be proved.'

'What about love, John?'

'What about it?'

'What about it! You can't prove that love exists!!'

'Indeed, what about it? What, may I ask, what good does that do?'

I said I didn't know but felt it must do some good.

These sudden outbursts never lasted very long, however, and were so quickly relieved by that crooked smile that his hare-lip forced upon him, but these sudden changes meant that we all had to be very careful what we said. He, himself, was very aware of these sudden outbursts, and that it made him a very lonely person; but for a long time it seemed that there was very little he could do about it. I suppose it accounted for the fact that he was so happy to give me as much extra tuition as I liked. I also think that he liked me. That pleased me.

John's manner of teaching was unusual; not odd, but different. On the occasions when he'd written some complex problem on the blackboard, he would always write out the answer on the board as well.

'Now you all know the answer, so you now all have ten marks. There are another ten marks for anyone who can tell me why it is right.' And after writing the proof, he would always end up with the letters written large Q.E.D. or Q.E.F., whatever was appropriate. What seemed to give him the most pleasure was the final full stop done with vigour, almost as if he was attacking the blackboard. Turning to his pupils he would always utter the one word. 'There!'

Listening to John delivering his lectures was not everybody's cup of tea, but his dry and precise manner of delivery was something I enjoyed greatly in spite of that slightly acidic way he had of going about it. Following his manner, I had also got into the habit of ending what I had written with Q.E.D. or Q.E.F.

* * *

When Anna first saw these letters she wanted to know what they meant and I showed her where to look in the Abbreviations section of the dictionary. She found another group that I did not know – Q.E.I., 'that which was to be found'. So now I had three sets.

1. Quod Erat Demonstrandum,
2. Quod Erat Faciendum, and
3. Quod Erat Inveniendum.

Q.E.D., 'which was to be proved', and certainly John's pleasure;
Q.E.F., 'which was to be done', and seemed always to be my job,
And Q.E.I., 'which was to be found', and Anna's main delight.
'Squashed-up writing' was what Anna called abbreviations.
And for her mathematics was simply 'All squashed-up writing'.

Sometimes it was difficult to understand what Anna was saying. Her invented words took some getting used to. Once, in a moment of pride, I took some pages of her writing to show John D., eager to hear what he would say about them. I was angry when, a few days later, I collected them, and found that he, apparently tripped up by her 'talk', had simply corrected the grammar and spelling in red ink. She was never very good at spelling or grammar. She had her own way.

Anna had been with me when John had launched himself into his usual anger about religion. 'If there was just one religion,' he said, 'I might be tempted to study it, but there are so many of them it's as if everybody has their own God and *that*, Fynn, is really beyond me. If there is an answer, there can only be one.'

Anna had written down her own solution to this problem but John hadn't grasped it. He had simply busied himself with corrections.

'It's easy, Fynn,' she had said. 'One of the first things Mister God ever did do was when he made light, wasn't it?'

'Agreed. That's what it says.'

And then she reminded me of the thing we had done together when, with the aid of a prism, and a beam of light, we had made that little spectrum of light on the wall. That's what it was all about. 'The Catholics used the red colour, the Protestants used green, the Jewish people another colour, the Hindu people yet another colour to see Mister God by.' Of course there were lots of different religions, and Anna was never really certain that somebody might not suddenly find another with one more holy day to cut out of the week, so that she would have less time than ever to play with her friends. But it didn't really matter when you saw them all as beams of the one light. As Mum said, you are born into one religion because you have no choice, but you die with them all or nothing. John very nearly missed this other way of looking.

* * *

Anna's times at School or Church didn't always achieve those aims intended by Miss Haynes or the Rev. Castle. For that matter, John also came in for a good few 'Poohs'. Some of all this teaching was not bad, but some of it was just downright 'daft, wasn't it, Fynn?' Poor old Rev. Castle most definitely was not pleased one bit to be so loudly 'Poohed' in the middle of his sermon, and the way he had peered at me over his spectacles made it look as if it was my fault. I did try to keep her quiet, but it never worked all that well. The Vicar had been telling the congregation the parable about the sower sowing the seeds. The fact that some of them fell among stones and others fell among thorns was a little bit too much for her. Her 'Pooh!' was startling enough, but her comment that he ought to be more careful was so loud that I'm sure even the statues heard it. It didn't help matters afterwards when she was heard telling me that this sower bloke was also a bit daft.

'He should have taken them stones out first. At least he should have dug them thorn things out, shouldn't he Fynn?' She almost convinced herself that the reason why grown-ups read fairy stories to children was because they, themselves, believed them!

I often taught Anna some of the things that John had taught me. She never was what you might call brilliant at mathematics, but she so often saw in it things that neither John nor I had seen, or at least not in the same way. For instance, multiplying two numbers together was fine if that was what you wanted to do. A bit of a bore at times and at times pretty hard to do. It was a great excitement for her when I showed her that 8 times 9 equals 72 was only one way of doing it. You got exactly the same result by dividing one number by the reciprocal of the other. The idea that you could 'do' multiplication by division was for me such an absurd idea that it just stuck with me. Of course, it was one of those things I had to teach Anna.

She did change the words a bit. 9 or $\frac{9}{1}$ became 'standing up' numbers and the reciprocal of 9 or $\frac{1}{9}$ was obviously 'upside down' numbers.

It made much more fun for Anna to do her sums with this wonderful new way. The old stuff of multiplying 9 by 8 suddenly became either $9 \div \frac{1}{8}$ or $8 \div \frac{1}{9}$. It didn't matter which way you did it, it didn't make any difference to the answer. Whichever way you did it, the answer was always 72 and it was 'the right way up' too. That certainly needed some thinking about.

$$8 \times 9 = 72$$
$$8 \div \frac{1}{9} = 72$$
$$9 \div \frac{1}{8} = 72$$

$$\frac{1}{\frac{1}{9} \times \frac{1}{8}} = 72$$

I don't remember if I had ever thought of what happens if you multiply $\frac{1}{9}$ by $\frac{1}{9}$, but Anna did.

'What happens, Fynn, what happens if you make them both "upside down" numbers and multiply them? $\frac{1}{8} + \frac{1}{9} = ...$? What happens, Fynn, what happens?'

The fact that it turned out to be a 0.013888888 was a bit of a disappointment to her after this new and wonderful way of doing it.

I waited for her next question. It took a long time coming, but eventually it came. Suddenly she launched both herself and her question at me.

'Is it, Fynn? Is it?'

'Is it what, Tich?'

'Is it an "upside down" number, Fynn, is it, eh?'

It was indeed a reciprocal or 'upside down' number of 72 ($\frac{1}{72} = 0.013888888$).

'Oooh! Fynn,' she gasped, 'ain't it good? Oooh! I'm going to tell Mister John next time. Do you think he knows about it, Fynn?'

'I reckon he does,' I replied, 'you can tell him about it tomorrow when we see him.'

John chuckled with amusement and delight at her 'right way up' and 'upside down' numbers. He had never heard them called that before.

'I don't suppose it really matters what she calls them, as long as she knows what it means.'

I left them to it for a few minutes. Anna was chattering away as fast as she could, and John was in his favourite armchair with a dazed but happy smile on his face. When I came back I heard him

say, 'Yes, my little maid, I'll remember, I will be careful.'

'What was all that about, John?' I asked.

He laughed. 'She just told me that sometimes the answer is "upside down" and that makes a difference and you've got to remember what you've done.' He poured himself a fresh tankard of ale. 'I never remember being so excited about reciprocals in my education. Perhaps, young Fynn, it's the names she gives things that I find so enchanting. "Upside down numbers" indeed! That does seem to fit so many occasions and situations, don't you think?'

'Think, John? I don't often get the chance to think when she gets started!'

'The answer might be "upside down",' he muttered. 'It so often is! Remember that, Fynn. The answer is sometimes "upside down".'

'Yes, John, I will. Sometimes I think it's me that is "upside down"!'

'Ah!' He laughed. 'She certainly does give it a new life, doesn't she?'

It didn't matter which way round you did it, the idea that it was possible to multiply by dividing and divide by multiplying was something entirely new to Anna. This must surely be real Mister God stuff. And then there was those logarithm things where you could multiply by adding certain kinds of numbers and divide by taking away certain kinds of numbers. John didn't see this magic as Anna saw it.

'You can do things like multiplication the ordinary way, you can do it by dividing and you can also do it by adding!'

That really was something to reckon with. So she plunged into mathematics with rare excitement. She never really did get into that Q.E.D. stuff. Proofs for her were a complete waste of time. There really was so much to find out.

After their first few meetings John had viewed her with tolerant amusement.

'She is so ignorant of the task ahead of her that she can't see the certainty of failure,' he had said. He was just plain puzzled by her. It was much later that he said, 'Well, I don't really know, whatever else might be said about her, she certainly does appear to proceed in a step by step fashion, even though I can't always follow her path!'

It was at this time that a curious magic happened between us: the 'which was to be proved' retired school master, the 'which was to be found' red-headed child, leaving me with the 'which was to be done' bit as usual; but that was all right. It was worth it! It was always a great pleasure to see these two together. John slowly became much more relaxed about things, and after a time he was even capable of playing pretend games, even though he never was able to stop being the academic. Being with these two didn't do me any harm either, even though I did get myself into a muddle at times. After all, I could ask, couldn't I? And I often needed to. I wasn't always sure about the answer, but I never went without one.

It didn't take John too long before he could empty all the contempt from the word 'brat' and fill it with love, in the way that Anna was able to empty the word 'sir' from its association and fill it with love. Neither of them, however, was able to get out of their own way of speaking. John often threw in a foreign phrase or two and Anna's choice of words was not always of the best. But 'brat' and 'sir' they became to each other for a long time and, for the most part, I was able to translate the one to the other.

On the occasions when there was nobody around to see it, John would often wear the red-beaded heart that Anna had made for his birthday. Making brooches was not a thing that John would ever attempt to do, and it was some long time before he gave her one she kept for very special occasions. John had chosen a plain little silver brooch for her on which he had had inscribed some words in Latin; of course, what else! QUOD PETIS HIC EST.

Anna would never tell anybody what it meant when asked. 'Ask Fynn. He knows.'

I did like saying, 'It means "What you seek is here"?'

At one time I thought of having one made for her myself, just to keep the whole thing in order so to speak. Mine would have been different, like QUANTUM SUFFICIT – 'As much as is sufficient'. If only I had known exactly how much! But I never did find the answer to that one.

That fact that much of my time was spent with books on mathematics, physics and related subjects, meant that Anna picked up a number of unfamiliar words, like 'electrons', 'polynomials', 'relativity' and 'quantum theory'. The fact that I never kept my books from her meant that she soon had words in her vocabulary which most people had never heard of or, if they had heard of them, didn't understand. Neither did she for the most part, at least, not in the way that would have allowed her to pass an examination. She simply sprinkled them about like salt and sugar. It didn't matter if the salt was where the sugar should have been. As a matter of fact I did not know all that much about them myself. But these words, in Anna's view, were the result of finding, and finding was to her all-important. A question mark was an invitation to finding. When she saw a chapter-heading IS THE ELECTRON DIVISIBLE ALSO? she knew it was important. When the author went on to say, 'Perhaps it is merely a coincidence that the person who first noticed that the rubbing of amber would induce a new and remarkable state now known as the state of electrification was also some great unifying principle that links everything together,' she realized he was a friend of Mister God, and she was quite certain that it was Mister God who made it all happen.

'Any mathematical book to be of any value has to be read forwards and backwards.' Nothing could be simpler, could it? So she tried it. It was something that was so simple to say and almost impossible to do, but in her own way she was often able to find some little gem out of the wreckage of instructions. She tackled this reading the book backwards idea with enthusiasm, even though to begin with she did think it was daft. It was easy for her to see that the best way to go about this thing was to prop a mirror on the kitchen table and read the reflection of the book in the mirror, not the book itself. It did seem to her to be a little bit like Mister God. After all, the Vicar never lost any opportunity to remind us that we could never actually see God, so the reflection was all that we had to go on. Mind you, it did mean that you had to be a bit careful!

I think that this was why she was so very interested in everything about her. For a few days I often saw her looking into the mirror, screwing her head to left and right. On my return from work one evening it was quite obvious that she was just ready to explode with excitement. The mirror was carefully set upon the table as she dived into her own private drawer and brought out a sheet of paper. It didn't seem to be all that important to me. She had simply written in large numbers $4 + 7 = 11$.

'So, what's all the excitement, about,' I wondered. 'That's pretty obvious stuff.'

'So what?' I asked her. 'What's that in aid of?'

'That's right, ain't it, Fynn?'

'Of course it is,' I replied. 'You know that. You didn't need to ask me.'

'Look,' she said. 'Look now.' She had turned the sheet of paper to face the mirror. The reflection now read $11 = 7 + 4$.

'That's right too,' I said before she had a chance to ask me.

'Um,' she said, 'but, Fynn, what else is eleven equal to?'

'Well, it could be $10 + 1$ or $9 + 2$, it could be …'

She interrupted me with, 'Couldn't it be squillions of things?'

'Yes, it could, couldn't it?'

'Fynn, that equals things makes it safe, don't it?'

'Safe for what?' I asked, getting a bit lost as usual.

'Safe so you can read it backwards like Mister God.'

Now I was completely lost. 'How come like Mister God?' What was so clear to her left me a wee bit in the dark.

'Fynn,' she replied with some exasperation, '"cos if there is only one way to go frontways to see Mister God and he won't let us and there is squillions of ways of going backwards, what then?'

There was not much glimmer of light, but enough for the moment. Doing something backwards and forwards might seem odd at times, but sometimes it did work and then well, who knows, things might happen. I liked the idea that the $=$ sign made it quite safe to go forwards or backwards, but I had never really grasped the fact that, of course, $4 + 7 = 11$ was, according to her, only right once when she read it forwards, but that there were squillions of answers when you read it backwards. $11 = 7 + 4$ or $8 + 3$ or … or … I was having enough trouble doing it the right way round! And I suppose Mister God just might have made it so that we couldn't see him frontwards in only one possible way, but that we had to look at him backwards like the reflection in a mirror. It did mean, as she told me, that there were simply squillions of ways to do it and that Mister God was in each way, and considering the fact that the little $=$ thing made it all so safe, that was fine.

'You'd better tell the Vicar,' I said, 'I'm sure *he*'d like to know.' She wasn't all that certain about that!

'I'm going to tell Mister John the next time I see him. Bet he wants to know, Fynn, bet he do!'

Over the next few days she did manage to tell this to the Rev. Castle and, for that matter, anyone else who would listen. The Rev. Castle had responded, 'There is absolutely no need for that kind of stuff in church, you know.'

She got a great deal more response from the milkman and the coalman and Bombom and Millie, but that was all right. In the next few days most of the railway wall was filled with little sums as she and her friends explored this idea. It didn't look like Mister God to me, but, according to Anna, it was, just the same.

It was after this that the whole idea of mathematics made sense to her and she plunged into my books with some urgency.

Her way of doing things often got me into hot water; like the time we had been turned out of St Paul's Cathedral. She couldn't understand how we were 'desecrating God's Holy Place'. After all, we were just pushing a prayer book around the black and white squares on the floor, and what was the harm in that? It's true that we had written some numbers in chalk on the floor, but as she pointed out, 'Fynn can get it off with his hanky', so why were we being turned out? This was God-stuff after all, wasn't it?

I was curious, considering the fact that John D. regarded the Bible as not worth reading as it was nothing more than a collection of fairy-stories, that he should be so offended when Anna

258

could so easily laugh at it. The Rev. Castle was even more put out. His word for Anna's laughter was that she was making a mockery of it and that really I ought to do something about it. For both of them Life was a very serious business. Everybody said how hard Life was. It was odd that two people so far apart in their beliefs should think of God in the same way.

'People get muddled up,' she told me.

'They must do,' I agreed, 'but about what?'

'Mister God and Old Nick.'

'Oh, do they? How do they manage to do that? I can't see how they make that mistake.'

'In Church the Rev. Castle keeps on saying that Mister God is always looking at me.'

'So, what's wrong with that?'

'I know that!'

'So?'

'Why does he say that Mister God stick me with a big sticker if I don't sit up straight and if I talk sometimes.'

'Suppose other people want to hear what he's got to say and that children ought to behave themselves.'

'Suppose so!' But obviously she didn't believe that was true. She tried to find the right words to explain to me what she was wanting to say, words that I could understand.

'I do try, Fynn, I really do.'

'Try to do what, Tich?'

'Try to behave good, and sit up straight, and things like that.'

'I know that!'

'But I don't always, do I, Fynn?'

'Not always,' I said, 'sometimes you are a blessed nuisance, but I love you!'

She nodded and smiled at me. 'So does Mister God too, don't he, Fynn?'

'Sure thing! I don't see how he could help it.'

'It's them bloody stones, Fynn. They get heavy. That's what they are like, *stones*.'

'What stones are you on about, Tich? What kind of stones?'

'All the things they tell you to do. *Them* kind of stones. That's what! And then they get so heavy, I can't do nothing. Mister God don't do that, do he Fynn?'

I was beginning to get the hang of this stones stuff. The Vicar was certainly full of 'do's' and 'don't's' and at times they did seem like heavy weights.

'It makes me laugh sometimes. It's funny!'

'Can't see what's funny about it. How do you work that one out?'

"Cos I can't do it. It's funny. I can't help laughing then Fynn.'

All this did sound complicated to listen to, but as far as I could see she wasn't far out.

The trouble with people like the Rev. Castle and John was that life was a deadly serious business, and so often they would load you up with dead weights and you certainly couldn't run and play. 'If you had to carry all them stones around with you! Mister God never did mean you to do that kind of thing, did he?'

As far as Anna understood Mister God, he never went around prodding people to make them fed up or frightened of him. What Mister God really wanted was to make you laugh – to laugh at your own mistakes. If you could do that, you really did learn and did not get tangled up in things you couldn't possibly do. 'It makes you laugh, don't it?'

* * *

It was about the middle of Autumn and I was just coming home from work. As I passed the Corner Shop I was hailed by Mrs Bartlett, our local shopkeeper, who, amongst other things, acted as a clearing house for telephone calls for those of us who had not as yet got a telephone. That meant all of us.

'Fynn,' she called. 'Got a message for you. The Professor's sister rang up this afternoon. The old chap's been taken bad and would you go as soon as possible?'

'Thanks, Missus,' I said, 'I'll get there as soon as possible after I've washed up a bit.'

'Hope he's all right. He's a funny old geezer right enough. Meself. I can't understand what he's on about half the time. He ought to learn to speak English proper. That's what he ought to do.' She chortled her next sentence, 'How do you fancy me as a Madam, Fynn?'

'Well, I don't quite see it myself, but you never know!'

'That's what the old gent called me. "Good afternoon, madam, have you by any chance got some French mustard?" And me with me curlers still in. "Madam" indeed! It made me feel a right fool, it did!'

Mum was never ever surprised at my comings and going. As far as I was concerned, there wasn't all that difference between day and night.

'Have you told Anna yet?'

'No,' I replied, 'I haven't seen her yet.'

'She went over with Bombom to May's house. I'll just tell her you had to go out. It's better not to say too much until you get home. Maybe it'll turn out to be nothing much after all. You can wake me up if you get home late. I'd like to know myself how the old fella is.' I promised that I would do that as soon as I got in.

Now Random Cottage, where John and Arabella lived, was various distances away, depending on the route you took and, of course, what means of transport you could use where. Trams and buses took a long time. But I had worked out a route using the canal tow-path and other short cuts.

As I rode along my mind was working nineteen to the dozen. J. D. was, after all, no chicken and well, maybe … I didn't waste my time in getting there. I just pedalled as hard and as fast as I could. There was nothing out of the ordinary that I could see as I made my way to the back door. Arabella was doing something in the kitchen. I rang the bell and waited. She greeted me warmly.

'Hello, Fynn. Hope I didn't give you too much of a scare. Thank you for coming so promptly. Go through to the study. John's there.'

I breathed a sigh of relief for nothing at all seemed to be wrong. It was, as far as I could see, much the same as usual. John was in his usual chair with his usual pint of beer.

'Hello, young Fynn. Pour yourself a pint of beer and sit down. Don't look at me like that,' he chuckled. 'You look as if you've seen a ghost. Drink up. Well, as a matter of fact, I did have a bad turn, but, as you see, I'm fit as a flea now.'

I was relieved to hear it and said so!

'I'm afraid, Fynn, that Arabella does get a little worked up about things, but there you are.'

It was just like John to think that some people got worked up about unimportant things. I did wonder, for a moment or two, whether I ought to say what was in my thoughts and decided that I must. 'You really must look after yourself.'

'No, no, Fynn,' he interrupted me, 'don't you start on me. You are far too young to tell me what I must or must not do.'

'Sorry,' I replied. 'You would not say that to Anna, would you?'

'That's an entirely different thing,' he said. 'You are beginning to think like me, so I feel free to correct you. Anna,' he continued, 'is far too young to want to offer me any advice. She has her own particular way of thinking and I do find what she says to be of some interest, even though I don't always understand what it is that she means.'

That I was beginning to think like him, I took to be a rare compliment, but it did seem odd to me that if I was more and more like him, why was it that he paid me so little attention or why was it that he was so interested in Anna's way of putting things?

'I had hoped,' he said, 'that you would have brought her with you. Didn't you think of that?'

'Of course I did,' I replied with a touch of anger, 'but I thought Arabella's telephone call sounded so urgent that you must be ill and, well ...' I was stumbling over my words.

'Pooh!' he chuckled, 'pooh and pooh again. You see, Fynn, it's never too late to learn.'

I was hurt by his remarks. 'If your being unwell is a pooh thing, I ...'

'Sorry, Fynn, forgive me.'

'There's nothing to forgive,' I muttered.

'I'm very glad you came. I did want to see you. I have been giving something a great deal of thought these last few days and I wanted to talk to you about the matter.'

I was very relieved at this. It sounded to me that he was back to his old self again, but I was totally unprepared for what he said next.

'Wouldn't it be nice if Anna could stay at Random Cottage for, say, a day or two?'

I was so totally surprised at this that I was quite unable to think of an answer.

'You look surprised, Fynn.'

'A bit,' I said.

'You know, I'm not the monster you take me to be. I too have a heart. The little one has never been frightened of me and that I find very pleasing.'

He did seem disappointed when I told him that I couldn't possibly give him an answer right then and that I would have to ask Mum and Anna. It wasn't very often that anybody ever said 'No' to him or didn't give him an immediate answer.

'I'll mention it, John,' I managed to say, 'I'll mention it and let you know later.'

'Mention it? Mention it, young Fynn? More than mention it. Give it some serious thought. I'm sure that a change of scene will do her good.'

I was beginning to feel that he was getting me into a corner and I was unable to get out.

'Think about it, Fynn,' he reminded me as I said goodbye. I promised I would as I mounted my bike.

I didn't hurry home that night. I was so surprised at the way things had turned out that I needed time to think, and also a pint of the necessary and a breathing space and time to sort out my thoughts before I got home. The more I thought about it, the more I looked at the possibility that he had arranged the whole thing, right down to Arabella's phone call. But no, that wasn't his way. There was something going on that I didn't know about.

I'd simply have to talk to Mum about this puzzling episode when I got back. It was nearly midnight when I finally made it home. Mum was still up waiting for me in the kitchen.

'Well,' she asked, 'what news?'

'False alarm,' I replied. 'He looked quite all right to me.'

She nodded her head as she said, 'A bout of indigestion probably. Can be nasty, that can be.'

I was still so undecided about the last few hours that I thought it might be better if I spoke of his offer, or was it a request, after I had slept on it. Anna was sound asleep so I wasn't going to be faced with an unending stream of questions this night. By the light of the street lamp, I could see her quite clearly and the only word that came to me at that moment was innocence. After an hour or two, that was the word that ended my waking hours. Whatever else, she was innocence. That was her.

Waking up to my early morning cup of tea brought by Anna, the word 'innocence' came into my mind. Innocence. What a nice word that was, even with all its risks. She sat on the side of my bed and kissed me with all the fire of a young child. Innocent certainly. And then it came to me that I had never realized what responsibility that quality placed on older people. Not that I had

any doubt about John at all. It was simply that I had no idea why John wanted to see her so much. Mentally, I added another word to Innocence and that was 'Trust'.

Over breakfast we talked about John's request. Mum didn't see that she would come to any harm, and after all it would certainly make a change to get out of all the smoke and dust for a few days.

'You don't suppose he's trying to change her mind about going to church, do you?' Mum asked me.

That was something I had never really thought about, but I was absolutely certain that he would never do a thing like that. As for Anna, the thought of seeing all the rabbits, birds and the odd deer was very pleasing to her. The fly in the ointment was being away from her friends ... Bombom, Matt, Millie and the rest of the gang. She gave it a great deal of thought. As I got ready for work, she made up her mind.

'Fynn,' she yelled, 'if you can come too, it would be very nice. Can you ask Mister John, and, say, Fynn, will you?'

I promised that I would get in touch with John before I returned home that evening.

'That's the best plan,' said Mum. 'I'd feel a lot easier in my mind to know that she wasn't alone with strange people in a strange house, and do try and find out why the Professor wants her to come, will you? I know she's as bright as a bag of buttons, but I don't know what she could possibly say that would be of any use to him.'

I promised that I would do my best to get answers to all of these questions and that we would talk about it more when I returned.

Anna walked with me to the top of the street. 'Fynn, when I get bigger, you can go to work on your tandem and I can drive it home and then come and get you, like the Posh people do, can't I, Fynn?'

'All in good time,' I replied, 'don't rush growing up too quickly, Tich.'

'I'm going to grow up like you,' she said. 'Just like you!'

I was certainly very pleased and flattered by her last remark but I couldn't help hoping as I pedalled along to work that she might grow up to be a bit better than I was.

I managed to finish off my work in good time that day and by six o'clock, knocking-off time, I was ready to go.

'What's the rush, Fynn? Wait for me and I'll treat you to a pint of wallop,' said Cliff.

'He wants to see his lady love. Who is it tonight, Fynn? Blonde or brunette?' asked Ted.

'Neither,' I replied. 'As a matter of fact, it is a red-head.'

'Oh!' said Cliff, 'you mean little Anna. Right, Fynn?'

'Right,' I answered.

'Keeps you busy, don't she. She'll wreck your love life if you're not careful What's she up to this time? What does she want now? A tin of canal water or have you got to pick a bunch of flowers for her?'

'Never seen one like her,' said Ted.

'Regular ball of fire, that's her!'

'She certainly is a real corker and that's a fact,' replied Ted.

'You're right there,' I said. 'What I want is forty-eight hours a day. Twenty-four hours just ain't enough.'

So I pedalled out to Random Cottage. I rang the bell at the back door. Arabella opened it.

'Fynn,' she exclaimed, 'you're a mess! Whatever has happened to you?'

It was then that I realized that I was still in my overalls and that I was not a very pretty sight to see.

'Come in, do come in. You'd better take off your shoes, though. Can't have you tramping all that oil onto my carpet. You can sit in the kitchen, but make sure you put that newspaper on the chair first. I'll fetch John for you and then I'll make you some tea. I hope you won't keep him too long. Our supper will be ready soon.'

I promised that I would be as quick as possible.

'Hello, young Fynn,' John greeted me. 'Whatever is amiss?' And after looking at me for a moment and wrinkling up his nose, he said, 'Is this the latest fashion that the young are wearing these days? You look a sight! What can I do for you, Fynn? Money or a new pair of trousers? Perhaps you'd like a bath?'

He was really going at it. He was in one of his sarcastic moods. I took no notice of him. I had heard this kind of thing all too often. I prayed that he would never have this approach with Anna. I did try to give her message to him as gently as I could, but it didn't come out quite right.

'Anna said she ain't coming unless I come too. So does Mum.'

He chuckled. 'Frightened of the ogre, is that it?'

'No,' I replied, 'that's not it, but, well, you can be a bit sharp-tongued at times and you know it. Anyhow, what do you want to talk to her about?'

'Trust, trust. Where is your trust, young Fynn? Surely you should know me better than that by now, young Fynn?'

He was beginning to make me ashamed of myself.

'Sorry, John,' I managed to say. 'It's just that she is so very young and if anybody was ever to hurt her, I'd, well, I'd ...'

'Break them in two,' he suggested. 'Don't worry, Fynn. I'd help you!'

'But, John,' I continued, 'whatever would you want to talk to her about? What you know compared with what she knows; it just doesn't make sense.'

'If that's meant to be a compliment, I accept it with pleasure.'

'Why, John? Why, then?'

'She's an exceedingly bright young lass and will no doubt reach a very high level, but it isn't that that puzzles me. She has caused me to look again at some of the things that I have missed. Now, now, Fynn. No revelation. No road to Damascus or anything like that.'

'What then?'

'Perhaps you've never noticed it, Fynn. It is simply the fact that she has this nice ability to use the right words for the right subject, unlike our local Vicar. I just like listening to her. She is one of the few people who makes me think, as you do sometimes.'

I felt a bit better after that remark; that sort didn't come very often from John.

On my way home I was at least satisfied that my dear old Master would be on his very best behaviour and that in no way would he cause Anna any distress. I was also happy to hear from him that he would break anybody in two if she was in any way harmed. It was a certain fact that she was a joy to listen to; that unending prattle and question, but I still had no idea exactly what it was that he expected her to say. Perhaps I might just understand more fully when we went to stay with him. Mum was very relieved when I had finished telling her about John.

'Well,' she said, 'that's all right then. What do you think about it all then, Luvey?'

'I'm glad Fynn can come with me. I wouldn't go else.' Then after a moment's thought, Anna said, 'Can't Bombom come too, Fynn? Can't she?'

'Well,' I replied, 'I don't really see how we could ask him to do that. Perhaps another time, if he asks us again. I could find out and then she might go with you without me.'

'Wouldn't go,' she said flatly. 'Wouldn't go without you.'

It's funny how good she could make me feel, and what's more I did know that she meant it, too.

'So,' said Mum, 'what's the arrangement then? Going on the bike?'

'Not this time,' I replied. 'We're going by car!'

'A real car, Fynn? A really real one?'

'Yes, Mister John is going to collect us here at ten o'clock next Saturday morning and he will bring us home about eight o'clock on Sunday evening.'

'Can I go and tell Bombom, eh, please? Can't Bombom and May come to Mister John's house on Sunday after tea and then he could bring us back all together, can't he?'

'Well, he could, I suppose. We'll have to ask him when he comes on Saturday. You are quite certain you wouldn't like Hec and Sandy and Doreen, Sally, Sarah and the rest of your friends?'

'Could they all get in the car, Fynn? Could they? Fynn, you're teasing me ain't you?'

I nodded. 'Off you go to Bombom then and mind you're back in ten minutes.'

She fled down the passage. It was always easy in our house to tell when Anna was coming in or going out. Her speed always made the gas light flicker.

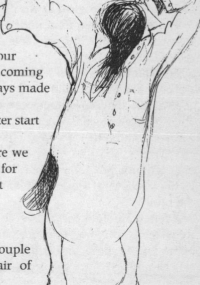

'I suppose,' said Mum, 'I'd better start getting some clothes together.'

Then 'Oh,' she said, 'what are we going to do about a nightie for her? I haven't got the time. Got any money in the tin?'

'About two pounds I reckon,' I replied.

'That'll do fine. I can get a couple for that. Better get her a pair of knickers while I'm about it.'

'Can't see her in a nightie myself. You know that she won't sleep in anything but my shirt.'

'I know,' she replied, 'but it is a special occasion and I wouldn't want to embarrass the child.'

'Take a lot more than that to embarrass her. She wouldn't turn a hair if she hadn't got a stitch to her back.'

'But still,' she said, 'they are not like us, are they? With that big house and all that fine stuff they've got.'

I laughed. 'Never thought of you as a snob. Couldn't live there myself. I'd be far too scared to touch anything.' By seven o'clock the next morning our clothes had been washed and ironed. 'Can I go in the street, please? I've got to say good-bye to Bombom and May.'

'Some people do sleep, you know,' I said. 'Even if you get up with the birds other people don't. Besides, we're not going away for ever. Off you go then and try not to make yourself dirty.'

'I won't,' she promised. 'Fynn,' she yelled, 'will you get my bag too, please? I might want something.' So I fetched her bag and placed it beside the case.

'Whatever has she got in there?' asked Mum. 'All her pencils and chalks I suppose. What would she do without them?'

By a quarter to ten that morning most of the street knew that we were to be away for two days, and had turned out to see the motor car.

'Hi Fynn!' yelled Millie. 'Off to the moon?'

'Looks like it, doesn't it!'

I was just about to light up a fag when the whirlwind struck me amidships once again. 'You won't forget to ask Mister John, Fynn, will you? And if he says "yes" you can telephone Mr Thackeray, can't you?'

At ten promptly John turned his car into the street. 'Can I get in the front Fynn? Do you reckon Mister John will let me honk the horn?'

A few more 'Can I's?' plus a couple of 'Do you think's?' and we were off. That was, of course, after she had finished her symphony on the horn, and with Anna directing John as to which way he must go, since she certainly wasn't going to let any of her friends miss seeing her in a car. With me spread out comfortably over the large back seat and Anna chattering next to John, we slowly went on our way. John was a very careful driver and he needed to be even more so at this moment, for he had to duck more than once as she flung out an arm to indicate some event or situation that we passed. 'Look, Mister John, look at that!'

'What's that, Mister John, what is it?' But he was fully concentrating on ducking outflung arms and trying to get us there in one piece.

We got there eventually. John was thankful that he had got home intact. He had never experienced that kind of journey before!

Arabella greeted us at the front door. Although we had been there a number of times before, we had always used the back door and she had never shown us the house. We had not seen more than the dining-room and perhaps had a passing peak at the sitting-room.

'Come along in you two. I'll show you to your rooms and then you can explore the house, but,' she added, 'please don't touch anything. We don't use that room,' she explained, pointing to a closed door, 'nor that one and that one is mine. You can look at it if you want to.'

We were taken upstairs. I had a double bed whilst Anna had a single. I helped her put her clothes away in the drawer.

'How did this get in here?' I asked her as she drew my shirt from her bag.

'That's for the night time, Fynn. That's the shirt you gived me.'

'Whatever happened to those two nighties I bought you?'

'Took 'em out!' she exclaimed. 'They were too nice for sleeping in. I like this best,' she continued, holding up the shirt. Arabella returned just as Anna was holding my shirt. It was a good one.

'Whatever have you got there?' she asked.

'For sleeping in, don't I, Fynn?'

I could do nothing else but nod my head.

'I'll find you an old blouse of mine,' responded Arabella. 'You can't go to sleep in a thing like that!'

Anna could. She liked it.

A few minutes later, Arabella returned with one of her blouses, all lace and frills in pink and white. 'You can have that,' Anna was told.

We didn't really have all that much to unpack, so we set off to explore the house. Everything was a bit of a mystery to Anna. She just did not understand why you went to bed in all that frilly stuff. 'I mean, what's the point if nobody is going to see it?'

And as for all those rooms that apparently were never used, well, I ask you, you just had to be a bit doolally to do a thing like that!

As for real hot water coming out of a tap! Just fancy not having to boil a kettle of water or light up the copper!

'They must be real millionaires, Fynn, mustn't they?'

'They are what people call "very comfortably off",' I explained.

I supposed her biggest surprise was that she was unable to find the bath hanging on the wall, in the back yard or anywhere.

'Don't they have a bath then, Fynn?'

So off we went upstairs again in order to see the bathroom. She tried as hard as she could to move it. 'It's stuck, Fynn. Help me.'

It was difficult for her to accept the fact that I wouldn't be able to move it either, for it was fixed. It took her a long time before she would believe that one!

For the next thirty minutes we just mooched about the house, looking at everything and in all the rooms that were not locked up. We saw the new-fangled carpet cleaner, the electric boiler, the solid fuel cooker and such like things. Anna walked with her hands held behind her back.

'What's up, Tich? Got a pain?'

'She told me not to touch anything, so I'm not.'

'I think she meant don't mess about with things.'

'I'm not going to,' she replied. Knowing her so well after these few years, I figured that there was a thing or two not to her liking. As we walked in the garden I said, 'Don't you like it, Sweetie? Wouldn't you like to live here?'

'Nope,' she snapped at me. 'I like it home with Mum better! I suppose some people might like to live here, but not me.' She continued to tell me why, before I had a chance to ask her.

'Fynn, it's all too sort of special and all those things that you have to look after that's supposed to look after you, well, well you just never get no time to play and enjoy yourself.'

I had never heard labour-saving devices spoken of like that before, but I suppose it might be true sometimes. She wasn't at all keen either that there weren't any trains passing the window, nor was there any street light coming in.

'I'm going to sleep in your room tonight, Fynn. That's what I'm going to do and then we can talk.'

I wasn't sure how Arabella would take all these criticisms about her house and only hoped she wouldn't ask any awkward questions.

* * *

Anna was surprised to find that John had another way of doing sums. He had told her mathematics was 'like playing a game'. That was new to her. She didn't understand. He explained the difference. 'When you play a game in the street, my little maid, you can't unkick a ball and you can't unthrow a stone. Once you've done a thing, there is no going back. But with sums and mathematics, there is always a way that you can go back.'

That afternoon he showed her two moving films he had made many years previously. I had never seen them. I didn't even know that his main hobby was making films. One was based on a game of draughts and the other was a game of chess. No people and no hands appeared in the film; just the pieces doing what they were supposed to do. It really did look like a game. Because he could vary the speed of the projector. He could make it look like anything from a pointless, dizzy muddle to a proper game. Anna liked it. It was just like being two different people, one seeing things fast and the other seeing things slow. It was no wonder

I got in such a muddle with all these different Annas knocking about. The one that saw things slowly, the one that saw things speeded up, to say nothing of the one on this side of the road and the one on the other. Her different perspectives were such that sometimes she reminded me of the story of Dick Turpin, who was seen to come out of the Black Swan Inn at York and ride off in several directions at the same time!

'Ain't God wonderful?'

Along with so many people in the 1930s, John was convinced that, given a few more years, Science would be able to explain everything that was worthy of explanation. He had little time or inclination to believe anything that wasn't capable of proof, or at least some sort of reasonable explanation. He held to this belief so firmly that on any possible occasion, he would launch into a lengthy talk on the subject, along with a total dismissal of the significance of the more gentle things of life around him. As I have mentioned, both his house and his garden were so well organized, with a place for everything and everything in its proper place, that anything slightly out of order was such a blight on the total organization that it had to be put right instantly. Anna viewed this order with suspicion and sadness.

'It's like bloody wallpaper. It's the same thing what just goes on and on! Don't it?'

As she was looking at the garden, John came up behind us.

'Do you like it, little one?'

'No!' She was never one to dodge the awkward things.

'Don't you like flowers, Mister John?' We were looking at blocks of red flowers, blocks of yellow flowers and that kind of thing.

John was more than a little perplexed. 'Can't you see that I do? I've spent a lot of time and money on this garden!'

'But not lo ...'

I knew she was going to say 'love them' but changed her mind and asked Mister John, 'Why don't you let them do what they want?'

'Why in heaven's name should a flower want to do anything? It hasn't the ability to *want* anything!'

Anna could contain her displeasure longer than most, but in the end she broke out with that scornful word: 'Pooh!' She turned away from the flowers and headed for what, according to John, was the untidiest part of the garden, the part that was going to be tidied up next spring and turned into a real garden. John and I followed after her.

'Don't you like my garden, my little maid?'

She shook her head vigorously. She had no need to think of her answer. That had been ready for a long time. 'Mister John, it looks like a war,' was her unflattering comment.

Poor John was completely taken aback. 'War?'

She nodded. 'All them flowers look like soldiers on parade,' she said and marched like a toy soldier around the border. John managed to restrain himself except for a little 'Oh!'

As we went in for tea, I hoped Arabella wasn't going to ask if she liked the house. I knew that there were a few more 'Nope's' lurking around somewhere. But she did ask. It wasn't a 'No' this time. She looked around the room and said, 'It looks like that enchanted castle. You know, Fynn, like the one in the book you gived me.'

I didn't remember the castle and I didn't like the way she dragged me into the discussion. It was a sure sign that something was going to happen. I got that itchy feeling again, but Arabella and John didn't understand the sign and they glowed to hear that they lived in an enchanted castle. They weren't quite ready for, 'You know, Fynn, that one where the people went to sleep for a hundred years.'

I wished that I was asleep too! She'd started it, so she could finish it, but no, she had got me into it and all I could do was to sit it out and hope that their looks would soon soften!

I never have been able to work out why it is that you spend years teaching children to be honest and truthful and then along come those times when you hope that they have forgotten that teaching! It happened to me often. I'd hope that she wasn't going to be too honest or too truthful, but she always was. *She* didn't mind one bit, but it often left me floundering. I suppose it's just one of those things you have to put up with. The order in John's garden and house was similar to the order in his mind. There was nothing random in all of this except for the name. For Arabella and John spring-cleaning lasted all year and every year. I must say I did enjoy the sharp edges of John's mind, especially when he launched into some complicated explanation, like the beauty of some involved geometric diagram or the shape of a

mathematical formula. This was always a pleasure to me, but it wasn't always so for Anna. The 'Skeletons' as she called these diagrams and formulae were all very well, but she was after the meat. She wanted to put clothes on the 'Skeletons' and that was what she was about.

We had listened to him for most of the afternoon on one of our visits. I wasn't doing all that well with his explanations. The idea that sooner or later the whole thing, atoms, stars and even Anna was going to be described by a few physical laws in a mathematical form, was a struggle for me. I had looked at Anna frequently, but she showed no sign of distress. I thought that by now we should have had an explosion or two, but they never came.

'Mister John,' she asked, 'will you know everything about Fynn and me too?'

'Oh,' he said, with some surprise, 'I'd forgotten you were there.'

This news was strange to her and it took her a couple of fizzy drinks and the odd cake or two before she managed to stow away the important bits of John's talk. She was always the master of the 'poor little me act'. It always left me feeling helpless, but I knew it was a danger sign.

'Mister John,' she said, 'I'm such a little bit of it all, ain't I?'

'Yes, my dear, as I am, and Fynn.'

'Here it comes,' I said to myself, 'I hope you're ready, John.'

'Mister John,' she said all too sweetly.

'Yes, my dear, what is it?'

'Why does such a little bit like me want to understand it all? It's such a big bit, ain't it?'

John tried to find the right words to answer her, but they just wouldn't come out. Anna wasn't at all frightened of bloody Skeletons and she certainly wasn't going to give up.

'What about them flowers then, they're littler than me? What about if the flowers want to understand too, what about it? That's why they want to play and you won't let them.'

It was more than a question, more like an accusation, and poor John didn't know what to do with it. It was quite clear to me the way he shook his head that John did not like that question at all. For him it wasn't a real question. It sounded all right to me and I wanted to know the answer. If it was all going to end up in a handful of laws, then it would be nice to know why a little bit of the universe should want to know and understand the rest of it. Perhaps I had simply missed a step or two on the way. It seemed to me that John had discarded Mister God so completely that I never did grasp the difference between a universe that understood itself and the Mister God that Anna talked about. It seemed to me, at times, that they were like a couple of bridge builders, trying to build a bridge across a chasm, and they had left me stuck in the middle, just hanging on with nowhere to put my feet

down. It was strange to be sandwiched between this pair, old John so full of knowledge and logic but so short of imagination, and that little red-headed imp, full of invention and imagination, but a little short on fact. But I really did want to know why the little bit wants to understand the big bit. Why should a daisy want to understand a star? So far as I could figure it out, the only thing that wanted to understand was the bit in the middle somewhere, the soul or the mind. There never was such an ill-matched pair as these two, but in some curious way they were able to spark each other off. Not that I'm complaining too much, mind you, but all this stuff was at times too much for me. I wasn't doing too badly with John's set of rules and his way of going about things, and I think I could just about manage Anna's set of rules, the red hot way, but it did mean that I was in danger of either being frozen to death by John or burnt alive by Anna!

*　*　*

There were many times when I reckoned that Anna must have had a little knob tucked away somewhere – one that I never found. If she had such a knob, I knew that the instruction would be 'Simmer gently until done and bring to a fast rolling boil'. But, as I didn't know where she kept it and neither did anybody else, there was always a danger of setting it at the wrong position, as I knew to my cost. For the last week or so it had been set to the simmer position. There was something on her mind. We were going off to have tea with John that afternoon, and, as we had plenty of time to spare, I took a more leisurely route on the tandem, just looking at things. John greeted us at the door. 'Ah! The little brat herself and young Fynn.'

'Sir,' she said.

I had finished that kind of thing some time ago. So, 'Hello John'.

On the table beside his chair was an open atlas. 'Bringing back old memories,' he said. 'I spent some time there.' He prodded his finger in the general direction of France.

'Where's "there", Mister John?'

He turned a few pages and prodded again.

'Can't see your house Mister John, can we?'

'Not on this map. I'll show you on another map.' He fetched a large scale ordinance map. 'There we are, just there. Just where that road is.'

Though she had got her own atlas, she had never seen one on a different scale before, and for the next hour or so John was kept busy with telling her about maps; that one of a scale of this many inches to the mile was either better, or maybe worse, than one of that many miles to the inch.

'Look, Fynn, look at this. Did you know that?'

'Yes,' I replied.

'You didn't tell me, did you?'

'You didn't ask.'

It was at about this point that the knob was turned to the 'fast rolling boil' stage.

'Mister John,' she so exploded it was almost possible to see the steam coming out of her ears, 'Mister John, if you could make a map squillions of miles to the inch and then one squillions of inches to the mile, you could see them things, couldn't you?'

'What things are they, my little one?'

'Them electron things wot Fynn reads about. Then you would know if you could divide them, couldn't you?'

John looked at me. All I could do was to shrug my shoulders. She hadn't quite finished yet. 'You could put it in yer ear, couldn't you?'

I never did find out why very small things always had to get put in your ear. Never mind. I suppose if you really could draw a map of the whole universe on that kind of scale you might easily put it in your ear.

John really should have left it there and got on with his beer. At this rate he might never finish it, but no, he just would go on telling her all about number scales, like in ordinary counting, where successive places were units, tens, hundreds, thousands, tens of thousands and so on, and the other ways where the successive places were units, threes, nines, twenty-seven and so on and so forth, to say nothing of all the other ways of doing it. It was the idea of reduction and enlargement that captured Anna's imagination, despite John's insistence that it was not possible to do that kind of thing because there are physical limits to what the mind can grasp. All he got was, 'In your head you can, can't you?'

There was really no answer to that one. I was pleased that it had been his turn and not mine to be the target of her ideas. I thought it was going to stay that way, but that was too much to hope for.

'Fynn,' she exclaimed, 'you can do sums with the angels, can't you?'

'I suppose you must be able to,' I agreed, 'but I don't know how.'

'You can find out, then, can't you? and then you can tell me, can't you?'

*   *   *

The problem with memories is not that they aren't true. It's just that there's so much of them to write down. All those things that have happened to me over the last umpteen years would take about ten or so times longer to write down than they took to happen. But then you don't have to put down the unpleasant bits, merely the nice bits; those little gems or words that were said all those years ago that meant so much to me then. I just don't know if they are as true as they seemed to me to be at the time. Old John's often-quoted saying that 'True mathematics is a lost art of civilization' or that 'Mathematics is nothing more than unconscious art'. Or Mum's remark that 'The brain is the organ of learning and the mind is the garden of knowledge'. These kinds of sayings still look fresh to me, even though my own garden of knowledge is always in danger of being taken over by the usual crop of weeds, and I find it takes me a long time to get rid of them. But I've never found a better way of saying things so I guess I'll stick with them.

And then there was that lovely but strange thing that Anna had said, and that I never quite understood. After a couple of years of pretty concentrated mathematical studies, she suddenly floored me one night with her usual mixture of maths and religion.

'Fynn,' she began, 'it's a funny thing, ain't it?'

'Must be,' I replied, 'but what is?'

'Religion.' She had thumped me on my head.

'How funny?' I asked.

A few more thumps. 'It reduces you in size and increases you in dimensions.'

'Hey, Tich, where did you get that from?'

'Saw it in one of your books.'

I was amazed that she had cottoned onto that, for it is the kind of thing that even if you don't understand you don't want to forget or throw away. It sounds so good that it might even be true; that is, if I can ever figure out what it truly means. Maybe one day I will, but in the meantime I'll keep it safe! There are so many words inside me. Things that either Mum or Anna or John have said. Things that really sound so good that I don't like to get rid of them, even though I don't understand them. But I will one day.

My life was now full of puzzles and riddles, like the occasion when John was trying to tell me the difference between applied and pure mathematics.

'Just remember, young Fynn,' he said, 'applied mathematics is when you search for the solution to the problem, but pure mathematics, ah! that is when you search for the problem of the solution.'

It was odd that he could so often say that kind of thing, but found it so difficult to understand Mum when she had told him that Anna wasn't looking for a needle in a haystack, but rather looking for the haystack in the needle. Even if she did change the word 'haystack' to 'God', I think I did understand. And, of course, Millie could also come out with the odd 'doughnut saying' that could so easily stand me on my head. But then I had known Millie for about ten years. She had a heart of gold and a wit to match. We have been talking about love. In view of the way that Millie made her money as a prostitute that might seem a bit odd to some people. I said that I found it very difficult to understand just what love was.

'You had better ask Anna,' she had said. 'I think it's got something to do with seeing in others the mystery of yourself.'

* * *

It was very early in 1935. At sixteen, I was among the oldest of John's students. In those days, most boys left school at fourteen years of age. For many it was a time to rejoice, to get away from school at long last. For others it was a matter of necessity to earn some money to help out the family. For them the lack of money was a perpetual worry. I was one of the lucky ones, with a small bursary and various odd jobs. Mum had persuaded me to stay on. She had a job, too. Although we had no money to waste we were a lot better off than most people. I was happy to continue my education, as by now John had asked me to demonstrate experiments in chemistry and physics against the background of his lectures. On this day he hadn't told me to prepare anything. He lurched in in his usual way.

'Today,' he said, 'I have good news for you. In a few months' time I retire.'

There was the odd subdued cheer from some boys, but for most of us it didn't seem possible.

'As from that happy date, Mr Clement will shoulder the impossible task of knocking sense into your heads, not that it will do any good. Some of you blockheads are so thick that I very much doubt if anything could penetrate those dark recesses of your minds.'

He was in his sarcastic mood again and he flowed on for ten minutes or so. 'Ah well,' he ended, 'it will no longer be my responsibility. In the meantime, we have much to do and do it you will.'

My world had suddenly shifted its orbit. I wasn't at all happy about this unexpected news, but at the moment I didn't know how John's retirement was going to affect me. It didn't seem possible that I wasn't going to see him every day. As my father had died so early on in my life it was John that I had taken my puzzles and problems to, and without him ... I guess I loved that old grouch, but I wasn't going to tell him.

We were to assemble in the big hall to bid him farewell and to see the usual presentation. I couldn't face that. It was too much. I didn't turn up. I wasn't going to cry, not in front of everybody. If I wanted to bloody well cry I'd do it alone. I had a very special place I went to on important occasions – one of the little bridges over the canal. Nobody used it very often. It was tucked away down a back street, with a nice view over the park. I had sat straddled across the parapet for hours doing nothing much. I couldn't think what came next. I knew that somebody had called my name but hell, so what?

'Fynn, Fynn, where the devil are you? Don't be a bloody fool. Speak up, Boy! Speak up! I haven't got all day to waste for an answer!'

The same old impatient Master walked over the bridge and stood beside me. 'What, no goodbyes, young Fynn? Aren't I worth a goodbye?'

'Bugger off!' I spat at him. 'Just bugger off.' I didn't mean to say that and I regretted my words immediately. I wanted to say something else but I couldn't. 'Who told you I was here? Why can't you leave me alone?'

'I asked your mother. She told me. It's a nice place to come to when you want to think, isn't it? As for your words, I do understand. I really do. Even at my ripe old age. I understand. My car is only just down the road. Let's go for a little jaunt, shall we, and we can have a long talk.'

Seated in the car he had taken my hand in his. He had never done that before. The only times he touched me had been with that three-foot length of bunsen burner tubing when he punished me, which was often.

'What's bothering you, Fynn? What's on your mind?'

With my hand in his I still couldn't say the words I wanted to. All I managed to say were the words of a child, a lost child.

'I won't see you again, will I?'

'Oh that,' he said, 'don't worry about that. I don't intend that to happen.' We drove slowly through the park and headed off across the marshes.

'What's your plan?'

'Suppose I'll have to get a job.'

'Don't be too hasty. There's plenty of time. Finish off your education and then wait until after the term ends. Mister Clement won't bully you like I have done and he really does know his subject. And as for not seeing me – you know where I live, you know my telephone number and it's hardly any distance at all to Random Cottage, and you can come and see me at any time at all. In fact, not only may you come, I ask you to come. You can still pursue your studies with me. You have the promise of good things and well … just come whenever you like. Is that what you want?'

That was what I wanted. It felt like old times again.

'I've packed my persuader,' he chuckled. 'I couldn't be without that.'

So it was that, although I didn't see John so often, I did see him for more hours in the week than I had previously done.

It was quite true what John had said. Mr Clement really was a nice person and certainly he knew his subject. I suppose it was because the persuader was no longer there that it happened that after a number of elaborate practical jokes and one thing and another, I was politely asked to leave the school. Had Old John still been there with his trusty persuader, I would have had to do my studies standing up. But it wasn't like that any longer. Things had changed a bit. With John, punishment was over and done with quickly, but being reported was quite another matter. We all missed the persuader and it really didn't hurt all that much. John had never said 'this hurts me more than it hurts you'. He knew better, and so far as he was concerned it was supposed to hurt and he was no weakling, especially not with the old persuader in his hand. I had complained on one occasion when it caught me in the wrong place and he didn't apologize. Not him.

'Last week,' he said, 'after that rugger match, you were not a very pretty sight with a missing front tooth, a beautiful black eye and a nose bleed. And you enjoyed yourself! I'm merely trying to give you more pleasure – something more you can brag about.'

Suddenly I was out to work, meeting other people and making other friends. And then there was Anna as well.

* * *

After a very few meetings with Anna, John was convinced of one thing, as he told me one evening when I had gone over to see him.

'This untutored and uncontrolled talent of Anna's really must be helped to develop in an orderly fashion.'

'Sure,' I replied. 'How do you go about doing that?'

'She needs proper teaching,' he said. 'I know you've done your best to help her, young Fynn, but you will surely agree that you haven't been trained to teach her, have you?'

I had to admit that the only training that I had had was as one of his pupils.

'I know that I taught you, but that was how to learn, not how to teach.'

I wanted to give John a good answer to that, but the words would not come. So far as I could make out, Anna and I managed to teach each other. We were both Students *and* Teachers, and the most important thing for me was to be the Student and her the Teacher. I didn't tell him that. It wasn't the kind of thing to say to a man with all that experience and knowledge, so I didn't bother to say anything.

'Although I am now retired, I am very willing to help her with her studies.'

'You'll have to talk to Mum first and see what she says,' I told him. 'And you'll have to talk to Anna, too.'

'No, Fynn, I will certainly talk to your mother, but you will have to persuade the child.'

I agreed to talk to Anna, but I wasn't going to press her into it. To tell the truth, I wasn't at all keen on this idea of John's but I would never stand in her way, if that was what she really wanted. I just wanted to do whatever was best for Anna.

It took us a few days to sort it all out. Mum finally agreed that it was worth a try for a little while, to see how it went. It was more difficult to talk to Anna about it. Her first response was 'No'.

'Don't you want to learn?' I asked her.

'Course I do.'

'Then why the "No"?'

The way she explained it all to me made it sound simple, and I reckon Mister God saw the sense in it too, but I had a feeling that John wouldn't. His insistence that everything had to be neat and tidy was matched by Anna's insistence that it shouldn't. They were poles apart.

Unlike John, I had given up any attempt to understand the way Anna's mind worked some time ago. I was content just to let things happen, and rescue her, if I could, from whatever muddle she might get herself into. When I couldn't, Mum was the one who understood her most. She knew that she might be hurt at times, but that's the way it had to be. 'There was really no safe way to grow up' as Mum put it in her upside down way. 'There might be a safer way than this to grow older, but there just ain't no safe way to grow up.' Both Mum and Anna did this kind of thing to me. They would so often answer my simple question, or puzzle, by a harder one and I complained. 'I'm surprised you haven't worked that one out yet,' she would say. She never did have much schooling, but she had packed a lot of experience into her life. How often she had laid her finger on my lips and said, 'No questions, wait. That is too difficult to do when you are young. That's what happens when you grow up. That's what life is for.' Poor Mum, she didn't understand, did she?

She very rarely got angry but she did one day in her own quiet way. 'You and your precious Master! The pair of you make me sick!! You *see* everything and *understand* nothing important!!!'

'Come on, Mum; easy. What does Anna do that I don't?'

She had softened my pain by cupping my face in her hands. She had smiled when she said, 'You never notice what you see most often. Neither does Mister John. Anna does.' She waited for a moment or two before she went on 'That's what's called "discovery".'

Having delivered herself of this little gem, she took a sheet of paper and wrote two words 'Look' and 'See'.

'There,' she said, 'the word "look" had got two eyes open and the word "see" has got two eyes half shut.'

I thought I could see what she was on about, but this wasn't the way that John had taught me. 'That's not scientific, Mum, that's just fancy.'

'They didn't teach you much, did they? Science is all right, but it's not everything.'

I wasn't going to argue with her, but I didn't agree with her.

'What is science,' she said, 'but the discovery of the rules behind the facts? It never occurs to your precious Mister John that there is something else.'

'What else can there be?' I asked.

'There's always the facts behind the rules and that's religion, that is.'

I nearly said they were just different sides of the same coin, but decided against it. I was almost certain to get myself into an even greater muddle. This was the problem when talking to experts in 'doughnut speech'.

*　*　*

When I got home it was all over. Arthur had arrived safe and sound, Nurse Turner was satisfied and most of the people who had waited around outside Mrs Jones's front door had left. The only person in the street who had only a vague idea of all the excitement and drama was me, and I was soon to learn.

'Fynn, have you ever seen a baby come out?'

'Out? Out of what?'

'Fynn, don't be silly. You know, born.'

'No, babies I never have. Kittens I have. Puppies I have. But babies never. Why?'

'Do you know what they do?'

'No, what?'

'They turn it upside down and smack its bum. That's what they do.'

'What would they want to do a thing like that for?' I asked.

'Don't know. The nurse didn't tell me. I wonder why they turn it upside down?'

This turning of a thing upside down was something Anna understood very well. It made you see things properly, so perhaps turning a baby upside down wasn't a bad way for it to start off its life. But smacking its bum she wasn't sure of. It was all real doughnut stuff. I wondered if John was ready for this kind of stuff. He surely must know about it. What would he do when it happened to him? I reckoned it was going to. John did seem to be very confident that teaching Anna was going to be a fairly straightforward thing to do. He was in for a surprise, I guess.

The first week went quite well. There were, of course, the odd hold ups but nothing much except the full blast of her puzzles on our way home.

*　*　*

On those journeys I always took the safe route because the way Anna wriggled about on my handlebars made the canal route tricky.

'Fynn, Mister John took my picture today and, Fynn, I really and truly was upside down. Everything is.'

John's large plate camera definitely showed things to be upside down. Either that, or she was. And, at that time, she didn't know which. What with being upside down sometimes and back to front in a looking glass, it was going to take quite a bit of working out and if John wasn't very careful, he was going to find himself turned inside out too!

'Know why it's upside down and inside out, Fynn? You know why?'

'Tell me when we get home, not now, or you'll have us both base over apex in the middle of the road.'

Little things like that were of lesser importance to her than telling me why everything, everything was upside down. ''Cos,' she yelled, 'Mister God ain't finished us yet.'

'If you don't sit still,' I told her, 'he's never going to get a chance.'

'Fynn, when we get finished properly, then we will all be the right way up.' I was glad to know that. It was a real comfort to me!

Over our supper we were treated to her nonstop chatter on the finer points of dividing one fraction by another. All you had to do was to turn one of them upside down, or was it both of them? She couldn't quite remember and perhaps it didn't matter. It came as no surprise to her, this business of turning things upside down in order to understand them. She was an expert in that kind of thing, and so was Mum with her 'doughnut speech'. I was a little envious of John in his teaching of Anna, but I was comforted by her saying, 'He ain't half as good as you, Fynn, he gets a bit muddled'. I wasn't going to tell him that. He'd never believe me. If she wanted to tell him that he got a bit muddled she would have to do it herself.

The first week of his teaching had gone off fairly well, except, that is, the small matter of living upside down. He had had no experience of that. The second week didn't go at all well. In fact, it was a near-disaster for me. Anna had been showing him some of the interesting things I had shown her months ago. Things with numbers and a chess board. I had used her own words to explain to her, not the kind of words you would find in a text book. For John, the right word was very important, so when she called it 'the thingy that Fynn showed me', he almost exploded. I know I should have called it the binomial theorem, but I didn't. It didn't seem important to me then, but it did mean that I got the rough end of his tongue.

'Why in heaven's name did you teach her that, young Fynn? She's nowhere ready for that ...'

'I didn't,' I said, 'it just happened. What's the trouble, John, did she get it wrong?'

'No,' he replied, 'as a matter of fact she explained most of it quite beautifully in her own words, but you really must help her to use the correct words otherwise she will never be understood.'

I didn't bother to tell John about the time I had spent explaining to Anna how to use the word terminology: giving names to things and ideas in various subjects. It didn't take her a moment to jump from numbers to Mister God. All those various names he got called, like Allah, the Absolute, Jehovah weren't really all that important, were they? *She'*d stick to Mister God and words like 'thingy'. Most of her friends had at least three names, some even had four, so it didn't matter what name they were called, they would know that you were talking to them. If it didn't matter to her if she was called Anna or Tich or even 'the brat', it certainly wasn't going to matter to Mister God one little bit, was it? It was a lot of fuss about nothing. John was a little put out to be told that he only changed the names, whilst Fynn changed the numbers. She had tried to explain to him that every square on the chess board had its own name, which could be changed, and that depended on what you did. All that the numbers did was to tell you in how many different ways you could get there. It didn't really matter what you called it as long as you got there, did it?

Neither did he like it when I said that all I could give her was a sort of life-raft, even though it did have plenty of holes in it.

'What other bit of nonsense have you managed to teach her? What must I beware of?'

I did tell him that the thing she really wanted to know was how to do sums with the angels and perhaps even Mister God too, and since nobody knew just how many fingers an angel might count on she did understand how the various number bases worked, powers and indices and such like.

'Oh, does she indeed! I will have to see about that. No doubt she is very muddled about that. I really do wish that you had left that to me.'

He was soon to find out that doing sums was one thing which wasn't too difficult once you had got the knack. It was her questions afterwards that caused all the trouble. I tried to tell him about those fifty bald-headed men she had asked me about. There was this church and every Sunday fifty bald-headed men came in, each man had a number painted on his head, the numbers from 1 to 50. Up in the dome of the church was an angel with a camera, and every Sunday he took a picture of the numbers painted on their heads, and every Sunday they had to sit in a different order, which was all very well except that she wanted to know, if the vicar was thirty years old, how old would he be when these bald-headed men finally repeated the first pattern. I did work it out for her. As far as I could figure it out, this vicar

must have been 5.848864^{62}. So I reckoned that by the time the pattern was repeated he would be far too old to be much concerned with it!! He was going to be a very old man, older than Methuselah, older than good old Tyrannosaurus Rex. Why, if you added the ages of every living person, he'd be a lot older than that! Perhaps he might even be older than ... No! That's not possible. I knew her answer to that kind of answer.

'Ooh, Fynn, ain't sums wonderful!'

'Yeah, ain't they.'

Particularly if somebody else did all the hard work for her. It was good for me when she began to take over the hard work for herself.

From the Rev. Castle's point of view, numbers were totally unimportant and, as for John, since he didn't believe there was a God anyway, going to church was, for him, a complete waste of time. As for the bald-headed men and her other problems, it was simply a matter of combinations and permutations, which was all right for some, but they weren't Anna's words. It all left me struggling in the middle somewhere. What neither of them seemed to understand was something very simple. At least, it was simple the way she put it.

It was a different matter when she asked me to work it out in numbers. That took a long time. She knew quite well that if you did things with little numbers they had the habit of suddenly becoming very, very big numbers, and very, very big numbers were obviously Mister God numbers. For her they both seemed to be the same thing.

The six days of creation looked a bit different after she had finished with them. Not that anybody else was impressed by her ideas. You needed to be with her whilst she explained them to really understand what she was on about. I didn't know that Mister God only made three things on that first day. Although she had no idea what they were and even if there were more than three, it didn't really matter.

'Then he went to sleep,' she told me, 'and dreamed how he could arrange these three things in different ways. So the next day, when he arranged these three things, he ended up with six things and after that, of course, he had another little sleep and dreamed of all the ways he could arrange six things in their different orders.'

And she wasn't at all surprised to find that the answer was 720. She gave up there on the answer to her question: 'How many ways can you arrange 720 things – in every possible way?' This was a bit too much for her and it was for me too! What Mister God was going to do on the fifth and sixth days was something only he could do. The number was going to be so big that nobody could ever possibly work it out. It was no wonder he was tired with all them numbers and had a rest on the seventh day!

Though, for Anna, Mister God and very big numbers were the same thing, neither frightened her. They were both lovely and both very beautiful, so they had to be the same, didn't they? Whenever Anna really got into top gear, there was nothing to do but listen until she had finished or dried up. When she was in full flood the only place for her to be was sitting on my lap.

It was a bit of a surprise to John to find her suddenly on his lap. I know that he was pleased with that, but as a Teacher it wasn't the kind of thing that had happened to him before. A couple of hours of this was quite enough for anybody and John was no longer young.

'You'd better take her home now, Fynn, and bring her back tomorrow. I need time to recover. Although for much of the time I didn't know what she was talking about, I must confess I did like listening to her. It is, I suppose, just possible that her chatter makes sense and I wanted to hear more of it, but not now. So take her home and bring her back tomorrow.'

* * *

Mister John, as Anna called him, was playing an increasing role in the life of us all, so that the day when we took Mum along with us to see him could no longer be put off. So there we all were one afternoon, drinking tea in his sitting room, Anna between Mum and me on the sofa, and John on the other side of the room in his favourite armchair. It was an extraordinary gathering, with three people who were not afraid to say what they thought and who might, at any moment, say it. Of course there was me too, but since I was always being taught by one or other of them, I didn't really count. I was along to see fair play. Although I was fairly certain that this little get-together wasn't going to end up as a free-for-all or a battle royal, I was sure that somebody or other was going to make a mistake sooner or later. Mum was firmly convinced that most people just went on talking when there was nothing else to be said. She did manage to ask John if all this extra teaching was absolutely necessary.

'You wouldn't want her to grow up like a savage in the jungle, would you?'

Anna nodded her head and held my hand.

'I'm not sure of that,' replied Mum, 'not sure at all.'

'Oh, come, come, whatever makes you say that?'

'Well, I've never had your education, but it does seem to me that these so-called savages don't do so bad after all.'

'In what way is that?'

'They, at least, do manage to live with their devils and demons and survive, but we live with our successes and fail so often.'

What the answer to that one was, I never did know. Neither did John. His next shot also went a bit astray: 'Every day she is getting older and every day lost is a day lost for ever.' That was a very bad mistake for him to make. Nobody else in the room believed that one. That was pushing education far too hard.

'Lost days indeed,' Mum said, 'surely there is nothing worth having in this world that is not worth waiting for.'

Mum's calm and slow manner put John off completely. She just never seemed to be where he expected her to be.

For the next thirty minutes John and Mum tried to work out some scheme to further Anna's education.

'So,' said John finally, 'what are we going to do with this extraordinary little Miss?'

The 'extraordinary little Miss' giggled and pinched me.

'Why not ask her?' I suggested.

'Not yet,' he said. 'Are you an extraordinary little Miss?' he asked her.

'Am I, Fynn?'

'Don't know about that!' I laughed. 'You're a perishing nuisance sometimes and if *that* is extraordinary, then I guess you are!'

John frowned at my remark and showed his disapproval.

Eventually it was decided that I was to bring Anna to his house and whilst he was helping her with her various lessons, I was to help in his large garden, doing odd jobs about the place. So, instead of bagging up sawdust and that kind of job that occupied my spare time, he was to pay me more than my odd jobs did. That was fine with me.

John wasn't the only one to express strong views on how Anna should be taught. Any more of it and I would begin to think I had let her down. It seemed everybody who came in touch with her seemed to know exactly how it should be done. After a few months of this arrangement, John said to me over a glass of beer, 'You know, Fynn, there is only one way to teach Anna properly, at least to teach her in the normal way.'

'And what's that, John?' I asked.

'I'm afraid that you'll just have to find the largest possible box there is and keep her away from other people. It's something that nobody in his right mind would do, but I can see no other way. The habit of asking every Tom, Dick and Harry to write things down for her means that her little head is open to every opinion under the sun and every crackpot idea imaginable. She really need only have one good teacher and not these hundreds of poor ones. If only I was twenty years younger, I'd like to take her on regularly, not just for an occasional lesson.'

'John,' I reminded him, 'in case you have forgotten, you did teach me for nearly five years.'

'True, very true,' he sighed.

'So I can't be all that bad.'

'No,' he agreed, 'as long as you stick to one thing at a time you are not too bad.'

'John, do you remember the nickname you had?'

'Which one was that? I've had so many in my time.'

'The Black Knight,' I replied.

'Oh, that one,' he said. 'I could never understand why.'

'Oh come on, John. Surely you know why.'

'No, I don't.'

'The way that you would jump from one subject to another could be so very troublesome.'

'Oh that! But I did know what I was doing!'

'That's exactly what Anna does too and, as far as I can see, she knows what she's doing too. So maybe I've got a White Knight to teach me now?'

'Perhaps you're right, perhaps you're right, and I suppose,' he continued in his sarcastic way, his refuge whenever he was lost for words, 'I suppose you consider yourself to be the King.'

'Not me,' I grinned, 'not me. I'm just a pawn. My problem is just that I have to change colour so often.'

'Your usual clever stuff, young Fynn!'

'Got it from a clever teacher.'

'The thing I find so very puzzling about her,' he continued, 'is the fact that she will not loosen her grasp on anything, even rubbish, until she understands it, to her own satisfaction that is. If there is anything in this world that might make one say I believe in the human soul, it's the sheer persistence of the child that baffles me. I really don't think she would bat an eyelid if faced by the devil itself. Now look what you've done to me! I am becoming maudlin and sentimental and it won't do, Fynn, it just won't do. Do you know what she asked me last week? She asked me what I would pray for if there was a God and, heaven help me, I told her. You'll laugh at me, Fynn. I told her that in that case I would pray that my butterfly and moth collection could be brought back to life. It's the one thing I feel guilty about. There, you see, between the pair of you I'm getting a bit soft in the head, and I don't like it.'

*   *   *

Then came the day she ran into the garden calling my name. I did manage to catch her in my arms before she fell into a flower bed.

'Fynn, Fynn. Come quick. Mister John fell over and he can't get up.'

He didn't look all that bad when we entered the sitting room, a little pale perhaps, nothing that a tankard of ale wouldn't put right. But the Doctor, when he came, had other ideas. He was old, he was tired, he mustn't get excited and suddenly Anna's extra teaching came to an end.

'Will you please continue to tend the garden and do little jobs for me?' he asked.

'Of course I will.'

'Please bring the little maid with you whenever you come and a few friends too, if that is what she wants. They can play in the garden and Anna can talk to me and we can all have tea together later.'

Although Anna seemed to have a fairly firm grip on many ideas, she wasn't all that good when it came to adding up numbers. It isn't my strongest point either, for that matter. Perhaps it was my love of mathematics that made her feel that it was this subject that was very important to understand. The problem was that at school, it was just one tedious round of doing sums like adding, taking away and multiplying. Things like that. So far as she could see, all that kind of stuff didn't matter a hoot.

What she really wanted to do was to know how she could talk to angels, Mister God and, who knows, perhaps even people who lived out there in the stars. The difficulty was she just didn't know how this could be done.

'Fynn,' she said, 'how can you do sums with angels?'

I was slightly taken off balance by this question. I didn't quite see why angels would want to do sums. Anyway, I reckoned they didn't have time for that sort of thing. So I answered her with, 'Why would they want to do sums anyway?'

'Don't know,' she replied, 'but they might.'

'Suppose so,' I managed to say, 'but I honestly don't see why.'

She thought for a long moment and finally said, 'If they want to know how many angels there are, how they going to do it, Fynn, how?'

'Don't know, sweetie. I just have no idea. I'm sure they manage to figure it out some way.'

She wasn't very impressed with that answer, so she tried it a different way.

'Well, then,' she said, 'how do they know how many people they have to look after? How do they count, Fynn? How, eh?'

'Suppose they do it the same way you do. I reckon they count on their fingers.'

'Pooh!' was her reply. 'Angels don't have no fingers.'

We were getting nowhere very fast with this kind of a conversation, so it was about time it stopped.

'Well,' I ended up hopefully, 'I guess they just have to count on their feathers.' I realized as soon as I said it that it was a daft thing to say and I wished that I hadn't said it. She gave me one of her sad, pathetic looks and hurled another question at me.

'How many feathers they got then?'

'No idea,' I replied, 'I guess it must run into thousands.'

'Must be funny kinds of sums then.'

'I reckon it must be,' I replied.

Perhaps she realized that I was teasing her for, as usual, she ended up trapping me into doing something that I had no idea how to go about.

'Fynn, can you work out how angels do sums and Mister God too and those things out there.'

'Oi! Hold your horses! What things out there? Maybe there ain't things out there.'

That was a complete waste of time.

'But if there are, how do they count, Fynn? How do everything count? Can't you work it out, Fynn, and then you can tell me.' It looked as though she was giving me a permanent task.

I didn't give very much thought to the angels and their sums. If they really wanted to do sums, they could work it out for themselves. Except for Anna's constant reminder, I would have forgotten it altogether. Anyhow, up to meeting her, I had never met an angel, at least not to my knowledge, and as for Martians and other such creatures, I was completely certain I had never met any. But I did manage to work something out for her. Something that pleased her. Something that excited her. It was so obvious when I had finished it, but with no calculator or computer around then, it was a very dreary and tiresome business with all that long division.

Suppose that there is some angel or something out there with seven fingers to count on, all you do is to divide whatever number of fingers it had got, or whatever it counted on, by itself, like if it has seven fingers, divide seven by seven and of course, that's one. Then you have to divide 1 by the number of fingers. 1 divided by 7 is 0.142857142 and that is the magic number for seven fingers: 0.142857142. After that it's simple, even though it does take a long time. All you need to do is to divide that magic number by itself, which is of course 1, then you divide 1 by the magic number and that gives the answer 7. Then divide the 7 by the magic number, which takes you to 49. Then divide the number 49 by the magic number and that's 343 and then just keep on going x ... x^2 ... x^3 ... x^∞. Every number has its own 'magic number'. Just another case of turning things upside down. Good old God, he's done it again! For Anna, God was just fun – sheer enjoyment.

* * *

Anna's excursion into the Bible concordance and dictionaries wasn't always a great success. The words she most wanted just weren't there. She had looked for the word 'fun' for a long time, but it was nowhere to be found. She found the word 'play' all right, but it didn't seem to mean what it ought to. You could play the harlot or the mad person, but where were games and just pure fun? She very soon came to the conclusion that people in the Bible didn't really have much time for children. They always seemed to be killed off for some reason.

'Don't people like kids, Fynn?' she had asked me one evening.

'Of course they do,' I replied. 'As far as I'm concerned there's only one thing wrong with them.'

'What, Fynn?' she asked.

'Too many darned questions!' I replied.

'Oh.' She looked at me. 'What's that, Fynn?'

'They never stop asking questions,' I grinned at her.

She spent a lot of time looking for what she called the very important words in the Bible; kids' words, that is, not grown-up ones. It did seem so very strange to her that when you consider just how nice Mister God was, there ought to be many more laughing words and happy words in the Bible. But she could never find just the ones she wanted. The Vicar wasn't much of a help, neither was Miss Haynes.

'You're far too young to understand,' she was told. 'Wait until you grow up.'

'Fynn,' she asked, 'do everybody have to grow up before they know Mister God?'

'Don't suppose it works like that,' I murmured.

'Then how does it work, Fynn? How then?'

'Well,' I replied hesitantly, 'I guess the Vicar meant *understand* Mister God, not *know* Mister God.'

'Oh.'

'Sometimes, Tich, I think it's a whole lot easier for kids to know Mister God than it is for grown ups.'

'Why, Fynn?' she persisted. 'Why?'

I didn't quite know the answer to that one, so I just had to make it up.

'Well,' I began, 'I reckon grown ups have often got so many problems of their own that they just haven't got time to ... er ... er ...'

'Play?' she suggested. 'Play with Mister God. Eh? Play?'

'Something like that,' I said.

'Um. Grown-up people make church so, well, serious that they never have time to play, do they, Fynn?'

'I guess you're just about right on that one, luv,' I replied.

'Too busy trying to earn enough money to pay the bills I guess.'

Anna didn't really go much on the idea that people had no time to play with Mister God. So far as she could understand the Bible and all the church services she had attended, it was often more frightening than joyful and she lost no opportunity in saying so.

'Fynn,' she said, 'is that why Mister John don't like Mister God?'

'Well,' I replied uncertainly, 'I don't think Mister John doesn't like Mister God. It's just, well ...' As usual I was getting into very hot water and I just didn't know how to get out of the mess I was getting into. With her usual persistence, she wasn't going to let me off the hook. These kind of questions so often left me stunned. I never quite knew which way to turn. I tried to wriggle out of them, but she never allowed me to. My problem was always how to try to explain things to her without destroying her own happiness in Mister God. I didn't realize for a long, long time that nothing that I, or for that matter, anybody else, could say could possibly destroy ... it wasn't love, it wasn't awe, it was simply happiness. She just saw God as a being of pure fun. She talked to Mister God in the same way that she talked to me or her dear friend Bombom. She saw Mister God not in the way most people did, but simply as her best friend; the kind of friend you could just chatter with and tell a funny story to. You could show him things. Well, you could simply have a good old giggle with him. She never could understand why it was you had to creep about on tiptoes or that sort of thing when you went into church. It just wasn't her. She could well understand that you would have to do that sort of thing with very important people like Kings and Queens, but surely not with Mister God! All she wanted to do with Mister God was to throw herself at him, to explode with joy. It was this spontaneous outburst that grown-up people didn't understand and simply couldn't do. She reckoned that grown ups had just forgotten how to play and it was, as she said, 'about time they bleeding well did, and Mister John bleeding well didn't'.

I did try to explain to Anna that it wasn't anything to do with not liking Mister God. It was ... it was that John just didn't believe that there was a God to like or not to like. He was totally convinced that, given a few more years, the scientists would be able to explain everything in the universe. Trying to explain this kind of thought was going to be a bit more than I could manage. But she accepted this like a duck takes to water.

It was some days later that she returned to this matter. I was just about to tuck into my favourite supper of sausages and mash when the fork I was lifting to my mouth was halted in mid-flight by her hand.

'Fynn,' she said, 'you know why, don't you?'

'I know why what?' I managed to say, sneaking a quick mouthful.

'Why Mister John don't believe Mister God is there.'

I nearly said, 'Where's there?' but I didn't. I took another quick mouthful instead. I managed to say, 'No idea, Tich. Why doesn't he believe that Mister God is there?'

She gave me one of her impish grins of delight.

"Cos he wants to know how it all started.'

'Oh, I see, that accounts for it! Don't you, then?'

She waggled her head. 'No,' she said. 'It don't matter, do it?'

I just had to ask the next question. 'What do you want to know then?'

'How it all ends and how me and you end!'

It was a great puzzle to her. The mistake people made thinking they looked like Mister God. You end up with a patchwork quilt of a God, maybe black or white, red or yellow, and possibly some other colour, she hadn't figured out. And then, of course, did it mean that Mister God was tall or short, fat or thin? This image stuff was far too dangerous to play about with. You never knew what you might end up with. If it meant anything at all, it must mean inside not outside, even that wasn't all that important. The really important thing was that he could do what we expected he could do and that was, for Anna, all there was to it.

Anna never did quite understand what all the fuss was about or why it was that some people just could not believe that God was around. So far as she was concerned, it was a stone-bonking certainty. She was sure that it was because of those words in the Bible, the bit where Mister God says, 'Let us make man in our own image'. That's where it all went wrong. She knew a lot about images. The circus had revealed her as a short, fat dwarf or a tall, thin giant in the distorted mirrors. Images could lead you into all sorts of trouble and, after all, Mister God never did say if he was making us in his outside image or his inside image and, since nobody had ever seen him, how do we know what he looks like? As far as she was concerned he could look like a pussy cat if he wanted to, or even a sausage roll, it was us that insisted that we looked like he did and that was what got us all mixed up. So none of that stuff was for her!

One evening we bumped into Old Woody and the night people.

'He! He! He!' he chortled. 'If it isn't the little darlin' herself! Sit yerself by me, my little one, and get yerself warm. Good evening little Miss er ... er ...'

'It's Anna,' she said.

'Anna, of course. Little Miss Anna. The little lady whose name is the same backwards or forwards. How could I forget that? Have you found all your answers yet?'

'No,' replied Anna, 'not yet. Some, but not very many!'

'You mustn't fret about that. None of us finds many answers. Some of us none at all.'

Anna stood before Old Woody and said, 'Mister, can I ask you a question?'

'Of course you may, my dear. Ask away.'

She warmed her hands before the fire and said, 'Mister, wot's religion? Is it about Mister God?'

'Now that is a very, very big question and I don't think anybody really knows the answer to that.'

'But is it really about Mister God?'

'Hark at that!' chortled convict Bill from downunder. 'That's got you stumped. Pass the bottle over!'

'Well,' said Old Woody thoughtfully, 'I don't really think it is all that much about God. It's about something different.'

'Wot?'

'It's about an appointment that none of us have made. It was made for us.'

'Oh? Where we got to go to?'

'That's another question I can't give an answer to. It might be here, it might be there, but I'm certain we will know when we get there.'

'And will we see Mister God when we get there?'

'That's what I think,' replied Woody. 'He was the one that made the appointment. An appointment in time or space. I know not where, neither do I care, but it's there.'

I liked the idea of an appointment that I had never made, and knew that I would stop being asked questions. Sure, she would collect a lot of rubbish, but I didn't want her to miss the gems. Nor did I! Fair gems are only found in the dust.

'Little Miss Anna, did you find your answer as to what poetry is?'

'Yes, Mister. Fynn's Mummy told me.'

'And what did she say? Will you tell me?'

'It's the least said the better. That's what Fynn's Mummy said.'

'I like the sound of that, I do indeed! "The least said the better." Fynn's Mummy does sound a very nice lady.'

'She is,' said Anna.

'But who is Fynn?'

'He,' she replied, holding my hand.

'He's a lucky man.'

I nodded happily. 'I know I am!'

* * *

Anna's schooling never did go along with that calm and easy rhythm that most teachers wanted, but her education had taken wings long before I had ever met her. As Miss Haynes once told me, 'She always gets good marks but she never seems to pay attention to what I am saying.'

I wanted to tell Miss Haynes that she probably paid too much attention to what she was saying. But that would never do. Anna had looked up the word 'school' in my dictionary long ago: 'A place for the education of the young and a place where horses were trained.' As she wasn't a horse and certainly didn't want to be instructed, she didn't want to go to school. She'd rather find out for herself. School was a bit of a bore. As far as Anna was concerned, brains was the kind of stuff you could buy in the butcher's shop or, if you were lucky, have on toast for tea. Many of the old ladies firmly believed that the more brains you could eat, the cleverer you would become. And when Miss Haynes persisted in telling her to use her brains, Anna was more than a little suspicious. So far as she was concerned, the heart was the important thing, not the brains. It was, for her, very simple. She could easily accept that brains could find out things, but the heart was something else altogether: 'That makes you understand things, don't it, Fynn?' The whole business of brains caused me no end of trouble.

'No, dear, you won't grow up to look like a sheep if you eat sheep's brains, nor a cow, nor a pig either.'

'Will I get cleverer if I eat them brains, Fynn?'

That was another thing I didn't know about, but Anna could make it all sound so simple. She had no difficulty in accepting that eyes, ears and noses and the other sense organs are what puts stuff *into* your brain, and she was equally certain that the *heart* was what you used to get it *out* again when you wanted to look at it. Poor Miss Haynes! Ideas about some things got 'Poohed' out of existence, and she lost about five points on that one, but then she was always losing points. Pity she didn't know it. Not that John did much better either. He was always losing points. It was comforting to know that I didn't lose as many points as either Miss Haynes or John. I lost some, but not as many as they did. What Miss Haynes and John simply did not understand was that it was all very well sticking stuff into the old brain box; the real problem was how to get it out again. You did so often

tend to lose the important stuff, things that you ought to be able to find, but where were they? As Mum so often told us, 'If you haven't stopped during the course of the day, you haven't done anything worthwhile'. As somebody or other has said:

> *What is this life if full of care*
> *We have no time to stand and stare?*

Mum was never against learning or education except, as she would say, 'Too much learning makes people lose heart' and, for her, losing heart was the greatest tragedy of all. Whatever else I might say about Mum and Anna, that's one thing they never did. They never lost heart. It was stopping and looking again that did the trick for them. A trick that I hadn't quite mastered.

* * *

I did enjoy the cool wind of John's approach to things, but I also enjoyed the warmer breeze of Anna's innocence. As far as I could see, the only way to go on was to accept both sides and get on with it. At least I wasn't the only person in the world to be fuddled with life! It wasn't the thought of all this extra learning that she was going to get that finally persuaded Anna. Rather, it was when John had said that on some days her friends Bombom and May could come with her in the long school holidays. After forty years of teaching, John had got the strange idea that children's minds were for filling up. He seemed to think that her habit of standing with her hands on her hips and head tilted to one side and red hair streaming, was a sign that she was ready for more facts to be poured in. I really did try to tell him that the real reason was so that the things that she didn't want to know could pour out! But he didn't believe me. He'd just have to find out for himself. Miss Haynes had tried long enough, goodness knows, and all she managed to get was a lot more grey hairs! My idea was to let Anna have a taste of everything in her own time. We had been to synagogues, churches and various kinds of chapels, and wherever we went there was always somebody who could tell you exactly what God was, what he was thinking and exactly what he wanted; and many of the books in the library weren't all that much help either.

People seemed to know everything there was to know about Mister God and then promptly forgot about it. It was all very strange. She really wanted to find out for herself. And I really should have told John that almost everything was either a 'thingy', a 'wotsit' or a 'doings', but that was another thing I forgot.

I made her one of those devices that spun on its axis and made a series of still pictures look as if they were in motion. The book called it Phanakistoscope, and as it was difficult to ask your friends if they would like to see your Phanakistoscope, it ended up being called a 'thingy'; and everybody knew exactly what a 'thingy' was except, of course, the Teachers.

I always seemed to be making something or other for her, and I did wonder how John was going to manage on her continuous cloudburst of questions and answers. It was all very well if you could live underwater! I reckon some of Anna's Teachers simply got washed away in a flood of 'Why?', 'Where?', 'What?' It wasn't always possible for her to put her ideas into words. I often had to make guesses about things until she told me I had got it right.

And that isn't the kind of thing most people have got time for. Things were altogether simple for Anna; understanding something was when you could play with it. 'Like Mister God,' she told me. He was always ready to play hide and seek, blind man's buff and all that kind of thing. He'd just creep up behind you and ask the question, 'Guess who?' The fact that at many times he could look like a tree, or a cat, or even a Phanakistoscope was really neither here nor there. You may not always know where Mister God was, but there was one thing that she was certain of, that he always knew where she was, and that was enough for her. Mum put the whole thing in a nutshell when she told John, in her own doughnut speech, 'She's really not looking for a needle in a haystack, you know. It's more like she's looking for a haystack in a needle.' You can't always work that kind of thing out instantly. It takes a time before it makes sense and I reckoned that was where John might have a bit of trouble.

* * *

It always gave me great pleasure to see John and Anna together – the old 'un and the young 'un. After the initial hesitation they had struck up a deep friendship. It didn't make my life any easier. In fact, it made it a darn sight more complicated, but that was fine with me. One of the problems was the fact that whatever Anna wanted to say or do, she said it in the simplest and most direct way possible. 'I want to have a pee, Fynn, a piddle, a piss.' It was all the same to her. I suppose it was a question of age and upbringing, but it was a lot different to John's, 'Fynn, I need to relieve myself'. John would so often hide what he wanted to say behind some Latin phrase or in some other language. So it meant that I had to speak two languages, his and hers; and on many occasions, act as an interpreter. It wasn't that I couldn't understand either of them, that was simple enough, but understanding them both together, that could be a bit tough at times! Most times, I was able to listen and understand John and Anna well enough, even though it might be a bit of a struggle. It was when they got together that I so often found myself in a flat spin. Like a spectator at a tennis match, my head was going from left to right, from right to left. Normally I could manage it. The problem was when my head was going right at the same time as my eyes

were going left, that caused me confusion. I wasn't made to do that kind of thing and I complained, but they both ignored my complaints. There was John who maintained that the things that mattered were the things we knew, the public things. Anna reckoned the only things that really mattered were the things we didn't know, the private things. Me? Sorry, I'm a stranger here!

As usual it was Mum who gave me the clue I needed. She told me that Mister John needed to know the biggest part and Anna wanted to know the smallest part. Put like that it made sense. After all, what do you expect from the sort of Mum who worked a sampler, as a young girl, which read 'Too much of anything kills the joys of having enough'. It hung over her large brass bedstead. I had learnt that she would never have had the usual sentences like 'Jesus loves me' or 'Bless this house'. When you come to think about her sampler, it makes sense and it worked out with John and Anna too. Once I had got that secret, things were a lot easier to understand.

The large telescope in John's garden impressed Anna well enough, and well, all them stars and things, you'd have to be a bit of an idiot not to wonder at it all. But it was a pity, wasn't it, that you had to squash those five or six daisies in order to do so. There were so many times when I was uncertain if I was being stretched or flattened! It's a bit difficult to put it into words, and each time I try to do so, it can sound sillier and sillier. The only way that I could put it was that while John had spent most of his life trying to fold the whole universe into a manageable packet, Anna was, in her own way, trying to unfold the daisies to fill that empty space that John was creating. I said it was too difficult to put it into words, but it was something like that. All this remind-ed me of the story of, I think, the Rev. Sidney Smith, who said to his Bishop, 'Is it not strange, my Lord Bishop, that you, because of your gravity, will ascend to heaven, whilst I, because of my levity, will descend to hell.' For I felt suspended in the middle, going up and down like a yo-yo!

When I repeated this one afternoon John's response had been, 'Are you sure it was Sidney Smith who said that Fynn?'

'I'm not sure that it was!'

Anna thought that it was worth a snigger but really not all that important. But me, I thought it was good and I knew that some-body had said it. And it certainly wasn't me and I don't think it mattered anyway. It doesn't to me. I don't give a fig who said it. It had been said and that was good enough for me.

And then there were mirrors. I use them when I shave, but I had spent hours and hours with John learning about geometry and mathematics of single and multiple mirrors, and then more and more hours learning about the magic of mirrors.

In those days I had a book entitled *The Mathematical Analysis of Knots*. So far as I was concerned a knot was what I did when I tied up my shoes or my tie, but I read that it was more than that. The simple once-over knot, called the clover knot, went one way, but its mirror image went the other way. I never realized that. The fact that the knot and its image are called an 'enantiomorphic pair' was interesting. Not that I used that word very often. And then the book went on to say that 'amphicheiral' meant fitting either hand, that socks were amphicheiral but on the other hand, gloves and shoes were not. Oh! Where did this 'other hand' come from? That's another thing I had never noticed. I nearly gave up when I was informed that something about these knots could be expressed analytically in its simplest form by the relation that follows:

$$x=1 \ y=1 \ x=1 \ y \ x \ yx=1 \ y=1 \ xyxy=1 \ x=1 \ y=1 \ xy=1!$$

I was impressed to know that this was the simplest way of expressing it!! And I was glad to know that I had learnt to tie a knot a long time before I had read the book! Otherwise I doubt if I could ever have tied up my shoes! But it reminded me so much of John and Anna. Was it just possible that they were reverse images of each other.

* * *

It was a day like any other day at home when it started. No green clouds, no manna from heaven, not a shower of pound notes to be seen anywhere, just a smiling-faced Anna with a morning cup of tea and the sound of the milkman, the train going by, the usual factory chimneys giving out the smoke and soot. As I said, it was just plain usual, absolutely nothing to raise the flags about, but it turned out to be the day when 'it' happened.

I was going to do a bit of digging for John, and Anna was to come with me. I took the tandem into the street, pumped up the tyres, checked the brakes, tested the lights. Just the common or garden ordinary things. Nothing special. I had finished the digging around about lunchtime, listening to Anna's chatter. Arabella asked us to stay for lunch, so that was fine. After lunch, we sat in the sitting-room and talked about nothing in particular, Anna looking at a large picture book, Arabella busy mending something. John and I each had a pint of beer and were just idly talking about this, that and the other. Nothing of great importance, but whether trees might have any means at all of communication with each other.

'No,' he had corrected me, 'they don't know each other, that would be too much. They can't possibly know anything, they were not made that way.'

'There might be some possibility that they could communicate with each other in some very primitive way. I wonder what they would talk about if they could?'

'The usual things, I suppose,' giggled John. '"The weather is not quite right", "the children are more like mother than father", just silly normal things.'

I'm certain that Anna had not heard a word of this conversation. She was far too busy with her book. Arabella paid us no attention at all. This kind of conversation was so far beneath her as to be almost out of sight. You see, normal, just plain every day normal. Anna drifted over and sat on the arm of my chair.

'Hi, Tich,' I greeted her. 'What's to do? All right?'

She nodded and smiled at John. She walked around the room once or twice, stood in front of me just looking, and suddenly without any warning flung herself into my arms. Of course we were alarmed. It was so unlike her, even Arabella unfroze a bit and was ready to give out with the comfort. I held Anna tight in my arms for some minutes until she wriggled free and there she stood, grinning down at me.'

'You scared me, Tich,' I said. 'You sure you're all right?'

'I'm good, Fynn. I'm good. Just want to say something to you, that's all.'

'Sure thing, luv,' I answered her. 'Fire away. I'm all yours.'

It was then that 'it' happened. The moment when that sitting-room held one very certain child and three uncomprehending grown ups. She uttered no more than fifteen ordinary words and the world seemed to stand still. All she said was, 'Fynn, you have to know much more to be silent than you do to keep talking.'

John looked at me in a dazed fashion. Arabella stopped her mending and stood up. 'Well,' she said, and nothing more. John was struck dumb.

There were no words that I could find for that moment either. I did manage to find my tongue a few minutes later, but all that I could manage to say was, 'Where did you find that one from?'

'Dunno, but it's true ain't it, Fynn? Ain't it true?'

'Suppose it must have come from one of the people she's always pestering to write it down big. I can't see how else she could have put that sentence together.' And I never did find out how she came by it. Perhaps she worked it out. I just don't know. I do know that John never ceased to quote it to people. It had a profound effect on him. 'It was then that it changed,' he would say.

As most of Anna's little stories and her workings out were done sitting on my lap or when she had gone to bed, I knew them all by heart. Most of them had a little sting in them somewhere, but not everybody saw it. It was after we had finished tea one afternoon when John said, 'Will you tell me a story, little one? I have heard a lot about your stories.'

'Yes, Mister John. What one shall I tell you?'

'Whichever one you like.'

'Would you like me to tell you about the mice, or the one about heaven?'

'I think,' he said, 'the one about the mice would do very well. You can tell me the one about heaven another day.'

'Say when you're ready then, Mister John, and then I'll start.'

'I'm ready, Anna, so you may start.'

'This king,' she began, 'had lots and lots of jewels and crowns and things like that. Then one day the biggest diamond of all fell out on the floor but nobody could ever find it again. The queen couldn't find it and the princess couldn't find it. Just nobody could find it, so in the end they all had to go to bed. Now in the middle of the night, a little mouse was looking for something to eat and he saw this diamond where nobody could find it and he tried to push it to the hole where he lived, but he couldn't move it a bit. So then he went to find his friend to come and help him, and they pushed and pushed and pushed and they couldn't do it. So they went to get some more friends to help too, but they still couldn't move it. So they called for some more friends to come and then there were hundreds of mice, all pushing this diamond and in the end it started to move and they all pushed all night long and in the end they pushed it down a hole and nobody ever saw it again. It was lost for ever.'

'I see,' said John, 'so that is the end of that little story, is it?'

'No, Mister John. That's only the start of it. I haven't finished yet. You've got to wait for the end of the story and I haven't got there yet!'

'I'm sorry, Anna,' he said a little abashed, 'perhaps I'm a little too impatient.'

Her 'Yes, Mister John,' turned him a deep crimson.

'Please go on.'

'Well then, the mouses couldn't find it either, cos it had fallen down a very deep hole and they couldn't get down it. Then, Mister John, one of the mice said to the first mouse, "What did we all push it for?" And do you know, Mister John, nobody could tell why they had worked so hard! Nobody could say why they did it at all! You couldn't eat it, could you? And nobody knew what you could do with it. It was a very silly thing for all them mouses to do, wasn't it, Mister John? And it was only because a king wanted to look important first of all. And that's the end of the story of all them silly mouses. But it's like people too, ain't it, Fynn?'

I was used to being given the hard bits to sort out afterwards, so I was ready for any question that John might ask. I think he got lost with all those mice dashing about, for he never said a word until Anna had gone out into the garden.

'I suppose, Fynn, she's saying that many people do useless things and have no idea why they are doing them. Is that it?'

'You said it, John, not me,' I laughed.

'Then why didn't she talk about people not mice?'

'Perhaps, John, if she had talked about people, you might not have believed her. It's a lot easier to believe mice are silly, rather than people.'

'Perhaps you're right, Fynn. I really must wait for the end of stories, mustn't I?'

* * *

Of all the odd jobs I did in my spare time, the one I enjoyed the most was driving the Baker's horse and van back to the depot, little more than four miles away, and I could earn anything between two shillings and sixpence and four shillings a time. Money for old rope. There was nothing difficult in driving Old Tom. He knew his way home better than I did. On some occasions, when the driver, after a night out, didn't feel up to it, I did take on the whole round. I could make as much as 12/6d for that, which wasn't bad going. Tom was so certain of the delivery round that he always stopped at the right pavement. With both front legs on the pavement and neck outstretched he waited for his titbit, a nob of sugar, a carrot or an old stale bun. He would not move until he had been given it. If Tom had been able to count money, I would have been out of a job. I often told him he was just an old flea-bag, but he didn't understand me, or if he did, he took no notice.

He was living in clover with all these extras and he got all the pats and strokes. Nobody ever did that to me. His attitude to me sometimes made me feel quite useless. Fred had told me often enough, but somehow I always forgot when the time came. 'Never turn your back on him, that's the one thing he doesn't like.' I could take his harness off, give him a brush down, feed him and water him and then turn away to lock the stall. He'd put his head in the small of my back and, with a twist and a shove, send me flying across the stable. If he had any sense maybe I could have reasoned with him, but he never could understand me, not even when I called him a flea-bag. That dratted horse could make me feel so small at times, especially when the others laughed at the number of times he bowled me over.

There was one November day when I was certain that my shrinkage was beginning to show. We had one of those November fogs, not the ordinary ones, but a 'pea-souper', those fogs when you took two steps outside your front door and were immediately lost. Nobody could see the street names and the street lights were nothing more than a greenish fuzz. It wasn't that you couldn't see your hand in front of your face, you just couldn't see it anywhere. This particular evening it was so thick that you could have nailed a plank of wood to it, or leant a ladder against it and climbed it. Some of the kids could make a few pennies on nights like this. With a paraffin lamp they could walk the curb directing a lost bus or a lonely car or two. Nobody knew where they were.

'Am I all right for the Broadway, mate?'

'Don't know, chum, I think it's the other way, but I'm not sure.'

Eventually I did find my way back home.

'What a night!' I complained to Mum. 'It's a real stinker!'

'Glad I'm in. It's not a night to be out.'

'What's for supper, Mum? I'm just about ready for it.'

'Fred Cooper's not well,' she said. 'He's got bronchitis. Can you take the van back to the yard for him?'

'Right,' I said, 'but I must have a cup of tea first and I'd better put something warmer on.'

'His Missus left something for your trouble.'

She had left me five shillings.

'No trouble, Mum,' I said. 'Buy yourself a tiara or something.'

'A couple of bags of coal would be nice,' she replied. 'What with the winter coming on that'll be right handy.'

'Good idea. I'll put it behind the clock for you.'

'Can I come with you, Fynn?' asked Anna.

'That's fine with me, but you'd better ask Mum.'

'Well,' said Mum, 'as long as you keep warm and don't do anything silly, yes.'

'How will you manage to get home if it's as thick as all that?' Mum called after us up the passage.

'Don't worry about that, Mum,' I said. 'We'll sleep with the horses if it doesn't clear soon. They won't mind.'

'Right,' she replied. 'I'll see you when I see you. Take care!'

We closed the street door and headed up the street. The fog was just as bad as it had been an hour ago.

'Can Bombom come?' asked Anna.

'If she wants to, of course, she can.'

In a few minutes, I was joined at the top of the street by Bombom, May, Nipper and Anna. Millie was by the lamppost talking to a couple of her friends.

'Where you lot off to?' she asked. 'Taking Fred's van back to the yard for him? He's got his chest again.'

'Like to come for a ride, Mill? You might not get back till the morning and if it goes on like this, you'll have to sleep with the horses.'

'I'm game. Lead on.'

In no time at all we were outside Fred's house.

'I'll just pop in to have a word with Fred. You might as well put Tom's nosebag on until I get back.'

'He can't go out on a night like this, Fynn. It'll kill him,' said Mrs Fred.

'Thanks for taking Tom back for me,' said Fred when I went in. 'Perhaps you'll do my round for me in the morning if I don't get in.'

'Sure I will. You get some rest.'

'Tom will see you back safely.'

'Right, Fred. I'd better go now. I've got a van load of kids waiting for me.'

'That's good. It'll be company for you. Oh Fynn, there's cold pies in the locker. You might just eat them between you.'

Outside the kids were waiting for me.

'Fynn,' laughed Millie, 'we've got a lost Copper who wants a lift to the station. Any chance? It's PC Laithwaite.'

We moved back the way we had come and I stopped the van next to the King's Head. 'Gonna buy some fizz,' I said. 'Back in a tick.'

As I clambered back onto the seat, I heard a lady say, 'I didn't know it was going to be like this, did I?'

'Now we are in a fix,' came the man's voice. 'I can't possibly drive the car back in this.'

'That's Mister John, Tich,' I whispered to Anna. 'Hop down and tell him.'

'Hello, Mister John,' I heard her say.

'Well bless me. It's the little maid herself. Are you lost too?'

'No, Mister John.'

'We are and I don't see any way of getting back.'

'Ask Fynn. He can do it for you.'

'Fynn! Where is he?'

'Up here, John,' I laughed. 'Would you like a lift home? I'm going your way.'

'Oh Fynn, could you really find your way in this?'

'Not me,' I replied, 'but Old Tom can.'

It was arranged that Danny would drive John's car back, following Old Tom and the van. Arabella wasn't at all certain that she was ever going to get home again and, as for sitting behind a smelly old horse, well 'the indignity of it!' Anna did manage to tell her that even the King and Queen did that kind of thing. She started to tell us that riding in a coach with smart horses pulling it was one thing, Old Tom and the Baker's van was something entirely different. We did at last manage to convince her that it was Tom and the van or nothing. She wasn't certain that I could manage either: 'I must sit with my back to the horse. I really couldn't bear to watch.' I told her that I couldn't see either, and that didn't help a bit. The fact that she would have to rely on a mere horse, a dumb animal, to get her home was almost too much for her.

At last we managed to get away, Old Tom plodding his steady way along the road. There was nothing much I could really do, with Anna beside me on the box and the rest of the passengers packed in the van. I asked Anna to get a cigarette from my pocket and lit it. When Arabella saw that I wasn't holding the reins in my hand, she nearly had the vapours.

'Fynn, do be careful. Don't let it run away!'

'Run, Arabella? Old Tom hasn't run for the last ten years. He's got too much sense for that.'

Poor Arabella, for all her learning, really didn't know very much about ordinary things like the way Old Tom was clever at cutting across the tramlines, which could be a little tricky at times. I never managed to work out exactly how he did that, but I never knew him to make a mistake except on the one occasion some time ago when I had pulled the rein too much. That was the time when I nearly had the van over, but since then I just let him get on with it at his own pace.

PC Laithwaite dropped off at the Station House without my needing to stop. I asked Millie where the cold pies were to be found, but Arabella would have none of it.

'Is Danny still with us?' I asked.

'Yes, Fynn,' said Bombom, her mouth full of pie. 'Fynn!'

'Yes?'

'Can I come and sit between you and Anna?'

'Sure thing. Just clamber up.'

She hadn't been with us for more than a minute or two when Tom came to a stop.

'Fynn,' Bombom said, 'now the horse is lost too.'

'Is he lost, Fynn? Do you know where we are yet?' Arabella piped up.

'He's having a drink,' Bombom told her.

'What's that noise?' asked Arabella.

'He's having a pee too,' explained Anna.

Now I knew exactly where we were – the horse trough by the canal bridge. We weren't doing badly at all. We ought to make it in about thirty minutes.

As we travelled westwards away from all the factories, the fog thinned out just a bit. Not that I could see all that much better, but at least the street lamps no longer had that greenish tint to them, and it wasn't too long before I pulled Tom to a stop.

'Where are we now?' Arabella asked.

'Home, Arabella. Safe and sound.'

She could hardly believe it was true. I had to refuse her

invitation for a hot drink. She was a little surprised when I told her that we couldn't stop, for it was about time Old Tom was tucked up in bed. For John and Arabella all animals were dumb creatures. She didn't want to believe that it was Tom who had got her home safely, dumb or not.

We made it to the stables in less than fifteen minutes. The fog here had lifted considerably. I took the harness off and wiped it down, gave Tom a good brush down and instructed Millie and the kids how to find his food and water and just where to put them. Then I led Tom to his stall. I was very careful not to turn my back on him that night, but I think he had had enough of that day and didn't give me any trouble at all. It didn't take us long to make up a comfortable bed for the night. Armfuls of hay, a number of horse blankets and the odd bag of oats, and we were ready for sleep. Even Anna was reduced to a sentence or two.

'Fynn, Jesus was born in a place like this, wasn't he?'

'Don't think it was as nice as this,' I yawned.

'Oh, don't suppose so.' A little chorus of good nights were exchanged and I think the last thing I remembered was her 'Good night, Mister God.'

I woke up next morning with somebody trying to poke my brains out with a straw in my ear. 'Hi, Fynn, time to wake up!'

'Millie, what's to do? Stop poking my ear, will you? Where have the kids got to?'

Peals of laughter from outside in the van yard told me all I wanted to know. 'What day is it, Millie?'

'Saturday ... all day long.'

'That's something,' I said. 'Any idea what the time is?'

'Just after six. The church clock just struck.'

'Suppose we'd better get a move on then. Has Fred been in?'

'Haven't seen anybody at all.'

'Give me a hand, Millie. I'm stuck.'

With her help I got to my feet. So far as I could figure it out, I had only stopped for five or six hours out of the last thirty-six. I was a bit washed out.

The foreman and a couple of ladies were in the yard with the kids, who were filling themselves with cakes and tea.

'Thanks for bringing the van back. There weren't all that many who made it last night. A regular stinker wasn't it? I've had a message from Fred. He says if you can do his round for him today he can bring the van back tonight. The fog has cleared up nicely and it looks like it's going to be a nice day. I've made the Saturday book up for you, and your young helpers are packing the van now. Perhaps you had better look it over so that you know where the stuff is.' He slipped a ten shilling note into my hand, 'Thanks,' he said, 'once again.'

'I must have a drink and a bite before we set off.'

'Mary,' he called, 'you can bring the young lady too.'

Millie arrived looking spic and span as usual. 'Surprising what a lick of powder and paint can do for a girl, ain't it, Fynn?'

'You look all right to me without it.'

'Thanks, Fynn. Don't stop, tell me more! You'll get yourself a bad name one of these days, Fynn.'

'How come?' I asked her.

'If the street ever gets to hear that you spent the night in bed with four young ladies, your name will be mud!'

* * *

The name of John's house, Random Cottage, had puzzled Anna for a long time. It didn't seem to mean anything at all. If it had been called 'The Larches' or 'Hill View' or something like that, that would have been fine. She could have understood that. But 'Random', I ask you! What did that mean? She told me that the very next time she saw John, she was going to ask him why.

I had been puzzling my head all week long over some bit of mathematics that I could not understand. Come Sunday afternoon I decided I was going over to see John before my head finally came off its hinges. Anna was off somewhere playing with her friends. Going to John and back certainly wouldn't take more than a couple of hours and I'd be back before supper. I would sneak off while she was busy. The street was full of kids playing their various games. As I made my way to the top of the street, 'Game of cricket, Fynn?' asked Heck.

'Not now. Going to be busy for an hour or so.' I had to dodge the skippers, the gobstone players and the odd ball players. I had almost made it to the top of the street when I was nearly knocked flying by Anna.

'Where are you going, Fynn? Going to John D.? Going on yer bike?'

'Not this time. Going to run along the canal. See you in a few hours time, Tich.'

I ran slowly the last few yards to the top of the street and I was just about to turn the corner and head for the canal when the quick patter of feet pulled me up short, to say nothing of the persistent cries of 'Fynn, Fynn'. Two young bodies thumped into me, Anna and Bombom.

'Fynn,' said Anna, 'why is it called that?'

'Why's what called what?'

'Mister John's house, why is it called that?'

'I don't know. You'd better ask him when you see him next.'

'You ask him,' said Bombom.

'What's it mean, Fynn? What's it mean?'

'Tell you when I get back,' and I started off again.

'Meany,' said Anna. 'Fynn's an old meany.'

After the space of a breath or two Bombom joined in the chorus. The two of them ran after me with their chorus of 'Fynn's a meany, Fynn's an old meany'. I could have got away from them quite easily except that I was hailed by Millie.

'Hi, Fynn, what's to do? Pinched the kids' sweets again?'

'Where did that idea come from?' I asked.

'The way you're being chased,' she gestured with her arms.

I turned to look. They hurled themselves at me. Being caught off balance I ended up none too elegantly or gently facing down in the road. I really could have got up except for Millie's foot which pressed me flat again. If nothing else, I was now looking upwards, not with a face full of gravel.

'There, there, Fynn. You'd better have a rest and get your breath back! Can't have the old 'uns too excited now, can we?'

My intention was to chase after her, but with her foot firmly on my nose pressing me back, it was difficult for me to do anything as she counted '6 – 7 – 8 – 9 – OUT'.

'You'd better give up, Fynn. You'll never win with the kind of kids you run around with.'

By this time I was encircled by faces looking down at me.

'You kids mustn't bully Fynn, you know. He's not as young as he used to be. What's he been up to? Pinched your lollies or summat?'

'He won't do something for me, that's what!' said Anna. 'He's a meany!'

'May you be forgiven, you little perisher!' I managed to say before Millie's foot pushed me back again.

'Ask him again, Anna,' giggled Millie, 'ask him while he's help-less. The way he's going on he'll probably never get back today. Get knocked over by a train or something. Go on, ask him again. I'll hold him still,' and she applied a little more pressure to my face. 'Ask him while he can still breathe.'

It was just another one of those occasions that I wasn't going to get out of. I had better made the best of it. What the passers-by thought of this little episode, I don't know. I didn't get any help. I was a little anxious when the large dog joined the circle and then happily went off in search of his favourite lamppost.

'Come on, Anna, ask the question. Fynn's coming back to life.'

'Fynn.' She spoke my name in that kind of apologetic melody that only children who know they are on to a sure thing can manage.

'Mercy, I give up! What means what?'

'That "Random" word. That's what's what. What does it mean? Ask him!'

'O.K. Mill, lift the foot and let me up.'

'Always told you it was no good trying to be a genius. You'll come to a sticky end if you go on like that, Fynn.' I didn't think that John would mind my telling him that he never had this kind of problem – when I got there!

On my feet at last I made threatening signs at Millie, a promise to strangle her.

'No violence, please Fynn. Only trying to spread a little light on things. Wouldn't mind knowing what it means myself. Give with the wisdom, what does it mean?'

'Well, it's a sort of ... it's a kind of muddle, I guess. Sort of no shape to it.'

'Gawd blimey, Fynn! What, you mean it's a lot of fuss about nothing?'

'Ain't intelligence wonderful?' she said to the world at large.

It wasn't exactly what I had wanted to say. It really needed a little more thought.

Lying with my face pressed into the gravel, I had got a gleam of an idea. 'Don't worry, Tich, I'll ask Mister John and I'll tell you what he says when I get back.'

'Oh no you don't! You can't wriggle out of it all that easy. It's now or you don't go!'

'Yes, master. The genie of the handbag is now about to do its stuff! That's if I can find the darn thing. Where did that darn pen go to? Never can find the blessed thing when I want it.'

It was Bill who spotted it first, plunged his hand into Millie's bag and produced the fountain pen. I took a peek into the handbag.

'Cripes, what's all this junk for? You could start a shop with this lot.'

'You stick to what you think you know, genius, and keep your nose out of my bag. It's got nothing to do with you. Ain't that right, kids?'

'What about a sheet of paper then? And you might as well dig out the table and chair too while you're about it!'

She swung her handbag at me but missed, which was a good thing considering all the stuff she had got in it.

'Paper,' I demanded. 'Paper.'

She took a bag of apples out of her other shopping bag and handed them around and gave me the bag.

'Don't I get one?'

'Not till after. If I can understand what you're going on about, you might.'

I shook the pen vigorously over the paper bag, which was soon covered by a multitude of spots. 'That,' I said, handing the bag around, 'is random, well more or less. It gives you the idea. There is no real order. It's kind of messy. There is nothing much you can say about it.'

'Bet that took a long time to figure out, Fynn!' Millie said.

'Couldn't do it meself! Takes brains that does! I'm just a dummy! Thrilling. That's what it is! Reckon I won't sleep for weeks after all that excitement! Takes real brains to do something you can't talk about! You must do it more often! Give your brains a rest!'

'Moron,' I yelled over my shoulder as I fled.

I decided to anticipate her, and more than an hour later I reached Random Cottage. After I had explained the reason and asked Anna's question, he answered with, 'Just luck. Nothing more than that. One of those long lost relations that fairy stories tell you about. Nothing more. I was very lucky. It's as simple as that. It was a whim, a fancy, that made me give it the name "Random". Odd, isn't it?' he continued, looking around the house. 'It pleases me to call it that. There is nothing that I can say about the word. Chance, nothing more.' Everything in his house and garden was so well ordered that the word 'random' was a joke, and he smiled whenever he used it. When I returned home, that paper bag with all its dots was spread out on the table with Anna's head down over it. I told her of the conversation I had had with John and got nothing more than 'Oh'.

'That's the last of that,' I thought. Little did I know how wrong I was! For after a few days, that paperbag with its dots was now a large sheet of white cardboard with even more dots. Except for the occasional, 'You can't say a fink about it', which could have meant anything, nothing more was said for a while. I was nearly trapped into asking her what it was that you couldn't say anything about it. I didn't because there was no use messing about asking silly questions if I didn't know what she was on about. After the umpteenth time of hearing that 'you could say nothing about it', it was about time to ask my question.

'Sorry, Tich, no idea what you're talking about. What you on about?'

'You know, Mister John's house.'

'Random Cottage?'

She nodded. 'You know, you said you couldn't say much. You know, about the word "random".'

'You mean that one?'

'Well …,' when she said 'well' in that way it was about time to duck. She darted to the cupboard and pulled out the large sheet of white cardboard which was now covered with circles and a few coloured dots. After a time to get her thoughts sorted out, she stabbed the red dot with her finger: 'That's you, Fynn, that is.'

'Oh, I see. Can't I be something important for a change? Something vital?'

'It is, Fynn. It is something important. And that's me,' pointing to a blue dot.

'Nice to have a bit of company. I was beginning to get a bit lonely.' Her smile was comforting, but the sharp intake of her breath meant that I was getting a bit too frivolous. This wasn't the time to be funny. This was going to be serious stuff. She moved to the Welsh Dresser and got my best brass geometry set. Nobody else would dare do such a thing. That was strictly hands off! Whatever it was that she was going to say was obviously so important that she didn't ask. She just looked at me. I did nod, but that was just for the sake of appearance. Sitting opposite me she opened the lid. Her hand hesitated and she gave me that look – the look of something important to come. 'Can I, Fynn? Can I?'

I nodded. She drew out the largest compass in the box, the one with the extending legs. After waving it about like the sword Excalibur and carefully inspecting the point with that air of concentration and revelation to come, she turned her gaze on me. 'This,' I thought, 'is going to be good.'

'Fynn,' she said, pointing at the red dot again, 'that's you.'

'I know, you told me.'

And with that, she stuck the point of the compass in me, the red dot I mean. I couldn't help it, it just came out. 'Oi! That hurts!' That remark wasn't worth noticing. She was busy opening the compass until the writing point met one of the dots, and with the sharp bit still stuck in me, the red dot, she drew a circle. So far so good. It was more than an hour before she had finished doing the same thing for each one of the other dots and there I was, right in the centre of all those concentric circles.

It was about time she recognized how important I was, but she hadn't finished yet!

'Fynn, all the other dots want it too. They want them circles too.'

It was a funny thing how Anna's dots or blobs always seemed to end up being more human than humans. At least they did know what they wanted.

'I done that too! I done it! I'll go and get it!'

Yet another sheet of white card was laid on the kitchen table. It was a bit different but the point was lost on me. In this one all dots' wishes and wants had been fulfilled, for now each and every dot was firmly in the centre of its own private nest of concentric circles.

'Good, ain't it?' she asked.

'Very good,' I agreed I nearly said it, but I had noticed something that I hadn't accounted for. Simple really when you think about it, but I had missed it. For one circle of every other dot passed slap bang through the middle of me. There was the dot called Anna, Mum, Millie and, since everybody is a dot, you too!

'What's all this mean, Fynn? What's it mean?'

I hesitated. The idea that was going through my head made sense to me. At least, it sounded all right, so I said it.

'What it looks like,' I said, 'is that every dot can be seen in two ways. Either it can be the centre of everything or' – and this was the tricky bit – 'every dot is a special, no unique, meeting point of one circle of every other dot.'

I got a kiss for that. I had no words for her.

'Like Mister God, ain't it? It's funny when you know how.'

'Plain funny how everything is like Mister God.'—

'Took a long time doing it, that did.'

'I bet it did!'

'Me bum went to sleep.'

'It's surprising nothing else went to sleep, the way you sit.'

She could always, and for that matter often did, mix God and bums and the strangest of things in one sentence, but then I really don't suppose Mister God minded at all. After all, he had been around a fairly long time.

The Rev. Castle didn't get the point and really wasn't impressed. As for John, he said, 'She doesn't understand the difficulties yet. I see what she is getting at, but that is pure cheek, it's not mathematics!' He didn't understand that it wasn't meant to be mathematics. All she was trying to do was to talk about something that nobody was supposed to be able to talk about, and as far as I could see she had done just that. The idea that everything could be seen either as the centre of all things or as a unique meeting place of everything else was all right with me. I felt I could stick with that one. It was time for lots and lots of tea after that.

* * *

It wasn't that the people in the street were poverty stricken, nothing like that. It was simply the fact that they didn't always have enough money and there are plenty of disadvantages in that state of affairs. But there were a few advantages – like knowing each other, helping each other, making do, the necessary inventions of living. All these things were about as normal as breathing. It was one of those things that John never fully understood. Perhaps in the long run it didn't matter one bit, except for the fact that many things had to be done another way and Anna was an expert in doing things another way. Many of her thoughts had to be seen in 'the other way' and if you didn't know 'the other way', it was quite easy to end up wondering what had happened and what had hit you! The Sunday that she spent the whole service drawing little circles in the air with her forefinger was one of those occasions. The Rev. Castle wasn't at all pleased with this activity and told me so, and John simply saw it as the idle doodling of the young. I was asked, no told, to do the same thing in the same direction.

She crossed the road, skirting the tram and dodging the odd horse and cart, and stood opposite me, still drawing her little circles, as I was doing. She managed to persuade some passer-by to copy her in this circle-drawing stuff and sped back to me. I was still busy drawing little circles in the air.

PC Laithwaite grinned at me. 'Nice to see you occupied for a change', was all he said. He had soon got used to the fact that if Anna was around, somebody near to her was almost certain to be doing something out of the ordinary. Maybe even a little crazy. More often me or Millie.

Miss Haynes never did understand why Anna would often stop and slowly spin around. It wasn't anything new to John. He had spent many hours talking about it, but her ideas about this circle-drawing were not the same as his. She told him quite simply and clearly that it was like being two people. He tried to give her the proper explanation, but whatever anybody else might say it was like being two people. Maybe even more than two and that was definite. After all, if on one side of the road you had to say that the circle was going one way, but on the other side of the road, that invisible circle was going the other way, of course it was like being two people! Once she asked me what a 'vicious circle' was and other little gems that grown-up people talked about, like reading between the lines, which was rather daft because there wasn't anything between the lines, anybody could see that.

* * *

It wasn't often that I made the journey to Random Cottage alone, and when I did I spent more time talking about Anna than I did in the garden. John wanted to know everything she had done since he last saw her: what she had said, what her latest ideas were. Most times we arrived with her sitting on my handlebars or, if Bombom was to come with us, then we'd go by bus, and whenever the weather was fine and warm, they would sit at his feet and he'd listen to their chatter. And as he grew stronger, he would often join in their little games.

'Nothing too strenuous, John, remember what the Doctor said,' Arabella reminded him.

'Bosh. Fetch me a drink, will you, Fynn, and one for yourself and find something for the children.'

Since we had been going to John's house so often he was never without a plentiful supply of drinks for the children.

There were many times when I thought that Anna ought to have been born a mountain goat, the way she could jump from one subject to another which so often confused her teachers and got me into hot water. For one thing, there was this large building site up by the bridge. Everybody complained about the mess it was making, the inconvenience it caused. There were piles of bricks, pipes, planks of wood, cement, sand and a lot of rubbish too. You'd just never think to look at it that somebody knew that the mess was going to be a building at some time. That was the way she saw her schooling and all her various explorations. Some things were good and she wanted them, but others were not so good and she had no use for them. Her teachers didn't really understand, but in the end it was going to turn out to be a 'Who knows?' and I was prepared to wait. It was bound to be something splendid and that was good enough for me! It was funny with grown ups, they were always throwing the most important things away. For instance, that dandelion that John had dug up.

'Can I have it please?'

'What do you want a thing like that for? There's too many of them. They are nothing but a nuisance.'

That wasn't what Anna thought about them. They really ought to be somewhere nice, so she planted it in a flower bed in the park. It didn't last very long there either. And then the Rev. Castle was almost outraged to find Anna planting this dandelion in the churchyard and he told her so in no uncertain terms. It wasn't all that long ago that he was telling the congregation that God saw that it was good and she completely agreed with him. If only grown ups could have seen things as she saw them, things would have been a lot easier, but they didn't and Mum ended up with the best weed garden in the country. Surely you'd have to be a real idiot not to say that weeds were truly beautiful if they were looked after properly and it was Anna's pleasure to do so.

In spite of Miss Haynes' anguish and John's concern about her disorganized mind, she continued to look for those things that Mister God saw were good. The fact that they sometimes turned up in the most unlikely places didn't really matter at all. After all, things always grow in the cracks in the wall, on waste land and in all sorts of unlikely places, and it really wasn't right to pull them up. All things were bright and beautiful, she felt, if you only stopped to look at them. And why did we have to spoil Mister God's fun? He must have thought it was important. So Anna's ways of going about things were just that bit different. Maybe if John had been woken up in the middle of the night, as I had been so often, he might just have come to an understanding of Anna's way a lot sooner than he did. But he was woken up only once at two o'clock and I got blamed for it. If only Anna had been able to read my night-time dreams as easily as she seemed to read my day-time thoughts, I feel sure that she wouldn't have woken me up so often. I never did get to the nice part of the dream. It would have been nice to hold all the money in my hand just for once, the money from the inheritance that the nice solicitor told me about, but that never did happen. I had to wake up to 'Fynn, what's a moron?'

'Fynn, what's a moron?' she thumped me on the chest. ''Cos Mister John said I was one.'

'Not you, Tich. Maybe me, but not you.'

'He did, Fynn. He said I was a moron. You've gotta tell him not to call me that. You've gotta tell him so!'

'Sure I'll tell him the next time I see him. I sure will tell him.'

'No, now Fynn. Tell him now.'

'I really don't think he'd like being woken up this time of night.'

'Don't care. Tell him, tell him I'm not a moron.'

She sounded so near to tears that there was nothing else to do but tell him now. As we headed for the nearest telephone box I tried to convince her that he wouldn't say a thing like that.

'But he did, Fynn. He really did!'

I reckon anybody who called a little girl like Anna a moron deserved to be woken up, no matter what the hour. Anyhow, he did have a telephone next to his bed. He didn't even have to get out of bed to answer it. Not like me, I had to get dressed and walk nearly half a mile. Anna tried to get the number a couple of times and at last the operator made the connection. I pressed myself as near to the ear piece as I could. I could hear his bell ringing and very soon I heard his voice.

'Hello, John Hodge speaking.'

'You do it, Fynn. You say it!'

I shook my head. 'It's your fight, you do it!'

'Mister John,' she bellowed down the phone, 'it's Anna.'

'Hello, Anna. What do you want? Are you all right? Is Fynn all right?'

'Yes, Mister John. He's here. He wants to talk to you,' and with that she thrust the telephone into my hands with a little sob.

'What's all this about calling Anna a moron, John? I wouldn't do that. She says you did and she's very upset about it.'

'Put her on, Fynn. For goodness sake, put her on!'

'Anna, my dear,' he said, 'I would never call you a moron. I couldn't do that!'

'Yes, you did, Mister John. I heard you say "She's the only two-legged moron that you had ever met"!'

'No, no, little Anna, you have made a mistake. Not a moron, I said you were an oxymoron. Will you put Fynn on. I had better explain to him.'

'Stupid men,' came a voice. 'You ought to know better than to frighten a little child.'

'Madam, will you please get off the line. This is important.'

'You bet it is,' said the operator. 'You both deserve to be locked up, confusing the kid with your stupid oxy stuff. She ought to be tucked up in bed. My advice is to take her home and give her a good cuddle.'

'Madam, please get off the line.'

'Fynn,' he said, 'the word is not moron. It's oxymoron, you know, oxymoron.'

Oxymoron wasn't a word I used every day of my life. It wasn't a very useful kind of word. The only time I ever remember using it was in an English lesson many years ago.

'Let's go and get a cuppa, Tich,' I said. 'I think we need one.'

'Is it all right then, Fynn? Did he mean it?'

'He didn't say what you thought he said. He said a different word.'

'What word?'

'He called you an oxymoron.'

'Is that word bad, then?'

'Not really. It's what is called "a figure of speech". Drink your tea while it's hot.'

Somewhere at the back of the old brain box I remembered an example.

'It's like when people say "hasten slowly" or like when people say "a living death" or something like that. It is two words that contradict each other separately, but put together make sense. It's something like that. That's what Mister John called you, not a moron.'

'Oh,' she said. 'That's different. That's all right, I thought he said something else.'

'Them things,' she said, 'you gotta be careful, ain't you, Fynn? I'm an oxymoron, ain't I, Fynn?'

She told the coffee stall owner too. 'I'm an oxymoron!' I don't think he really cared a bit.

'I'm tired,' I complained. 'Can I go back to bed?'

I was glad that she thought it was a good idea too!

Mum called down the stairs as we got into the house.

'Where have you two been off to? It's nearly morning.'

'Been killing oxymoron,' I yelled back.

'That's nice,' came the answer.

It wasn't until I was once again in bed that it came to me just how strange this night had been. 'The pointed conjunction of seeming contradictories' was the dictionary definition of an oxymoron, so I guess John wasn't so far out after all. She was an oxymoron, sort of, and, for that matter, put together they made another one. All I was left with was the fact that 'you've gotta be careful'.

More and more I was getting the feel of it. Being by now so used to the way both expressed ideas, I was able to translate John to Anna in a way that she could understand, and I could do the same for John when he was finding it a bit difficult. I must confess, I often found it difficult too. Whatever it was that was so perplexing him was causing him no little pain and confusion, but one thing was for sure, he was beginning to lose that acid touch in his conversation with her, that exasperation which he had so often shown; that sharp edge in him which could hurt so often was beginning, slowly, to take on a more gentle edge. And as for Anna, she was losing none of her magic, but in some ways developing better ways of saying exactly what she wanted to. Not much, but a bit. Partly, I suppose, just because she was growing up. Poor John was really having a rough time of it. There was no sudden revelation to him, no blinding illumination. It was all a very slow progress and all with the greatest difficulty. In what direction, he did not know. For that matter neither did she and, least of all, me!

* * *

John decided that Anna ought to be given the benefit of his knowledge of things, so it was arranged that we pay a whole day's visit to the various Museums of South Kensington. I didn't like to tell him that we had already been there and that she didn't think much of them.

So it was that a little group of kids, about eight, waited for him one morning. I had asked Millie if she would come along to help out. I didn't fancy the job of chasing the kids around the Museum. She agreed.

John arrived, ready to stuff our heads full of information. In the centre of the large entrance hall to the Museum was a large model of a human flea, bigger than Anna herself. She circled it, giving it a wary glance. The shake of her head indicated that she didn't think much of it and wasn't at all interested in whatever John, or anybody else, might have to say about it. I did mention to John that they did at least have something in common, that both of them made me want to scratch something. I couldn't reach, but he simply frowned at me.

After months of Anna I knew all about this need to scratch when she got going, but John hadn't learnt that yet. He would, given time. But after years of being taught by John, I wasn't going to protect him from her kind of torture. He was old enough to look after himself.

'Fynn,' he asked, 'has Anna been to the Hall of Dinosaurs?'

'Don't know. I don't think so.'

'Well, in that case we must go along to see them. I'm certain that she will be impressed.'

We saw the bronto things, the stego things, the icthyo things, and other things that nobody but John could pronounce, and finally ended up in front of good old Tyrannosaurus Rex. John poured out facts and figures about old Rex, but his millions and millions of years didn't impress any of the kids at all.

'Wouldn't like to meet him in the dark,' said Millie, and Bombom's 'Blimey!' exhausted her comments. May's cry of 'Coo ... ee!' echoed around that hall and turned a few heads for a moment. Well there isn't much you can say about such a thing as old Rex, is there? 'Strewth!' just about sums it all up.

We moved off to look at more wonders, with John still giving out with his hundred-million-years-ago facts. I knew how easy it was to lose Anna and, for that matter, get lost myself when she was doing a bit of thinking and, as she wasn't with the rest of them, I had to go back to look for her. I found her swinging her satchel, dwarfed beneath good old Rex, all teeth and claws. From the way she was swinging her satchel and the look she gave it, her thoughts were pretty obvious. If she wasn't frightened of Old Nick himself, she certainly wasn't frightened of old Rex.

'Don't you start on me or you'll get a good slosh with me bag.'

She smiled at me and wrinkled her nose as I stood beside her, and we went off in search of John and the others. When we found them, John was busy trying to convince May that this exhibit was called a Duck-billed Platypus and not a plat-billed-ducky-bus. In spite of all his insistence, it remained a plat-billed-ducky-bus for ever more!

After an hour or two it was decided that it was about time we went into the gardens to eat our sandwiches. John sat on a bench beside me, and the others on the grass. He wanted to know what Anna thought of all those dinosaurs.

'Did you like them, little one?'

'Um,' she replied.

'Did they frighten you?'

She wagged her head.

'What did you think of them?'

She thought for a moment or two and, looking him straight in the eye, said, 'No meat!'

It wasn't what he had expected to hear, and he launched himself into the task of telling her that the flesh had decayed millions of years ago. That didn't get much further.

'Um, I know that, Fynn told me.'

He didn't know that 'no meat' was important to her.

'Do you think the little maid is enjoying this, Fynn?' he asked me. 'It's not too much for her, is it?'

'Don't think so, John. I'm sure she's taking most of it in.'

'She seems so quiet, not like her usual self. I wondered if she was feeling unwell.'

'Don't take any notice of that, John. She's thinking, that's all. Trying to put it all together, trying to work it all out. She's often like this.'

'It would be nice to see inside her head for a while.'

'I shouldn't try that one, John, if I were you. You'll never find your way out again and I'm not sure there's all that much space left, with all the stuff she manages to cram inside her noodle!'

'Perhaps you're right at that. The thing that really puzzles me, young Fynn, is how anyone, faced with this evidence, could possibly believe that the Bible was right. How the creation story can stand up against all these facts is beyond me.'

'I don't see that the Bible tells you much. It merely creates moods.'

Neither of us had noticed that Anna was standing nearby and must have heard what he had said, but she said nothing at all, nothing but a sniff.

'Will you and Millie be able to take care of the children for thirty minutes? I have a little business to attend to.'

I did managed to convince him that we had done this kind of thing before and that they would be safe, even if Millie and me weren't!'

'We'll be off to the Science Museum next, John. See you there in an hour or so.'

'Right,' he answered. 'I'll find you somewhere.'

The kids found this much more interesting. All those buttons to push and a whole row of historical lavatories, where they could pull the chains much better than all the dead things. Dead birds and stuffed animals were all right as far as they went, but not as much fun as the buttons that made the wheels go round, model trains, model cars and all that sort of thing. They were obviously so engaged in button-pushing that they wouldn't miss me.

'Millie, d'you mind if I lose myself for a while? I'd like to look at a display.'

'Sure thing, Fynn. Where you off to?'

'Next floor up. There's a display of mathematical models I'd like to look at.'

'Might have known it,' she laughed. 'Trust you.'

I hadn't been there very long before Anna's red hair wriggled under my arm. 'Fynn.'

'Hi, Tich! What's to do? Run out of buttons to push?'

'No. Wanted to be with you, that's all. Wanted to ask you something.'

'Sure, ask away.'

'I don't think Mister John believes in Mister God, do you Fynn?'

'Not sure,' I said, 'but I don't think he does.'

'Oh.'

I did try to tell her that not everybody in the world believed in Mister God, and that many people believed in something altogether different. That was difficult to explain and she did not believe me anyhow. For a little while she walked around the cases with me, looking at the various models, trying to get inside them in her imagination.

It was not long before John reappeared. 'Glad I found you here, Fynn. I want to show you the exhibit over there. The Bush Differential Analyser. A very interesting device, really most interesting. What it does is ...'

But he never did get around to telling us about it, and Anna wasn't much interested whatever it might do. There were questions she wanted to ask John and that was what she was going to do. I don't suppose that anybody had faced her questions so directly. She just hit him with them: 'Mister John, why don't you believe in Mister God then? Why don't you?'

It wasn't often that John was lost for words, but he was on this occasion. He had to sit on a nearby seat. 'Sit next to me, little one, and I'll try to tell you.'

I wasn't certain how this was going to turn out at all. I wanted to be near her to give her support if she needed it. She had never heard him on the subject before and it was quite possible she might need a hand. I had quite forgotten the look she had given old Tyrannosaurus Rex.

I had never seen John be so gentle in all the years I had known him. He tried to explain so very simply that he couldn't possibly believe that it was all made in the way the Bible said. She listened without saying a word. He ended with, 'so you see, little one, why I can't believe it. I'm sorry, but I can't.'

For a long time nobody said a word. Anna, with her head hung down, was busy studying the floor. I hoped she had not been too hurt by what John had said and, from the looks he was giving me, it was obvious that he regretted the need for his words, but for John, the 'truth' was all-important, no matter what the consequences. So there we sat, not knowing what to say. As she raised her head I did notice that little smile that she reserved for her 'I haven't finished yet' times, so there was a lot more to come.

'How many pages in the Bible, Mister John? How many pages?'

'Pages?' he said. 'Pages. I'm really not at all sure, but I suppose it must be around two thousand or more. Why do you ask?'

'How many pages when Mister God made the world, then? When he made it all.'

'Not many. I don't think it was more than five, if that.'

'That's like them skeleton things, ain't it Fynn? It don't matter do it?'

Since I didn't know what would come next, and the fact that I was always being dragged into this sort of thing, there was nothing much I could say.

'It's all them other pages, Mister John. It's all in them.'

'What is, my little maid? What's in those pages?'

With a kind of 'I told you so' flourish, she ended up with: 'All the meat to put on them bones, them skeletons.'

All that John could manage was, 'I see. I must remember that.' John was somewhat put out to have all his facts and figures so easily dismissed with the words 'no meat', but she wasn't talking about the flesh of those long-dead beasties. It was something else entirely. I hoped she wasn't going to start on that ... I had had that one for weeks.

So far as Anna was concerned, her 'no meat' referred to all those equations and formulae and things that John had taught me, and that I so loved messing about with. She had told me quite clearly and simply that all that kind of stuff was just a lot of old bones, skeletons. Not that she had anything against them at all, but the really important thing to do was to put meat on them. She did manage to tell him: 'They ain't got no outside, Mister John,' and after a moment, 'no insides, too.' You've got to admit that it's difficult to get very excited about something that has got no outsides or insides.

*　*　*

For a few weeks the kids' conversation had been all about the coming bonfire night and how many fireworks they might have. It was to take place on Moonground, that place that the adults insisted on calling 'the dump'. For the kids, it was a place of imagination and invention, a place where the normal rules were changed to who-knows-what – like all scrap heaps, it was simply a jumble of the junk of living. There were times when I thought of it as a place where the ordinary rules had failed. It had been called Moonground for as long as I could remember. The adults knew it as a place to be avoided, a dangerous place, an eyesore, a place which somebody really ought to do something about! I had been trying to persuade John and his sister to come to see the kids and Moonground, and eventually it was agreed that we would all meet at seven o'clock on Bonfire Night. I always found it a slightly odd experience, standing in the middle of Moonground, for not too far away we could see the tower of our parish church where the Rev. Castle talked about another land where the rules were different, and where everything was very much better, because Jesus had stood the old rules on their head. Moonground was such a place, where the rules were both different and better. That was why grown ups did not like it. They felt uneasy because they did not know the rules, and they could not play with Mister God. They couldn't see it with different eyes.

'People see it with the same eyes,' Anna had told me. 'You've gotta see Moonground with different eyes.'

I simply hadn't got the heart to tell her how difficult that was for most people. So I shut up.

So it was that Danny, Nob and I spent many hours struggling to collect whatever was burnable and making a reasonable bonfire, whilst the kids were busy scrounging pennies: 'Spare a penny for the guy, Mister.'

Some of the older boys were busy making hand-warmers. A well-made hand-warmer was important for the coming winter months. Any person with a safe and well-made hand-warmer was always the centre of a huddle of kids. Some liked a large size cocoa tin with air holes punctured at the bottom and a lid that could be securely closed. This, fixed to about two feet of wire and a wooden handle, and you were ready to go. Once the paper, wood and coal in it were lit, a few energetic swings and twirls made it ready to warm the coldest of hands, and whoever had one was 'Tops'.

Come the appointed hour we all gathered at the end of the street, the older boys carrying large biscuit tins full of fireworks, and four or five swinging hand-warmers, like incense, as if they were in church. As we were going to Moonground along the Canal, Sally had decided we ought to take a few paraffin lamps to light our way along the towpath.

'Couldn't get no spuds, Fynn,' yelled Heck. 'Mum didn't have no money.'

'It doesn't matter,' I said. 'We'll get some at the coffee stall.'

'Got a bag of "stickjaw"', chipped in Bunty.

'Good thing, too,' said another. 'It might stop you talking for a little while.'

'Oh, you're a rotten thing, you, you're rotten!'

'Anybody got anything else?' I asked.

'A bag of peanuts ... '

'I got some toasted coconut squares', said another.

We were slowly collecting a small feast.

'Ain't you got nothing, Fynn?' asked Kath.

'Sure I have,' I replied. 'Got some bars of chocolate and a bag of wine gums.'

'You got anything, Mill?' asked Nipper.

'Sure have,' replied Millie. 'It's for grown ups like me, not for kids like you lot.'

'I'm grown up,' cried Kath. 'Ain't I growed up? Give us a look,

Mill. What you got in the bag? Eh?'

'Just you keep your nose to yourself. Keep your nose out of my bag.'

'Betcha it's booze, ain't it, Mill?'

'Betcha a million pounds it's whisky ... I betcha.'

'What's it taste like, Mill?'

'Gi's a taste!'

'Nope,' laughed Millie. 'Nothing doing. It's just for me and Sally. You've gotta keep the damp and cold out when you're as old as me.'

'How old's our Millie, Fynn?' asked Anna.

'Search me, Tich. I've got no idea.'

'I'n she old like wot she said?'

'Betcha she's fifty,' chimed in Heck.

'Can't be,' cried another. 'Betcha she's not older than thirty-five, ain't you, Mill?'

'Hold it you lot,' complained Millie. 'You'll have me in a wheel chair if you lot go on like that. If you really want to know, I'll be twenty on Christmas Eve.'

'That's rotten, that is, ain't it?' said Rose. 'You get one present and not two, do you?'

'Gonna have a party, Mill? Can I come?'

'... and me?'

The continuous chatter of the kids spilled into the cold night air, the mist rising from the Canal and the breath of all the excited kids wove patterns in the light of the lamps, like newly formed ghosts. The shapes, unable to sustain themselves, disappeared. As we approached the bridge to cross the Canal we could see our bonfire on the other side. A rocket hurled itself into the sky, trailing its lace-tail of sparks.

As we approached the fence which we would all have to wriggle through by the light of the fire, I could see John's car parked at the far end of Moonground. I had forgotten that entirely, and wondered how he had managed to get it in. No doubt Danny or Sam had figured out some way of doing it. The early ones had certainly made a good bonfire. As we searched for an easy way in, we were confronted by PC Laithwaite on the other side of the fence.

'This way,' he said, 'and mind how you go. Glad to see you're all sensible this year. None of your dangerous backyard fires like last year. It's about time you older ones started to use your loaf,' he remarked, directing that one at me. 'There's hope for you yet. Come in and enjoy yourselves and mind you make sure the fire is well and truly out before you leave. I see young Fynn is with you. Oh, how are you Millie? Nice to see you get a night off then.'

'I wouldn't miss this little shindig for all the tea in China,' replied Millie.

'Sadie and Sally's here too.'

'Do you good,' he replied. 'Off with you and have a nice time!'

Arabella came to meet us as we wandered towards the fire. 'I've brought some baked potatoes with me,' she said, 'and enough sausages to feed an army. Hope I've done enough,' she remarked, looking around at the kids. 'You'll only need to warm them up.'

Anna and I went over to greet John.

'You came, Mister John. That's nice.'

Danny had made John comfortable on the rear seat we had

taken out of an old wreck of a car a few days ago.

'Hello, little Anna,' replied John. 'Come and sit beside me.'

She did more than that, much to his surprise, for she gave him a hug and a kiss, as did Millie and, encouraged by this display of affection, the other kids decided it was about time they joined in too. What with the red glow of the fire and the glow of his own pleasure, he looked happier than I had ever known him to be.

It was when Millie, the gentle tart from the backstreets, handed him a double whisky, that he nearly came apart at the seams.

'Have a tot, Prof.,' she said, 'keeps the cold outta yer bones.'

For a moment or two he was quite undecided what to do, but finally he said, 'Will you come and sit the other side of me, Miss Millie?'

'Sure thing, Prof.,' she said. 'I'd luv to,' and plopped down with a flurry of skirts and legs. Poor old John. It must have been many years ago, if at all, that he had met anyone like Millie and he shifted a bit to make more room for her; but he had not reckoned with Millie! For she tucked an arm through his with 'Us old 'uns gotta keep each other warm, ain't we Prof.?' Dear Millie. No matter how she earned her living, there was an innocence about her that it was impossible to miss. John smiled and relaxed, and there they sat, the loving pair, the earnest Professor and the questioning Anna.

Suddenly the night sky was afire with multi-coloured lights and showers of brilliant sparks.

'Watch this one,' warned Danny as an extra large rocket climbed rapidly skyward and blossomed into a shower of coloured stars.

As the sparks slowly faded, Millie said, 'It's good to know the stars are still there when all the fuss is over, ain't it Prof.?'

He nodded, and turning to Anna, he asked, 'Are you enjoying it?'

'Yes,' she replied, '… but …'

'But what?'

'Mister John, what happens when the stars go out? What happens then?'

After the fireworks had finished and the fire had died down to a large mound of glowing embers, Danny and Sam went off to the pub for some bottles of pop and such stuff for the kids. We all sat around on old oil drums, packing cases or whatever could be found, reheating our baked potatoes and sausages. The kids began to sing. It amused me that they knew the words of the ... well ... naughty songs far better than the other ones. Soon Moonground faded into strange odd lumps, lit only by a few gas lamps from the street nearby, and the stars took on that strange nearness of a cold frosty night. John had been asked more questions in the last two hours than perhaps he had had for the last two years.

'Mister John, why are some of the sparks of them fireworks green and some of 'em blue?' and 'What makes rockets go up? What, Mister John?'

By this time Anna was lying almost full length, staring up into the stars with that silence which so often heralds an outburst of questions. I edged towards her, expecting at any moment to be asked impossible questions. But I was to be spared it this night, for her questions were aimed at John.

'Mister John,' she asked, 'how many stars up there?'

'I think,' he said after a moment's thought, 'there are about three thousand stars that you can see and many, many more that you can't see even with a telescope.'

She tucked that bit of information away somewhere as she silently rehearsed the next bit.

'Mister John,' she said, pointing upwards, 'if you join a line from that star to that star and then to that one, and then to ...', she rattled off more stars. 'If all them stars were joined up by little lines,' John was giving nods of his head.

'Yes,' he said, 'I've got that.'

'What then?'

John was preparing to give some astronomical explanation.

'Then it makes my face, don't it,' she asked everybody in general.

I think John's lower jaw dropped an inch or two and I must say I reckon I had joined up a few stars the wrong way round, because I couldn't see it.

'Why ain't it *my* face?' exclaimed Bombom.

'It is too. It is your face too, Bombom,' replied Anna. 'It's everybody's face if you do it proper, ain't it, Mister John?'

Poor old John, he could do nothing more than nod his head! She hadn't finished yet.

'How many different faces in all them stars, Mister John? Eh?'

It wasn't the kind of question that John wanted to be exact with.

'So many,' he said finally, 'so many you couldn't count them.'

'More than everybody in the world?' she went on.

He could do no more than nod silently. We were all silent as we looked for our faces in the stars.

'You wouldn't get my old man up there,' giggled Heck.

'Why not, Heck?' I asked.

'He's so bloody ugly, Fynn,' laughed Heck. 'He'd frighten the life outta everybody. But he's a good 'un, a good 'un for sure!'

Sam had gone across to John's car, to get it into the road. A few of us carried the old blanket and hamper that Arabella had brought with the various goodies in.

'Did you like it, Mister John? Good, wasn't it? That blooming big rocket, betcha it nearly went up to the Moon, betcha it did. Didn't it, Mister John?'

'A long way,' smiled John. 'It certainly went up a long way.'

I was glad that he didn't launch into some mathematical calculation in order to give some more accurate estimation of just how high it had reached. He shook his head and, to my complete surprise, said, 'Perhaps it did go up as high as the moon.'

'Told you so ... told you, didn't I?'

Something had made him see the magic of this night and not simply the facts. As we walked, John put his hand on my shoulder.

'You must be tired, John,' I said. 'Can I do anything?'

'I'm not really all that tired,' he replied, 'more ... well, more thoughtful.'

'What about?' I asked.

'Looking back.'

'Oh!'

'Did I? It's too long. I can no longer remember. Did I?'

'Did you what?' I asked.

He gave a long, long sigh. 'Did I ask so many questions when I was that age? I can no longer remember that far back.' He paused for a moment. 'Where does the magic go to, I wonder? Where? Where?'

I didn't answer that one, for in the first place, this wasn't the moment, and in the second place, I didn't know the answer.

They were just about to drive off.

'Bring her to see me. Bring her often ... little Anna!'
I promised I would.

* * *

From somebody or from somewhere Anna had very early on
picked up the idea that answers came first and questions came
later. This wasn't the way I had been taught and it certainly
would not do for Old John. Mum had perfected this way of living
for a long time, so when Anna and Mum came together, they
were a well matched pair! It was a little tough on me, for I never
really knew if I was coming or going, and, more often than not
I found myself trying to go both ways at once. That can be a
little painful at times.

At times I did complain that Answers really ought to come
after the Questions, but I never did make much headway with
this approach. I was smiled at. Being smiled at in that particular
way could be very tough to take. It could reduce me in size
immediately.

'There is mess in every order,' Mum said, 'and an order in every
mess, but whatever order you may find or whatever mess you
make, it's yours – nobody else's!'

It was not unusual for some people to liken Anna to something
or somebody that they understood. 'She's like a jackdaw or a
magpie, she picks up these things.' I did it myself, I likened her
to an angel. Not that I knew all that much about angels, I can't
remember if I've ever met one or not, but I was a bit surprised
when John likened her to a rifle. That stumped me completely!

'Have you ever fired a rifle, Fynn?'

'Nothing bigger than a peashooter or a popgun. Why do you
ask?'

'She reminds me of one.'

'A bomb I could understand, I feel as if I've been blown up at
times!' I replied, 'but a rifle, never.'

I don't think he liked what he had said. He was struggling for
words.

'Hell! There are times when she appears to have a foresight and
a backsight. Don't be so dense, young Fynn. You sure know what
I'm driving at.'

'You've lost me, John, give with the explanation.'

'I suppose what I am trying to say is that you align with the foresight and adjust with the backsight.'

'Sounds all right to me,' I said, 'but what's to do with it?'

'Not much, I suppose, except she knows exactly what she's aiming for. I wish I could say the same for myself. She causes me to have the strangest thoughts. Idiot thoughts. Things that I know can't be true, but they're there.'

Now I was in a muddle. He seemed to be thinking like Anna and I said so.

'Perhaps you're right, Fynn, perhaps so.'

'Does she ever give you the feeling that she is ...'

'Is what?'

'A detached part of your own memory? She does me. I'm losing my grip on things.'

'Not you, John. Not you!'

'Often she reminds me of my own childhod, my own memories, my own muddles.'

'Muddles I can understand,' I said. 'She often stands me on my head.'

'Now you're laughing at me. You're not to! I don't like it one bit.'

'Sorry, John, but you did it often enough to me.'

'I know,' he said, 'but that was different. I was a lot older than you and it was, after all, my duty to teach and yours to learn. She can give me a positive mental itch at times, and I just don't know how to scratch it. Mental indigestion, I suppose, but Fynn ...'

'Yes?'

'There are times when I think she may be right, not in the bigger things, you understand, but in the smaller things. If only she could explain herself accurately it would help.'

'It would help me too,' I laughed, 'if you could tell me what you're on about. I'm lost.'

'Has she,' he asked, 'assaulted you with her very, very, very world?'

'Oh that one,' I said, 'I got that one in the middle of the night weeks ago! The very, very, very small and the very, very, very large. Something she picked up somewhere. Perhaps somebody wrote it down for her, or maybe one of my books ...'

'That I can understand, but where did she get the idea that the rules were different? Did she work it out or did somebody tell her? She's right, you know.'

'That puzzles me far less than the fact that she looked up the word "very" in the dictionary. I did many, many years ago. It's not a word I use often. Do you know the meaning of the word?'

'Never given it a thought. I just use it.'

'Only that it means real or true, and that's what I'm not at all sure about.'

John was now spending as much time with the kids at our home as I spent at Random Cottage. It was strange to see this retired teacher sitting on an old crate or the old car seat which was always called 'Mister John's place'. In no time at all he was perfectly at ease with Millie and her pals at the top of the street. No longer did he judge them or criticize them. Certainly he was saddened by the fact that they had chosen that way of making money because they could see no other way of helping their families out. He put it correctly, when he said to me, 'You're very lucky to have such good friends.'

And I was so lucky.

*   *   *

I'm fairly sure that I had never heard Anna use the word 'preface' in any of her chatterings, but she certainly understood that the beginning part of a book told you what the book was going to be all about, and that was just the skeleton, wasn't it? It was the rest of the book, 'the meat', that helped you to understand it all. So when John told her that he couldn't believe in Mister God because he just couldn't believe the beginning, she wasn't all that surprised. Just saddened. She had seen shelves and shelves of books in his study, so he must know that the beginning bit was only the skeleton, mustn't he? He did agree with her when she explained it to him, but it didn't help him all that much. It was funny how grown-up people did that kind of thing. They just didn't bother with all the nice meaty bits, but they were always ready to fight each other about the skeletons. Like the Rev. Castle. He always talked about Mister God as if he was like a very strict Head Master with a cane in his hand, just waiting to punish everybody. It was no wonder his sermons were so often punctuated by her overloud 'Pooh!' So far as Anna was concerned, Mister God was definitely and positively cuddly. It makes a difference if you start off that way.

'It isn't that I think she's right. It's what she says, young Fynn. Nothing like that at all, but then ...'

'I know what you mean, John. It's always "but then" with her!'

'She puts so many different things together in one idea that, to me, it's just a muddle.'

'To me, too. I never know for certain if Im up or down.'

'But then she always wriggles out of her muddle somehow.'

'It's the way she has of saying things.'

'I find myself waiting for the next bit. I'm surprised to find I'm holding my breath and I haven't done that for many years.'

When talking about Anna, I so often find I run out of words. I don't know what to say next. I did manage to say: 'She just sees things in a different way, that's all John.'

'Maybe, maybe, except that she has the knack of making things look beautiful. Even her own complicated muddles. She puzzles me, Fynn, and I don't mind saying it. The most I would like to say about the little maid is that she makes me stop and think again. Does she ever write stories, Fynn?'

'Yes, quite often.'

'Perhaps she might write some for me sometime?'

'Why don't you ask her yourself? Better still, why don't you ask her to tell you one of them.'

'Perhaps I will.'

*　*　*

That winter didn't treat John kindly. On too many occasions he had to stay in his room with some bug or other, which meant our visits were far less frequent and much shorter than usual. But on those occasions when we did manage to have a little chat, he appeared to be very much more thoughtful. His decisive, cold edge was no longer there. He seemed far more inclined to listen, rather than to launch into some complex lesson as to the nature of things. I'm really not certain how he would have taken comment on his change. 'He's more cuddly', Anna had said.

I'm not certain that I would have used those words but change there certainly was. He no longer had that unshakeable certainty. He was more given to listen to other views and, most curious to me, he asked questions, which was something I rarely heard him do. On those occasions that I did manage to get a question in,

the answer was often, 'I'm not sure, Fynn', or, 'I don't know'. On a number of occasions when we had been talking about one thing or another, he had turned away from me and said to Anna, 'What do you think, my little one?' I had the distinct feeling that he was wanting to capture some of Anna's fire or some of her excitement of the nature of things. Maybe I was just letting my imagination run loose, but it certainly seemed that way to me. I was beginning to feel that it was her that he really wanted to talk to, not me. For in many ways we were far too much alike for me to be of any help to him at all. My main contribution in this threesome was as a sort of interpreter.

For much of the time I don't think they were all that aware that I was even there. Old John was even beginning to giggle. Not the kind of giggle you did behind a raised hand, but a full-blooded giggle of joy. At the start of these giggles, he had often apologized, but now he would take her by the hand and let go. It was good to see the pair of them laughing so happily together. There were secrets between them that I was unable to share. For they divined in each other something that I was unable to reach. In spite of all their laughter, though, I felt that beneath it all John was having a pretty rough time. He was wrestling with something and I didn't know what it was, and neither John nor Anna was prepared to tell me. Not only was I often asked to go and do something else, things which so far as I could see were completely unnecessary, but I was also firmly told to take my time about it!

'Go and get some doughnuts at the shop, Fynn. I'm sure Anna would like a doughnut or two for her tea. I certainly would.' I was completely unable to tell him that there was a bag of doughnuts in a tin in the kitchen. So off I went and left them to it. I didn't really mind all that much doing these little things, but I was taken aback when, after a bit of shopping and after I had put the tea tray down in the drawing room, he turned to me and said, 'Doughnuts, Fynn? You should know by now that I never eat the things. Isn't there a jam tart in the kitchen or just a plain bun or something?'

I very nearly told him that not only were there jam tarts, there were plain buns, fruit cake and at least six more doughnuts in the kitchen, but I didn't. It didn't really seem worth it!

* * *

It wasn't that Mum was so much better than anybody else that made her so different. She wasn't beyond the odd cuss word now and again, and her temper on those few occasions when she lost it was really something to see. That was the time to duck! No, it was altogether something different – simpler.

In her view, the reason why this old world got itself in such a tangle wasn't because people either did or didn't believe that there was a God. It was quite simply the fact that everybody wanted to do more than God. As she put it, 'Nobody ever told you that you've got to do more than God, did they?' I had never heard it said and it certainly wasn't that Mum didn't work hard, she did. But she always kept time for herself, time when she just liked being with all those crazy things that went with just being. She could simply turn off. Anna could do it with ease. Turning off came naturally to her, but with me it was hard work. It took me a long time to learn that. As Mum put it, how could you read a book if there were no spaces between the words? and music would sound like I don't know what without its own intervals!

* * *

The New Year had arrived for me almost unnoticed, except for the fact that we were all going to be a year older. Anna was fast growing up, both in her size and her pursuit of beauty. I had recently bought myself a tandem. It would be much safer to make our journeys on that than to have her perched on my handle-bars, where her continuous wriggling about was a bit of a hazard, to say the least. That year Anna was going to be seven so we decided that we would go off to see John and show him our almost new tandem. It hadn't taken much to alter the rear seat and the handle-bars, and we were all set for off. I don't think she had really noticed the pedals and that they were there in order to help the thing along! I really didn't mind at all, doing all the pedalling, and she found it easier to look at things as we went along much better than when wriggling around on the handle-bars.

John gave it a really close inspection as he walked around it.

'You may find this difficult to believe, young Fynn,' he said, 'but I was once very good on one of these contraptions. Once the weather gets a lot warmer you must let me use it for a little ride.'

'I'll steer it, Mister John,' said Anna.

'I think,' he replied a little doubtfully, 'we had better wait until you are a bit older.'

'I'm nearly seven,' she replied. 'That's old.'

'Seven!', he said. 'That's old is it? Well, well, well. I'm nearly …' He started to give his age and then thought better of it. He merely said, 'That makes me very old, then.'

I went into the house with John for a pint of refreshment, leaving Anna to wander around in the garden. We both raised our tankards and wished each other a 'Happy New Year' and then he said, 'That little one out there has made me realize something I really ought to have known. It's an error that I really can't account for.'

'What's that, John?' I asked, quite uncertain as to what this terrible error might be.

He chuckled deep in his throat before he answered. 'I suppose I had assumed that the mind was a sort of array of little cupboards, each one clearly marked with its particular subject.' He ticked off a number on his fingers – 'Mathematics, English, Science, Geography, and … maybe Religion too.'

I didn't think he wanted any answer to that one, so I just waited for him to continue. 'You can see my point, young Fynn, can't you?'

I shook my head.

'Well, maybe not, but I'll teach you this. After listening to little Miss Chatterbox,' he said pointing to the window. 'I've begun to think that you can't organize your mind in the same way you can order your books. It just doesn't work that way.'

I did know the next question to ask, but I never got the chance.

'No, Fynn,' he continued, 'whatever goes in the mind must, I suppose, be, to some degree, altered by what is already there.'

'Sounds all right to me. I'll go for that.'

'This attitude of wonder and excitement that Anna has is something that I think I've never possessed. It makes a difference, you know. Fynn. It prevents you keeping everything apart. I won't say that I think she's always right in what she says, but I do admit that I was wrong in dismissing it all too easily. What a mix up. It is all a mix up, to be sure, Fynn. Like everybody else I have not been without hope, but I need to be convinced. Not that the little maid has convinced me, but it's the silly little things that she says that make me doubt my own doubt. A few days ago I asked her how did she know that Mister God was true and that he was really there. She simply said she could feel him because he is warmer than me. 'That's why, if Mister God wasn't different, I wouldn't know, would I?'

'I did ask her about Satan. "Old Nick is colder," she had said. You know, Fynn, the way she has of putting things does make sense. I suppose my mistake has been that I have never really put it to the test. Perhaps I ought not to quiz her too vigorously, Fynn, but she does have an answer to all my questions. Not that I understand her answers!

'I asked her, "Where do I find Mister God?" Her answer didn't give me any comfort at all! Her answer to that little question was "in people's puzzles". What do you make of that one, Fynn? I suppose she could be right. There I go again, Fynn, I do get too technical at times, but I have no other way. It's difficult for me to think about something that is not open to inspection. All you are left with is to say what Mister God is like, and the little maid can be quite convincing there. All her dratted circles and colours make a nice point. I've always found that the usual talk about God leaves God as a remote and abstract thing, not the warmth that Anna talks about. I suppose if you are able to involve something in everything and that everything's in that something, that has to be the answer to Mister God. She seems to be able to do that with such ease and I must say, I like it. Sorry to sound so clinical, Fynn, that's the way I am, I'm no expert. On the other way, I need a great deal of practice. She always reminds me of an insurance company, if you see what I mean.'

The remark was beyond me.

'It's the ignorance of the one thing that can, if you go about it in the right way, lead to knowledge of the many things. There I go again, but I do find her way most compelling.'

John did have a rough time with Anna, with what he called the 'invisible stings of childhood' and his wish to see things with other eyes.

One thing was certain. He had changed a great deal.

Tea didn't take long that afternoon. All she really wanted was to get into the garden.

'Well, well, well, what caused that little eruption?'

'I don't think anything caused it,' I said. 'It's just one of those things that happen now and again. I think I need something stronger than tea. A pint might be better, or maybe even two.'

'It might at that, Fynn, it might at that. It was as well I retired when I did. I was really getting too old for it. The thought of the brat every day of my life was ... well ... too much. No, not that, Fynn, let's say very rich. She never leaves you with nothing to think of, does she?'

'That's for sure. How do you like the thought of sticking the universe in your ear, John?'

'Not a pleasant thought, to be sure, but I see no way of getting out of the dilemma. Perhaps we really are the wrong size after all. I must give it some serious thought.'

'While you are thinking, John, spare a moment to think about my problem too. How the devil do you talk to angels?'

'Not talk, Fynn. Do sums. There's a difference. Perhaps not much, but there must be one.'

We did have another pint before we left and had it not been for my passengers there might have been one more.

'Good luck with the angels, Fynn!' he said as we left. 'I have great faith in you and know that you'll manage something to her satisfaction.'

'Nuts!' I said and we were off.

* * *

'Growing up,' John said to me one evening over a pint of beer, 'Growing up – what the devil does that mean?'

'Don't ask me. If you don't know by now I don't know who does.'

'Gently, gently, my young Fynn. Please don't rub it in. It must have something to do with understanding, I suppose. Otherwise, what else?'

'Perhaps it ought to, but it doesn't always turn out that way, does it?'

'Conformity to other people's ideas, that's what it is. Conformity!'

'Oh! What brought that on?'

'The little maid. I have been thinking a lot about her recently. I still don't understand her. Perhaps I never will.'

'Perhaps we aren't meant to,' I replied.

'Meant, Fynn, meant! Don't give me any more of that gush. Nobody means us to be anything except us and none of us are very good at that. Conformity is just too much to pay for the pleasures of living. I know that I'm much older than you, young Fynn, and I just don't like it. Not one bit. The little one has got something that I haven't got and it's puzzled me for weeks.

I know what it is. It's something I lost too many years ago. Something I should have guarded with my life. I never realized that until a few weeks ago. Conformity robbed me of it and I never noticed until now.'

'What is it, John? What did you lose?'

'A vision. Just that I had one once, but not now. Sometimes little Anna's chatter reminds me of it, but it's not there any longer, I'm afraid.'

'A vision, John? Don't we all have them?'

'I'm sure we do, but conformity knocks it out of us and then it's too late.'

'Not with you, John. Not certain what you're saying. What do you mean?'

'Exactly what you have said. You don't know what I mean. The little one would never make that mistake, she would know.'

"That's beyond me, John. You just confuse me and that's not like you!"

He chuckled. 'Haven't you ever noticed, Fynn, that a vision, like love, has its own language that you can never find in a dictionary. The little one knows that so she has to invent a way of words that is different. I hear what she says well enough and I listen well enough. Perhaps I hear it too well and I correct what I hear, but there are so many times when I just don't listen. Perhaps that's the difficulty of growing older, hearing – but not listening. Blasted kids,' he grinned, 'they listen, but so seldom hear! Remind me again of that saying that your mother so often uses.'

'What one is that John? She uses so many!'

'The one about stopping.'

'Oh, the one about if you haven't stopped in the course of the day then you just haven't done anything worthwhile. Is that the one?'

'Yes, that's the one. It's crazy, just plain stupid, until you stop and listen and then it makes sense.'

'That's what we call "doughnut speech" at home.'

'Who called it that name?' he asked.

'Anna of course, who else?'

'That's exactly the point I'm driving at. With a vision, you are forced to invent words. I had forgotten that that's why you have to listen so hard. The straight and narrow sounds all right, but if you're not careful, all you learn are the tricks of the trade and nothing else. I used to think at one time that everything could be written into a book, but now I'm not sure. Books might contain what you need to know, but where, oh where, do you find what you want to know? I'm very tired of tricks, Fynn, and I envy you more than I can say.'

'Why do you say that, John?'

'Both your mother and the little maid have a vision. It might make life very difficult for you, but don't lose it. There sure must be more than words to it all, Fynn, don't you think so? There are times when I am of the opinion that they are more of a hindrance than a help. What is there other than words? There's nothing else to use.'

'I know Anna's answer to that, John,' I replied. 'Beauty.'

'She might have something there at that, but we still need words, for how else can we share beauty?'

'You'd better ask Mum about that. She reckons that when you come face to face with beauty there is nothing else to do except remain silent.'

'Your mother and the little maid have an answer for everything. It is just possible it's right, but it's so difficult to remain silent you know, young Fynn. You may think that I am against the Bible entirely. I'm not. I do admit to being puzzled about the first and the last chapters of the Bible, but everything else I understand up to a certain point. It puzzled me when I was a child and it still does now. Fynn, answer me one question and then I'll be satisfied. Who was God talking to in the first chapter of Genesis?'

'Nobody, as far as I know,' I said.

'I'm glad you don't know either. It always puzzled me when God says "Let us make man in our own image". Who was this "us" He was talking to? That's where I must have lost my vision. I think it's puzzled me all my life. It was very early in my life I resolved to dispel the mystery of it and preserve the wonder. I don't think I've made a good job of that. It depresses me, but then I am encouraged to read the lines "and God saw that it was good". Perhaps it means beautiful. Do you think so, Fynn?'

'Could be, John, could be. I don't really know.'

'I'm always so happy when you bring the little maid to see me, you must do it more often. No, no Fynn, don't say it is because I'm old and she is so young. It's not that at all. Nor do I understand her chattering, but every once in a while she uncovers a beauty for me that I had lost. Do you understand what I'm saying, Fynn?'

'I think so,' I replied.

'The nerve of her! The last time you were here she told me I was wrong.'

'How did that come about?' I asked him.

'I happened to say that she was magic.'

'So?'

'Her answer was so hard to believe that I thought for a moment that she was regarding herself too highly, much too highly, but I was wrong.'

'Come on John, let's have it. What did she say?'

'"No Mister John," she said, "I'm not magic, I'm a miracle!" What do you make of that?'

'Just being her normal self, I suppose.'

'No, you're making the same mistake as I did. "Miracles", she told me, "was when you said sorry to Mister God and he took you back to find what you had lost." I'm not at all certain about saying sorry to Mister God, but there is a lot of truth in taking you back to find what you have lost, so who knows, maybe she is a sort of miracle. So, Fynn, bring her as often as you can.'

There was no doubt about it. John had changed a lot since I had first met him. He was certainly a lot mellower, although with me he could still be tough and still the same old stringy John that I had first met. With Anna he was much gentler, which was strange, because it was me he ought to have been gentle with. He just didn't know how tough Anna really was! Like so many people who spent much time with Anna, they so often got it wrong. Sure she was sweet, sure she was all the things that you might drool over in a child, but when, like me, you could be woken up at any time of night to talk about "them things" you began to see her in a different light. At three o'clock in the morning, to be faced with the question, 'Fynn, them things you were talking about yesterday – what does it do?' or maybe, 'What does it mean?' She never did realize that at that time in the morning I had enough problems trying to figure out what I was, let alone trying to explain what 'them things' were, particularly when 'them things' could be almost anything from a rice pudding to

a volcano. I didn't see her as sweet at these times, but I didn't really mind. In fact, once I got over the shock of having my eyes opened, I really enjoyed it.

It was often in the middle of the night that things really happened. To wake up to her 'Fynn, Fynn ... the Vicar!'

'Eh! What? What about the Vicar. What's he been up to?'

'Why does he have to protect Mister God so much and make people frightened?'

'No idea, Tich.'

'Why does he protect Mister God so much and attack people?'

'I've got no idea.'

'Why does he do it then?'

'Dunno!'

That wasn't my idea of a good night's sleep, but that was the way I got used to my nights, and this was one of the things about her that very few people knew, and as for her prayers that I heard every night, I often wondered what the Rev. Castle might say on that subject!

'Hello, Mister God. This is Anna talking', which was a nice way to start. There were also times when it seemed to me that it was her way of letting Mister God know who he was talking to. Her next words might easily begin, 'Now look, Mister God ...' or 'Look here, Mister God ...' She could just as easily give him a good scolding or tell him how wonderful everything was. I reckon you had to be pretty sure of Mister God to start off with 'Now look, Mister God, you mustn't blame him or ...' Anna was certainly sure about Mister God. So sure that the occasional ticking off was quite all right. It was at these moments when the sweetness that other people saw in her could turn her into something tougher than anybody realized. When John had spoken to me of Mum's and Anna's vision, he made me a little itchy. Visions were something I knew very little about. So far as I was aware, we were a little short of visions, visitations, voices and such like down our street. Everybody was far too busy doing lots of things with so very little to expect such wonderful happenings. When John had told me just how much he enjoyed being with her and listening to her chatter, he then said, 'She probably is the complete eclectic.' He made it sound as if she had got the measles or the plague or something like that. That was a new one to me. I had to look it up in the dictionary. 'Eclectic' meant picking up those things that please her most, but what was wrong with that? It was true she picked up things, she picked other people's minds or other people's ideas, whatever pleased her. What John didn't realize then was that that was the easy bit. What she was then doing was re-arranging the bits she picked up or the bits that pleased her and, in due time, she would present this bouquet to Mister God. Not just a bunch, but a proper bouquet, one of the best arrangements possible. That's where she was a toughy. That took time. Sometimes what she wanted was hard to find.

* * *

On the day of the Sunday School outing, that once a year scramble for the kids, I was unable to go along with them. I had to work a few hours' overtime that Saturday morning. I did manage to get all the kids to the appointed place in time and we waited for the char-a-banc to arrive.

'Sorry you can't come, Fynn,' said Millie, 'but we've got enough of us to look after this lot.'

After work I decided to spend a few hours with John. I did like talking to him and he was glad to see me when I arrived.

'Glad to see you, young Fynn. By yourself?'

'Anna's off to the seaside with the kids from the Sunday School.'

We talked about this and that, drank a few pints and munched a few sandwiches, but Anna crept back into our conversation.

'Fynn, I'm never really sure if she's teasing me or not.'

'I know what you mean. It's not that what she says always makes sense, far from it. All the same, I know what you're going to say, John. You must not, or cannot, ignore it or dismiss it completely.'

'That is exactly it! She so often mixes up her subject matter so completely that I am not always certain what she's up to.'

'I've been there before,' I said.

'Often, nevertheless, Fynn, in spite of what you and I might call a muddle, she does paint a most captivating picture. One that I wouldn't miss for anything.'

'Don't worry, John, she won't let you miss anything!'

'You know my views on religious matters?'

'I have heard, John. I have heard!'

'It's her attitude to her precious Mister God that puzzles me so much. Of course, Fynn, it's none of my business whether anybody believes in God. By all means, if that's what gives you comfort ...'

'Not comfort, John,' I managed to say. 'That's easy. It's joy, and that's not easy.'

'As I was about to say, Fynn, she seems to know her particular God so well that I can't ...,' he paused for a long moment, '... can't tell them apart! It's always struck me as strange, Fynn.'

'What has?'

'The fact that the less you know anybody, the greater are the differences that you can recognize, and conversely, the more you know a person, the more you realize just how alike you are.'

'That's an interesting thought, John. It makes me wonder, if Mister God realizes just how alike he is to Anna he might have a bit of fun for a change.'

'If I was a church-going man, Fynn, I might say you were being sacrilegious, but as I am not a church-goer, I merely say that you're being facetious. Did it ever occur to you to wonder why I singled you out all those years ago?'

'No, but I did often wonder why it was always me that ended up with so many beatings.'

'Oh that! It never did you any harm. I singled you out, for, in many ways, you reminded me of myself when I was your age.'

'In what way was that, John?'

'Cocksure! Just bloody cocksure! Perhaps we just grew up too fast. You know, Fynn, bearing in mind what I said a few moments ago, you are beginning to sound like Anna at times. What a terrifying prospect for you, young Fynn.'

'How's that, John?'

'To have both me and Anna inside you at one and the same time! No wonder you get so muddled at times. No offence meant, Fynn, no offence. Don't worry! They seem to fit well enough. I'm happy.'

We talked in that fashion for hours.

'Fynn, it would be nice if other people could see me as you and Anna do. Most people see me as a cantankerous old Grouch. I suppose I am. When are the children back from their outing?'

'They are due at the church at six o'clock.'

'Ah,' he said. 'You can put your bicycle in the back of the car and I'll drive you there. I'd like to see the kids again?'

So, at the proper time we ended up at the church and, after a short wait, the char-a-banc arrived. In no time at all John found himself in the middle of a tangle of kids.

'Hi, Fynn,' said Millie. 'I'm done to a frazzle. I'm worn out!'

'How'd it go, Mill?'

'Like clockwork, like clockwork. My bloody spring's busted.'

Slowly the kids found their mums and left, and I walked over to John and Anna.

'Fynn,' he said, 'I have suggested to Anna that she might like to come to my birthday party next Saturday, if that is convenient to you, that is. She can bring a few of her friends too. Not too many, of course, I really could not face all that lot.' So the time and place was arranged and he went.

I was completely unable to suggest to Anna any present that John might like to have. Not with the money that was available, that is. So far as I could see, there was nothing much he didn't have. I had to leave it to her.

That week was a frenzy of activity. Whatever it was that was going on I was not allowed to see. I often saw Millie and Anna sitting with their backs to the railway wall, busy doing something or other, and in the kitchen, things were hurriedly put away. I got many a secret smile from Millie and Anna, but that was as far as I got. I knew that Millie was coming to the party and Bombom, May and Bunty, and that was as far as I knew. And I was told that we were going by bus, so we could sit upstairs in the front. Of course, there was no other way to go, not when you were nearly seven, that is. So armed with the fare money that I had given her, we boarded the bus and in due time we arrived at Random Cottage, polished and all shined up. John didn't try to shy away from Mill's warm kiss or from the rest of the kisses from the kids. After all, this was a very special day. The sitting room was full of people drinking cocktails and eating 'funny things on sticks'.

'I know you, Millie, would like a large whisky, and a pint of my special for you, Fynn? And for the children, there's lemonade, ginger pop and that kind of thing. What would you like to eat?'

All the various bits and pieces on sticks, so easily and rapidly rechristened 'horses doofers', they didn't want. What they did want was toast and dripping, the meaty jelly stuff at the bottom of the basin.

Anna tugged at my arm. 'The present, Fynn, when?'

'Now,' I said, 'right now.'

And so John was wished 'Happy Birthday' and handed various packages and 'stickjaw' toffees. It was a pity that Bunty's offering of a bag of hundreds and thousands burst on its way to the table. Arabella's squeal alerted the whole company to this disaster, but we soon sorted that one out, and I took the kids off to the kitchen to hunt for toast and dripping, and in no time at all they were happily munching away. Considering how house-proud Arabella was, plus the fact that dripping has a habit of dripping everywhere, I decided that the place for us was in the kitchen out of all possible danger. It was there that John found us.

'I hope you've all had enough. Come along with me and meet everybody. Look, Anna,' he said, 'I'm wearing my badge,' and he displayed his large beadwork red heart. 'And as for your picture of me, I think that is wonderful.'

This was news to me. I hadn't seen the heart before, nor the picture. We followed John back to the sitting room.

'Have you had your toast and dripping?' asked a lady.

'Yes, tanks, Missis,' said Bunty. 'Wasn't arf good, too. It lines yer belly a treat that do.' They all laughed.

'And this,' said John, taking Anna forward by the hand, 'is the young lady who drew my likeness.' The likeness was of a face constructed from numbers and surrounded by hearts.

'How very clever of you to think of such an original idea,' said a lady.

'It's so like John. Nothing but numbers.'

'All them hearts are him too,' corrected Anna. John glowed at this and placed his new likeness on the centre of the mantelpiece.

The party went well and eventually all the other guests left, leaving us alone. As Bombom was mincing up and down with an empty cocktail glass: 'How original of you, my dear!', John was standing in the doorway. He did manage to move out of sight before he burst into laughter.

* * *

I had been in John's garden for near on a couple of hours. Arabella wanted that patch of thistles, docks and nettles turned into the usual well-ordered flower bed. I had managed to get it near to what she wanted, but by now even my blisters were getting blisters. It was time I packed it in. I was careful to tidy myself up, and put on a different pair of shoes so that I didn't tread mud all over the house. Anna and John were heads down, battling away over a game of draughts. John lifted his head and pointed across the room.

'Pour yourself a pint, Fynn. I can recommend the new brew, and you might just as well bring me one, too.'

I was thankful to get the weight off my feet, and sank into a comfortable armchair. I managed one long drink and then it happened.

'It's like Mister God, ain't it, Mister John?'

John didn't answer.

'Ain't it like Mister God, Fynn?'

I didn't move. After all, since, according to Anna, almost everything was like Mister God in one way or another, it came as no surprise to me to learn that playing a game of draughts was like Mister God. I didn't know how it was, but it really didn't matter, for in due time we would be told. John wasn't at all used to this kind of thing and showed his impatience.

'Get on with it, it's your move.'

'Fynn, if Mister John is Mister God and I'm me, this is where it starts.'

John had been called many things before, but never ever had he been called 'Mister God', and he didn't know which way to look.

'He always found it difficult to pretend.'

'Fynn, here! Look!'

There was little use in making a fuss, so I just got up and went.

'He's Mister God over there and I'm me here.'

'Yeah, I know that.'

I looked at John and raised my eyebrows.

'Fynn, don't you dare. Don't you dare say anything!'

I couldn't resist it. 'He's Mister God and you're you, I've got that bit. What's next?' I said.

'Then I'm going that way to him and he's going this way to me.'

'Uh, uh, that's the usual way it's done.'

'So it is a bit like Mister God, ain't it, Fynn? It's got to be.' She nodded her agreement with herself.

'Then what happens?' I asked.

She thought for a moment before she launched into the next bit.

'Fynn,' she exclaimed with excitement, 'if I get home to his side he's gotta turn me into a King, don't he?'

'What happens,' I managed to ask, 'if he gets to your side? How do you work that one out?'

'Well,' she replied, 'he can turn himself into anything he likes, can't he?'

Although this wasn't the kind of conversation John ever got himself involved in, he did manage to ask a question.

'Anna, my dear, what happens in the middle? After all, that is where the game is played '

'Course it is, I know that.'

'Well?' I asked.

She looked at John and me as if we were some form of idiot.

'Well,' she announced, 'you gotta be careful then, don't you?'

'It's all ready too simple when you know how, isn't it?'

'You finish off my game, Fynn. Must have a pee.'

John looked at me and laughed. 'How does she do it, Fynn, how?'

'Search me,' I said. 'I haven't found the answer yet.'

'She seems to be able to wriggle out of the most complicated situations,' he said.

'Well,' I added, 'there are times when she simply shifts it over to you. If you want to play you've got to be prepared for the changes.'

* * *

It was about the middle of October. The days were beginning to get noticeably shorter. I was having a chinwag with Millie and Danny at the top of the street. The gaslamps were never all that bright, and I didn't notice Arabella until she was almost on top of us. She very nearly tumbled and certainly would have done so, had Danny not held her up.

'Fynn, can you come? John wants to see you, I think he might die. Fynn, do you think that you could bring Anna, too?'

'I'm not at all sure. How bad is he?'

'I think he's very bad. The doctor is with him now. Fynn, please ask Anna. She wouldn't be frightened, would she? Not with you.'

'I'll go and ask Mum and Anna,' I said. 'Would you like to come down with me or would you rather stay here?'

Millie said: 'You stay here with us, Arabella, and let Fynn sort it out at home. You hold on here and I'll pop across the road for a whisky. You look as if you could do with a lifter.'

'How about getting you home after all this?' asked Danny. 'I've got my motorbike around the corner and you're welcome to a ride if you like.'

'It'll have to do, won't it?' she said.

I returned about this point with the news that Mum had said it was all right if Anna wanted to go. So Mum was already getting my tandem onto the street and Anna was putting on something warm. Danny went off to get his motorbike as Millie returned with the whisky and a stool for Arabella to sit on.

'Fynn,' she said, 'I think that we are going to lose him this time. He has had too many little attacks in the last few years, but this, Fynn, this one is big and I don't really know what to do.'

Mum turned up, pushing my tandem, along with Anna following behind. 'Anything I can do?' she asked.

'Wish I knew what,' I said, 'I don't think so.'

'If there is,' said Mum as she turned to go, 'give Mrs Bartlett a ring and I'll certainly do what I can. If you have to stop, that'll be all right. I know where you are, but do be careful on this dark night. Be careful and don't go along the Canal. Stick to the road. See you when I see you then. Take care.'

I promised I would. A minute or two later the roar and rattle of Danny's bike heralded the fact that he was nearly with us.

'Sorry I was so long. I had to find a cushion for the pillion seat. Sorry about the noise, Arabella, but the old exhaust is getting a bit dicky, but it'll get us there all right. Oh, and keep your leg away from it, it does get a bit hot. I can't think of any other way of getting you home.'

'This will do just fine.'

'It'll have to, Fynn,' he said. 'I'll get off now, so we'll be waiting for you.'

With one last adjustment of the exhaust they were off. It was a sober little group that listened to the fading roar of that engine. By this time there must have been twenty or so people huddled around that lamp post.

'Hope he's gonna be all right,' said Bombom.

'He ain't gonna die, is he, Fynn?' asked May.

'Don't know, luv,' I replied. 'We'll just have to wait and see.'

'He's a nice old geezer.' This was from Nipper.

'How long it'll take you to get there?' asked Millie.

'Ten, maybe fifteen minutes,' I replied. 'Suppose we'd better get off then. You on, Tich?'

'I'm ready, Fynn.'

'Hope it'll turn out all right, Fynn. Give him our love, if you can', said Millie.

I promised I would do that if I could.

'And, Fynn,' she yelled as we moved off, 'give us a ring if you need any help.'

I wanted to speed along as quickly as I could, but with Anna on the back, I had to be extra careful. What with all the tramlines, the dimly lit streets and those damn cobble stones I just had to concentrate. My passenger was silent for the whole journey. I was not used to this lack of chatter, but in the circumstances it was a good thing. It allowed me to give my full attention to getting us there in one piece. About two hundred yards from Random Cottage, we met Danny pushing his motor bike on the homeward journey. I pulled into the side of the road, 'Hi, Da. Trouble?'

'No. Thought I'd better push this old contraption away from the house before I start her up. She can make a bit of a racket at times. Wait a tick, Fynn, will you? I might need a bit of a push. There's somebody there, Fynn. There's a couple of cars in the drive. Don't know who. Maybe the doctor. Don't know. You're to go straight into the sitting room.'

By then his motorbike was shattering the night air. It really was about time he got a new exhaust. I waited a few minutes until the sound of his engine faded into the distance. It was a matter of holding on to something familiar for a while longer.

I leant my tandem against a tree in the garden and we headed for the house. We said nothing until we had reached the porch.

Anna was holding my hand. She spoke my name. 'Fynn.' It was the first word she had said for the last twenty minutes. Anna pulled her skirt and top straight and silently questioned me. I nodded. She gripped my hand tightly as we entered the sitting room.

I was a little surprised to be confronted by a man in clerical garb. He walked towards us with outstretched hand.

'Ah, John's protegé and his bright star!' He had placed his hand on Anna's head for this last remark. 'John Daniel never stops talking about you!' He shook my hand once again. 'Gerald Hodge.'

It was many months later that I was told that Gerald Hodge was John's younger brother. It hardly seemed possible. They were so different.

Anna had wriggled away from his hand and was sitting beside me. The brothers were so different from each other that the thought of them held my attention for some minutes. Gerald had none of John's sharp cutting edge, and never spoke with those attacking sentences that I had become accustomed to. The only thing they seemed to have in common was an air of certainty.

Gerald once more placed his hand on Anna's head.

'The bright star, the bright star … and a little child shall lead them.' I could see that she didn't really like the 'bright star' stuff, but she didn't say anything. We just sat.

Gerald said, 'He's told me so much about you both I feel that I know you well. He has never really loved many people, but I think he is likable.' Gerald oozed goodness.

It was a week or so later that it dawned on me that he had never used anybody's Christian name in those few hours at Random Cottage. I had been overwhelmed by his presence and had been able to say nothing more than, 'How do you do?'

Though it could have been no longer than ten minutes before Arabella came into the drawing room, it seemed like hours.

'Will you go in now? He's waiting for you. I think he's a little brighter.'

We started to make our way up to John's bedroom until Arabella told us that she had set up a bed for him in his study. I tapped lightly. I was relieved to hear the snap of 'Well, come in, come in.'

We entered, not quite knowing what to expect. John didn't look too bad, a bit washed out, perhaps. Anna had to hold his tankard of beer for him; he was none too steady.

'Not too long, I am a bit tired. I'm very glad you've come. Very. Do sit down, Fynn, for goodness sake. You make the place untidy. Sit on the bed beside me, Tich. I want to look at you.'

Anna grinned and wrinkled her nose.

'Well, brat,' he smiled at her, 'been talking to Mister God again?'

She put her head on his shoulder and whispered to him.

'So have I Tich, so have I.' I heard him say that distinctly; there was no doubt about that.

We stayed for a few minutes longer and then I got up to leave.

'It's best,' he said. 'I really do want a rest.'

Anna kissed him, 'Goodnight, Mister John. I love you.'

'I love you both. I do. You had better stay the night. You can use my bedroom. I'm not using it. You'll be alone upstairs. I don't suppose you two hunters will mind that, will you? Come and see me in the morning.'

We left him.

Arabella didn't object to us staying the night, nor sleeping in John's room. Nor did she tell us not to touch anything!

Neither of us felt like sleep although we were both tired. We stood by the open window in John's room and talked.

'Fynn, Mister John loves me and you, don't he?' she said. 'Yes he did, Fynn, he called me Tich. Did you hear him? And brat too!'

'Did you mind?'

'No, it was nice.'

We talked about little things for a while before we stretched out on the bed. Anna had her usual long conversation with Mister God, with my arm around her, and we slept. It was about midnight and I had been up since just after five that morning. Although I wanted to stay awake I couldn't. I slept.

It didn't feel as if I had had more than four hours' sleep, but I had. It felt more like four minutes. A knock at the door had shot me out of bed.

It was Arabella. 'John's gone, Fynn. He's gone. About an hour ago.'

So this was it, I thought. I didn't notice that Anna was beside me. She had heard it. It was odd that my first thought had been that I was glad that I was not the one to break the news to her. I was quite uncertain what came next. What to do?

Anna, in her magic way, just took over, or so it seemed. After all, seven was really a ripe old age, wasn't it?

'I'll go and make some tea,' and Anna was off to do so.

It was one of those things that just happen at times. After the strain of that night the fact that Anna was off to make some tea was a bit too much for Arabella. She just exploded into peals of laughter.

'Oh, Fynn,' she gasped, 'she is so ... well, what's the word, Fynn, I just don't know, she's ...'

'She is, ain't she?' I managed to say.

True to her word, by the time we had reached the kitchen she had prepared the biggest pot of the blackest tea that she could manage.

'Done some toast for you, Fynn. Couldn't find no dripping though.'

She was totally engrossed in cooking bacon and eggs for Arabella.

'I couldn't manage that. Not all that!'

No, but definitely no, Anna did not want to pay her last respects to John.

'You do, Fynn. He ain't there. He's with Mister God.' And that was that.

Arabella asked us if we would mind staying with her for the day. It was Anna's suggestion that we stayed the night too.

'Why don't you let Millie come tomorrow when we've gone home?'

'Well,' said Arabella, 'I don't know about that.' Then after a pause. 'Do you think it would be all right? Would she mind? I would like some company and she could help. You telephone Mrs Bartlett and tell Millie and Doody to come.'

That was the way that day progressed. We just did what we were told, whilst Anna whizzed about the kitchen producing a cup of tea every half hour or so.

It was early next morning before Millie and Doody arrived, and after they were settled in, I decided that it was time Anna and I were off.

'John left this for you, Fynn,' Arabella said, handing me a letter, and some books for Anna.

On our way home I did wonder just how Arabella would make out with two young prostitutes in the house. I felt certain that John would have chuckled about it.

Millie and Doody stayed with Arabella for about a week, doing or helping to do those things that had to be done. John's body was taken up to the North of England, where his brother arranged the burial in a churchyard for which he was responsible.

*   *   *

Anna was absorbed by her new treasures – those books that John had left her – astronomy, mathematics, and physics. For no reason at all that I know of I didn't open John's letter to me for about two weeks. My excuse was that I had been too busy. Maybe I had been. I don't know.

'Where's John's letter, Mum?'

'Under the clock on the mantelpiece. I put it there for safety.'

I opened it in the back yard. I reckoned that I wanted to be alone.

'My dear Fynn and Anna,' it began, 'I write to tell you what a joy it has been to know you both. You may be surprised to know that although I have had no sudden revelation or "road to Damascus" illumination, I have at least come to the realization that I made a gross error in dismissing religion too rapidly. Now I find that it isn't the cosy hideaway I thought it to be, but hard work. Anna my dear, how right you were! I did want to know how it all started and how right you were to want to know how it all ends. Anna, if you still have that display of those circles, will you enter me at some point as a blue dot?'

'My dears, I salute you and your friends.

'I salute the God-hunters. I can already hear Tich saying "but Mister John, Mister God is hunting for us too!" I do hope so. Good luck in your searching.

'I send my love to you both. John.'

Somewhere down the line I reckon there must be an affinity between Mister John's world and Anna's, but in order to solve their problems, they had to hunt in different fields, and each saw the other's as different. Perhaps most people need both. I certainly do.

Arabella sold Random Cottage and went to live with a cousin, I think somewhere in New Zealand. Except for a few Christmas cards, that was the last I heard of her. As for Random Cottage, it was lost, together with other houses, under a dual carriageway.

* * *

It was strange for me not to be able to share my thoughts with John any more. No more tankards of ale with him – those occasions when I spent a lot of time fending off the ice-cold logic of his attacks. Now I would have to sort out my own problems.

He had undoubtedly changed a lot during the years I had known him. Some people told me how much he had mellowed in his later years – or that he had become 'almost human' after his retirement. But it wasn't that, for Old John was always very much a human – he could be hurt. Mum had told me a long time ago that the effort he had put into hiding his hurt had made him a bit irritable. Maybe she was right.

'Why do you think he caned you so often – for the fun of it?'

'I hadn't given it much thought,' I replied.

'Simply to toughen you up?'

'Hold it, Mum. Hold it! I reckon I was tough enough for my age, don't you?'

'Oh, you were *strong* enough! Perhaps a bit too strong for your own good. But I don't mean that kind of strength. It's the other kind of strength I'm talking about. It was some years ago that Mister John told me that he was going to take you under his wing because you so much reminded him of himself at your age.'

'I know that, Mum,' I replied, 'he told me that too, but I never did know what he was aiming at. I don't think that I'm anything like John.'

Her eyes crinkled and she smiled. 'You're more alike than you know!'

'How's that, Mum? In what ways?'

'You are just a pair of big softies!' she laughed. 'And that's why he beat you so often, so that you wouldn't be too easily hurt.'

'Don't know about that, Mum,' I laughed. 'Maybe he wasn't much to look at, but he was strong and he certainly knew how to use the old "persuader"!'

'Oh, that,' she replied, 'that's nothing. You'll get a lot more hurts than that in your life. If that's the only kind of hurt you have in your life, you'll have it pretty easy.'

I wasn't at all certain that I had understood her properly and said so.

'It doesn't matter,' she replied. 'You'll learn!'

It was just another one of those occasions when I wasn't going to get anywhere.

'He did change a lot, didn't he?' I tried another tack.

'He certainly did that, he certainly did. He was a lot more content and happier in his last two years. It was good to see it.'

'It was a good thing that Anna came to live with us,' I said. 'I reckon she did him a power of good.'

Mum looked at me a long time before she asked, 'In what ways do you mean?'

'Well, all her chattering about Mister God helped him to change his mind. Don't you think so?'

She didn't answer me.

'I reckon he ended his life believing that there might be a God after all.'

'Well,' she replied, 'he was certainly no longer convinced that there wasn't a God. That's for sure.'

'I reckon he did believe,' I said.

'Perhaps. All I know for sure is that the last time he came here he asked me if I could lend him a Bible.'

'I'm sure Anna had a lot to do with that,' I said. 'She was like a … like a …'

'Don't,' Mum interrupted me. 'Don't say what I think you were going to say. You'll certainly be wrong.'

'How do you know what I was going to say? How could you know?'

'I can read you like a book. After all, I've known you long enough. There are times I know what you're going to say before you know yourself.'

'All right, then, tell me what I was going to say, if you can. Tell me!'

'A pound to a penny you were going to make the same mistake as your Aunty Doll and Mrs Weeks make, that Anna was sent by God or that she is a messenger or something like that. Come on, admit it!'

'Well,' I managed, 'not exactly that, but something similar, I suppose.'

'Thought so!' she replied. 'What a burden to hang around a child's neck! What a burden!'

'I can see that,' I said, 'but you've got to admit she is a bit different and I'm sure that she did help John.'

'Of course she did, but not in the way you think.'

'How then?'

Mum laid her hand on mine. 'To use his own words, his very own words when I last saw him, "Anna has shown me how useless it is to build Mind Mountains, and that to know God is altogether different from describing God". I wouldn't put it that way myself ...'

'"A Mind Mountain"? What did he mean by that?'

'Like your stupid wall. Even if you had leapt over it, it wouldn't have meant that you had grown up – only that you were bigger. That's a "Mind Mountain". So don't build any more!'

'In that case, I'll try not to. What was it about Anna? What has she got that I haven't? What did John see?'

'Well, number one, the night you brought her home you told me that she was lost, right?'

I nodded.

'If she was lost, I'm a Dutchman! Why, she's one of the few people who really knows who she belongs to, and that surely is not being lost!'

'You mean Mister God?'

I didn't need an answer to that question. I shouldn't have asked it in the first place.

'Number two,' she continued, 'is that she is too busy living to carry around with her any useless baggage. So don't you hang anything on to her what she doesn't need! Got me?'

'Got you, Mum.'

'I reckon that just simply by her chatter and her lovingness John saw another world that he hadn't seen before – not just the world of his own knowledge. I know how much you admired him but everyone has his limits, and I'm afraid dear old John really did try to go beyond his. After he'd known Anna a bit, I think he just stopped pushing at God and then stepped back a bit.'

'So what, Mum?'

'Well, I suppose you could say it gave God a chance to move

forward.'

'That's a difficult one for me.'

'Maybe, but I have a sort of feeling that that's the way it was.'

'I wish I knew why he had changed so much, Mum. I just wish I knew.'

'Maybe you'll never know that.' She smiled at me. 'God moves in wondrous ways.'

I had to be content with that.

Q.E.I.

Judge not the Lord by feeble sense,
But trust Him for His grace.

— 'Providence' by William Cowper

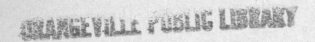